SOMEWHERE TOWARD

FREEDOM

SHERMAN'S MARCH AND THE STORY OF AMERICA'S LARGEST EMANCIPATION

BENNETT PARTEN

SIMON & SCHUSTER

New York   Amsterdam/Antwerp   London
Toronto   Sydney   New Delhi

Simon & Schuster
1230 Avenue of the Americas
New York, NY 10020

First Simon & Schuster hardcover edition January 2025

SIMON & SCHUSTER and colophon are registered trademarks of
Simon & Schuster, LLC

For information about special discounts for bulk purchases, please contact Simon
& Schuster Special Sales at 1-866-506-1949 or business@simonandschuster.com.

The Simon & Schuster Speakers Bureau can bring authors to your live event. For
more information or to book an event, contact the Simon & Schuster Speakers
Bureau at 1-866-248-3049 or visit our website at www.simonspeakers.com.

Interior design by Wendy Blum

Manufactured in the United States of America

1   3   5   7   9   10   8   6   4   2

Library of Congress Cataloging-in-Publication Data has been applied for.

ISBN 978-1-6680-3468-2
ISBN 978-1-6680-3470-5 (ebook)

All photos Courtesy of the Library of Congress

To Hannah & In Memory of
Ruth K. Parten
(1933–2022)

CONTENTS

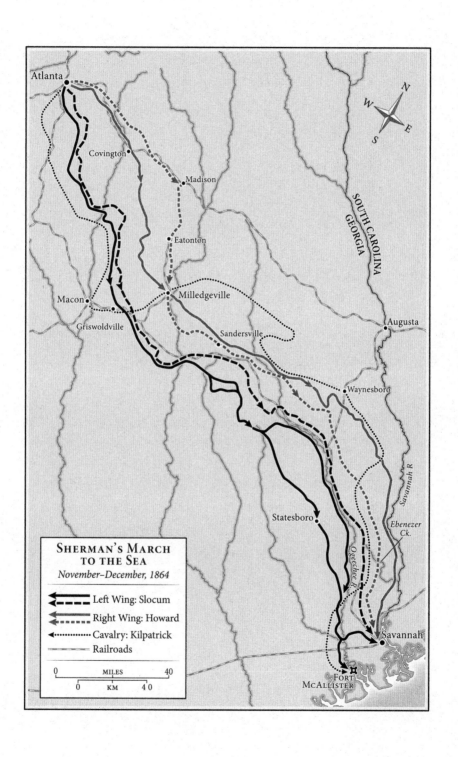

N
W   E
S

SOUTH CAROLINA
GEORGIA

Atlanta

Covington

Madison

Eatonton

Macon

Milledgeville

Griswoldville

Sandersville

Augusta

Waynesboro

Statesboro

Savannah R

Ebenezer Ck.

Ogeechee R.

Savannah

SHERMAN'S MARCH
TO THE SEA
November–December, 1864

Left Wing: Slocum
Right Wing: Howard
Cavalry: Kilpatrick
Railroads

0   MILES   40
0   KM   4 0

FORT
MCALLISTER

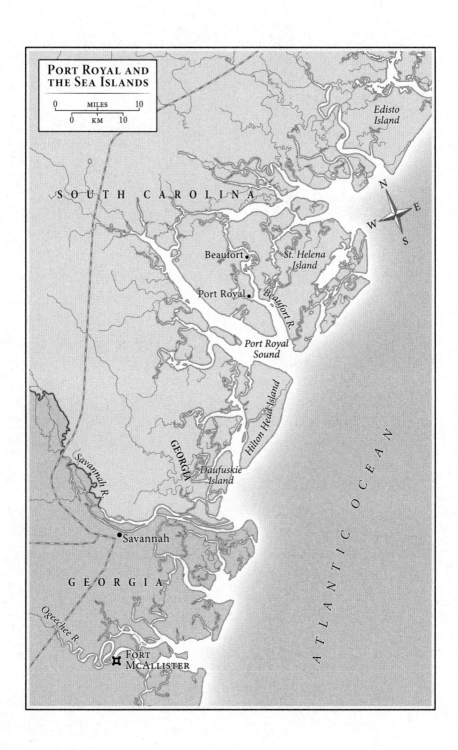

PORT ROYAL AND
THE SEA ISLANDS

0   MILES   10

0   KM   10

*Edisto
Island*

S O U T H   C A R O L I N A

N
W   E
S

Beaufort

*St. Helena
Island*

Port Royal

Beaufort R.

*Port Royal
Sound*

Hilton Head Island

GEORGIA

*Daufuskie
Island*

A T L A N T I C   O C E A N

Savannah R.

• Savannah

G E O R G I A

Ogeechee R.

FORT
McALLISTER

SOMEWHERE TOWARD

FREEDOM

INTRODUCTION

In the late fall of 1864, as General William Tecumseh Sherman's Union Army marched toward Savannah, Sally, a freedwoman, roamed the camps at night searching for her children. Ever since she and her husband, Ben, had joined the army on its March to the Sea, she had been asking everyone she met for "any clue" into her children's whereabouts. When she encountered freed people who fled to the army and joined the march just like her, she would scan their faces and scrutinize them closely, hoping that by chance she might detect some distinguishing feature: a smile, a scar, or a mannerism, something only a mother would know and never forget. Her evening rounds became a camp ritual. Everyone knew of her search, even the soldiers, though most felt that she might as well have been searching for a "needle in a haystack." In fact, all Sally knew was that ten years before, one of her children, her eight-year-old daughter, Nan, had been sold to the "lower country," and that Nan might be down there yet. Late one evening, as the army neared Savannah, Sally got the news she'd been hoping for. A friend told her that he'd heard someone call his wife "Nan" and the woman just might be her daughter. Struck by the news, Sally stopped what she was doing, praised God, and did what any mother would do: she started running.[1]

1

Sally and Ben had both been enslaved in Georgia, probably some-where near Atlanta. Little else is known about them except that earlier that fall their lives had changed forever. General Sherman's monthslong campaign for Atlanta had concluded in a decisive Union victory. The city was now occupied by the US Army, which meant it had become a refuge for enslaved people residing on nearby plantations, men and women like Ben and Sally. Sometime that fall the two had taken flight. They had escaped to Atlanta, attained their freedom, and then found work laboring for the army. Ben had become a wagon driver for the Twentieth Army Corps; Sally had become a cook for one of the offi-cers. When it came time for the army to move out of Atlanta in early November, they decided to go along. Perhaps they thought that camp life might better secure their freedom, but they must have also known that their journey could take them toward Savannah, to that place called the "lower country," where they might reunite with their long-lost daughter.[2]

Little did Ben and Sally know that in marching along with Sherman's army, they would take part in the largest emancipation event in US his-tory. In the coming weeks sixty thousand soldiers would march overland from Atlanta to Savannah in what's known as Sherman's March to the Sea. Though neither Sherman nor most of his men had any desire to turn their march into one of liberation, the enslaved people they met en route certainly did. From the very start and at every stop along the way, enslaved people fled plantations and rushed into the army's path. Men and women arrived at night or during the day. They came as families or as lone escapees. And some made long, circuitous journeys while others simply met the soldiers on the main road—or right there in the shadow of their homes. The movement was unlike anything anyone had ever seen. Soldiers described it as being practically providential. Enslaved people did, too. They hailed the soldiers as angels of the Lord and celebrated the army's arrival as if it were the start of something prophetic, as if God himself had ordained the war and the days of Rev-elation had arrived.

Some of the men and women who ran to the army took the occasion to do just as Ben and Sally did and march along. Indeed, wherever the army went—plantations, homesteads, roadsides in between—enslaved people packed their bundles, said their goodbyes, and marched off with Sherman's men. Some found work, often as cooks, laundresses, or laborers, and thus marched along with the main columns, but the vast majority who left traveled along somewhere at the army's rear, with long lines of formerly enslaved people sometimes stretching well into the Georgia countryside. Mostly on foot and with little to eat or protect them from the cold of a Georgia winter, those men and women essentially traveled as wartime refugees. And as Sherman pushed his massive army toward Savannah, those refugees would soon swell the army's lines, turning one of the war's great military campaigns into a march of liberation.

By the time Sherman's army arrived on the coast, as many as twenty thousand freed people followed—all marching, one soldier would write, "somewhere toward freedom."[3]

The story of Sherman's March has never been told quite like this. Instead, for much of the twentieth century the question has been whether Sherman's March represented an early instance of "total war"—or, said differently, whether Sherman's "hard-war" policies previewed the civilian horrors of twentieth-century warfare. Scholars now see the issue as mostly settled. As hard as Sherman wanted to make the war, he never targeted civilians outright, and his March was never as horrific as, say, the bombing of Dresden or the Rape of Nanjing. Yet for decades the question loomed so large that it continues to frame the history of the campaign. To write about Sherman's March has been to write about warfare; it's been to focus on the soldiers, on Sherman, or on how he endeavored to "make war so terrible" that generations would pass before the South ever considered rebelling again. As a result, we've typically imagined the March as a military campaign and with a few exceptions have traditionally treated it as military history.[4]

One of the principal claims of this book, however, is that to understand Sherman's March is to reimagine its history by seeing it for what it truly was: a veritable freedom movement. That was clearly how the enslaved people saw it. From the moment Sherman moved his army out of Atlanta, enslaved people across Georgia appraised the situation, knowing that wherever the army went, freedom went also. That calculation led tens of thousands of enslaved people to travel down roads and footpaths and creek beds, sometimes enduring incredible hardships, in an attempt to reach army lines. Yet it wasn't just the movement of enslaved people that made the March such a freedom movement; it was the movement of the army as well. The way the army marched—its speed, its breadth, and the intensity with which it broke the back of the planter class—cut out a space deep in the heart of Georgia wide enough for enslaved people to begin imagining freedom as something real, as something coming within reach, and as something that existed in the path of the March. That mix of movement, momentum, and meaning defined the entire campaign.

Another implication of this focus on the army has to do with how we view the March's aftermath. We often think of Sherman's March through Georgia as simply the Savannah Campaign—meaning the roughly 250-mile march from Atlanta to Savannah in November and December 1864. We also sometimes follow the march to Savannah but then quickly shift the story's focus to Sherman's next move: the army's push through the Carolinas and on to Durham, North Carolina, where Confederate general Joseph E. Johnston surrendered his army in April 1865. But the problem with this narrative is that it obscures what happened in January and February in Savannah and therefore misses the fact that Sherman's March initiated a sprawling refugee crisis along the coast of Georgia and South Carolina. The crisis began as an attempt to

resettle the freed refugees at a federal outpost on the South Carolina
Sea Islands and ended in tragedy: men and women died from sickness
and exposure; freed people landed in places ill equipped to support
them; and thousands of people found themselves experiencing freedom
in what were effectively foreign lands, in places far from home and in
unfamiliar environments.

This book tells a new story by bringing this history of the March's
aftermath to the fore. In doing so, however, it actually revisits a venture
that historians have been writing about for decades, a project known as
the Port Royal Experiment. Based on a set of barrier islands surrounding
a wide deepwater sound just north of Savannah, the Port Royal Experiment was an early model—or "rehearsal," as one historian described
it—of Reconstruction. Its goal was to begin the transition from slavery
to freedom by instituting a free labor regime on the region's abandoned
plantations. Its presence on the islands—indeed, its foothold—was why
Sherman decided to send the refugees there to begin with. But if we
accept the project's dubious label as an experiment, it's clear that Sherman's arrival in Savannah represented the uncontrolled variable that no
one had seen coming. The presence of so many refugees transformed
that self-contained outpost in an isolated corner of the war into the site
of a full-fledged crisis. Historians have known and written about Port
Royal, but the story of the Georgia refugees has largely gone untold.[5]

These arguments point to *Somewhere Toward Freedom*'s main argu-
ment: that Sherman's March was a turning point in the history of American freedom. I mean this, on the one hand, in a very real and grassroots
sense: it was the largest emancipation event in our history and one of
the largest in the rise and fall of Atlantic slavery. The army's movements
from Atlanta to Savannah channeled enormous force, enough to destroy
Georgia's slave system, pummel the planter class, and bring freedom to
some untold thousands of enslaved people. The collective movement
of so many enslaved people—first *to* the army and then *behind* the
army—did the same. It dismantled slavery from within, undermined

the Confederate project, and kept the idea of freedom at the center of the campaign. In fact, one way to understand the March is that it did in effect what the Emancipation Proclamation could do only on paper.

On the other hand, I mean this in a much larger and perhaps more abstract sense. The best way to describe it is that the March was, as Sherman himself once put it, like "a good-entering wedge." Because the army moved with such overwhelming momentum and because the freed refugees followed the army, the combination of the two had implications and aftereffects that expanded out from the source. Some of those effects were political in nature, having to do with emancipation on a national level; others were more humanitarian and had to do with the fate of the freed refugees. In either case, the result was a series of twists and turns that set the agenda for postwar Reconstruction. The history of the Freedmen's Bureau, the origins of land reform, and indeed the very meaning of freedom all have their origins in either the March or its aftermath. Though we've typically looked at Sherman's March only as one of the last campaigns of the Civil War, it was also an early battle of Reconstruction, a wartime crucible that went on shaping American society long after the marching stopped and the campaign came to a close.[6]

Over and over, in soldiers' letters and diaries, in war reminiscences and in official military reports, freed people expressed themselves through the idea of "Jubilee." It was the idiom of the age, the metaphor of emancipation, and it bounced like choral notes above the rough sounds of a marching army. Freed people celebrated Sherman's arrival in Savannah by singing the songs of Jubilee—often "The Year of Jubilee" or the "Jubilee Hymn"—and out on roads and along cart paths everywhere, freed people praised the army, claiming with "ecstatic exclamations of joy" that the day of Jubilee had arrived. Soldiers claimed it, too, and recognized that in marching through Georgia they were taking part in something epic, something that would change the order of history, which was why when the Northern composer Henry Clay Work sat down to salute the March in song, he wrote "Hurrah! Hurrah! we bring the Jubile! Hurrah! Hurrah! the flag that makes you free! So we sang the chorus from Atlanta to the sea, While we were marching through Georgia."[7]

Drawn from deep in the Old Testament, the idea derives its power and meaning from an almost celestial moment of rapture and release. According to its biblical origins, the Jubilee was a time when society would renew itself, a period when enslaved people would be freed, large estates would be broken up, debts would be absolved, and fields would go fallow for a full year while the earth regenerated itself. Sometime between the days of Leviticus and the firing on Fort Sumter, however, the idea developed an apocalyptic edge. It came to describe something prophetic and millennial, and it became synonymous with ideas of universal emancipation, a time when the world would make itself anew. Americans of every creed and color knew of the idea, but enslaved people in particular embraced it as a self-evident truth, believing that one day God would right the world of all its wrongs, starting by freeing them for all posterity. The idea therefore developed a special meaning within enslaved communities as a vision of emancipation, and nowhere within the landscape of the war was that vision as clear or as true as on the March.

Indeed, what President Abraham Lincoln described on a crowded platform at Gettysburg as the nation's "new birth of freedom," enslaved people all across Georgia celebrated as their "day of Jubilee," and this is why the idea is such an important metaphor. Refugees typically leave minimal sources; testimonies from freed people are few and far between. Despite the wealth of writing about the Civil War, sources detailing how freed people felt about freedom, how they imagined it, and what it meant to them are sometimes hard to come by. The idea of Jubilee helps fill in the gaps. It tells us that freed people imagined their emancipation as having world-historical significance, as being rooted in ideas of rebirth and divine justice, and as pointing toward a dawning of freedom that would mend the sins of American slavery. In that sense, the ages-old idea of Jubilee is an overarching metaphor for our Civil War, reminding us that underneath all the blood and gore, beneath the banners and flags, and despite all the myths and legends, the Civil War created a redefinition of American freedom largely led and articulated by people who had once been enslaved.

The fact that the idea of Jubilee came to characterize Sherman's March to the Sea only underscores how crucial the campaign was to both those processes: to the lived reality of emancipation as well as the larger redefinition of freedom.

Sally may have even had Jubilee's promise in mind when she dropped her things and praised God after hearing the news of a woman named Nan. We don't know. All we know is that in the blink of an eye, Sally "flew to where they were." The campfires lit the way. She ran past soldiers and tents, probably ignored shouts and jeers, and might have grabbed the wrong person once or twice. When she finally got near enough, the woman she believed to be Nan stopped and stared at Sally. Sally stared back. The two didn't know what to say or do; a decade had passed since Sally had seen her daughter, and her daughter had been just eight the last time she had seen her mother. It wasn't until the woman said that she'd used to live near Atlanta as a young girl that Sally felt sure it was Nan. She called Nan her child and said she'd been looking for her all that time. Then came the tears. The two hugged, kissed, and cried out in joy. Friends cheered as soldiers watched, and pretty soon the entire camp erupted in a riotous commotion. Sally then went to get Ben, and the whole scene repeated itself. The soldier who later narrated the reunion called it "the most powerful demonstration of human emotion" he'd ever seen.[8]

Sally and Nan enjoyed their tearful reunion while marching along with Sherman's army. They were, however, only two of as many as twenty thousand. Not everyone had the same experience. The idea of Jubilee may have promised a rebirth, but it also called forth more apocalyptic ideas of upheaval and strife. The reality of the March—of sixty thousand soldiers marching to the sea in the final full year of a bloody civil war—is that it was often loud and chaotic and always dangerous. Violence, or the threat of it, lingered around every bend in the road. Freedom—or something like it—was often more uncertain than certain. And calamity was never all that far behind. The March may have been the war's most revolutionary moment, an instance when the ground shook, tumult ensued, and freed people everywhere started realizing freedom as never before. But as the well-known New England abolitionist Thomas Wentworth Higginson once warned, "revolutions may go backward." They sometimes turn tragic. And by the end of 1865, a year after Sherman's army arrived in Savannah, the refugee story of Sherman's March did just that: it became an American tragedy.[9]

Ruins of a depot destroyed by the federal army during Sherman's departure from Atlanta.

Chapter One

THE VIEW FROM ATLANTA

On September 1, 1864, Sam Richards, a white merchant, saw the city of Atlanta explode. Around noon, rumors began circulating of a Confederate defeat on the outskirts of town. Confederate general John Bell Hood would be evacuating his forces at once, leaving William Tecumseh Sherman's Union Army free to take the city. Word of the impending evacuation set off a mad scramble among the remaining residents. Some packed their bags and evacuated hurriedly; others searched the town looking for food. "If there had been any doubt of the fact that Atlanta was about to be given up it would have been removed when they saw the depots of Government grain and food thrown open" and distributed by the "sackful and cartload," Richards wrote. Then the explosions started. Hood had ordered the burning of all remaining munitions trains, which caused whole railcars to burst like fireworks. One such explosion, Richards remembered, lasted for "half an hour or more" and was powerful enough to shake the ground and shatter the glass of nearby windows. Other, louder explosions continued throughout the evening, making the city feel as if it were stuck inside a roaring cannon. "This has been a day of terror and a night of dread," Richards wrote after it was all over.[1]

The next day, local officials surrendered the city to Sherman's army without a fight. The campaign was complete. After marching out of Chattanooga, Tennessee, earlier in the spring, after months of the Confederate Army's digging in and falling back, after more than a hundred miles of hard marching and continuous fighting, after fierce battles at places such as Dalton, Resaca, New Hope Church, Kennesaw Mountain, and Peachtree Creek, after countless miles of train tracks torn up and destroyed, bridges burned, farms desolated, and nearly seventy-five thousand casualties, Atlanta, one of the last great Confederate strongholds, had finally fallen. Soldiers from the Twentieth Army Corps were the first to arrive and make the city home. The rest began arriving shortly thereafter. Sherman, who remained headquartered at Marietta, a town just to the city's northwest, and wouldn't arrive for several more days, nevertheless announced the news of Atlanta's occupation on the night of September 3, writing "Atlanta is ours, & fairly won."[2]

By then Atlanta was already a city transformed. "It is strange to go about Atlanta now and see only Yankee uniforms," Richards wrote the following day. City Hall had been turned into the headquarters of the Provost Guard, an official army term for the military police. It was one of the few buildings left undisturbed, for in the search for liquor and tobacco, Sherman's soldiers had looted stores. "Such a state of utter disorder and confusion presented itself to my eyes then," wrote Richards, who watched as soldiers rummaged through his own store, breaking open everything and taking it as if it were a "free fight." Even more alarming, the forlorn prisoners who had once filled the city's jails and worn blue now wore a faded gray. Roughly 1,800 Confederate prisoners had been marched through the center of town while their blue-coated captors whooped and hollered. Even Richards's church had been taken over by an "*abolition*" preacher, sentiments that would have been grounds for an arrest and punishment only days earlier.[3]

That was perhaps the most stupefying change of all. Almost as soon as the occupation began, a spirit of emancipation swept through the city.

Atlanta was free, and neither Sherman's soldiers nor the city's formerly enslaved people wasted any time in demonstrating what that meant. Richards, for one, couldn't believe the "impudent airs" Atlanta's freed people put on in the face of their former masters. They "were all free and the Yankee soldiers don't fail to assure them of that fact," he wrote, noting that one freedwoman was "as independent as can be" and that two of the men he had enslaved had both escaped into the city. It was like that all over town. Atlanta, which weeks earlier had had thousands of enslaved people working on its defenses, was now a haven for freed people from across the region, with men and women pouring in from the surrounding countryside. As the dumbstruck Richards wrote, it was as if slavery had suddenly "vanished into air."[4]

Despite Richards's apparent disbelief, slavery's demise hadn't been quite as sudden as he thought. If anything, it had been a slow process that had begun once Union armies had begun invading the South in the earliest days of the war; yet that, too, understates the complexity of what the process actually looked like on the ground, particularly in places still experiencing the vortex of war. James M. Wells, a US cavalryman with a taste for adventure, had caught a glimpse of how complex the process could be some two months before Atlanta's fall while retreating back to the city following a failed cavalry raid on targets in middle Georgia. He and his men were facing a tall task. Georgia's scorching summer heat was in full blaze. The men were separated from the main body of mounted horsemen, and their only instructions had been to escape back to Atlanta by whatever means necessary. Though they had covered some of the terrain before, the good news ended there. Not only were the roads humming with Confederate cavalry, their horses were tired, they would soon need food, and the army's lines around Atlanta remained many miles away.[5]

Much to the benefit of Wells and his band, a group of enslaved women soon discovered the desperate cavalrymen and began acting as their guides. The women had no horses of their own, so the men rode while the women walked. The women guided them down creek beds and along footpaths so deep and dark that Wells likened riding along them to descending the depths of "some vast subterranean cavern." Oftentimes the glare of torches led the way, shining upon fords or foot trails that made the dense Georgia brush more easily passable, which must have added to the feeling Wells had while riding in the dark of the night. He couldn't help but appreciate the steely courage of the women, who navigated the "impenetrable darkness" and faced grave repercussions if caught by Confederates. Pretty soon, larger groups of enslaved people began following along, increasing the size of the band. The enslaved people were all "determined to flee the country with us," Wells remembered, though he left no indication that anyone ever did.[6]

He didn't get the chance to find out. Not long after meeting the enslaved women, Wells broke from the group during a surprise shootout with Confederate cavalry and was later captured, making him one of the many prisoners of war who never made it back to Atlanta following an operation sometimes remembered as Sherman's "big raid." The original plan of attack was for two cavalry forces to swing around Atlanta in opposite directions. General Edward M. McCook's force of Union horsemen was to ride west while General George Stoneman's squad of cavalrymen was to ride east. The two were then supposed to join forces south of Atlanta at Lovejoy Station in an attempt to cripple Hood's last remaining supply line into the city. If successful, the two cavalry forces would ride on to Macon, liberate the Union soldiers held there, and then head for Andersonville Prison, the great gulag of the Confederacy, which held as many as thirty-three thousand Union prisoners and sat in the state's southwestern corner near the town of Americus.[7]

The problem was that the operation had been a fiasco from the start. Stoneman ignored orders. Rather than linking up with McCook at Lovejoy Station, he bolted straight for Macon. That left Confederate cavalry free to consolidate around McCook's forces, leading to a standoff southwest of Atlanta near Newnan. McCook, caught off guard and exposed, had no choice but to retreat in a wild ride back to Atlanta that saw hundreds of Union cavalrymen either killed or captured. Stoneman, meanwhile, ran into trouble of his own just outside Macon. He encountered a large force of Confederate cavalry at Sunshine Church, and like McCook, he soon realized he was in trouble and ordered his men to make their own wild, lifesaving ride back to Atlanta, which was the situation Wells found himself in before being captured. But unlike McCook, who managed to escape capture, Stoneman did not. He and more than four hundred of his men, many of whom had been holding the line so others could escape, were taken captive, which put a final end to one of the most calamitous cavalry movements in the history of the war.[8]

Nevertheless, despite being a stunning failure, the "big raid" was one of the first instances in which Sherman's mounted wings dug deep into the Georgia countryside, carrying the war to communities well beyond Atlanta. For the unsuspecting, it was a wake-up call. A war that had once been distant and abstract was now up close and personal and looming all around. Militias took to arms, and whole communities stood guard. That meant "sleepless nights," wrote Dolly Sumner Lunt, a widowed plantation mistress from Covington, southeast of Atlanta. Stoneman's cavalry had been seen on the road, and Lunt had heard reports of stores being ransacked, railroads being destroyed, and neighbors taking flight. In Newnan, where McCook's raid came to an end, Fannie A. Beers, a nurse in a Confederate hospital, watched as Union cavalrymen clashed with Confederate horsemen. Locals rushed past her into the action while others fled. "There was no time for deliberation," she wrote. The war was fast extending its reach.[9]

For enslaved people, the raids carried a different meaning entirely. Some were rightly wary. Armed white men on horseback were specters that enslaved people knew to approach with caution. Yet the raids were also the army's first foray into the upper sections of middle Georgia, a part of the state where the lower Piedmont begins folding into the state's fertile plantation belt, home to thousands of enslaved people.

Blue-coated men penetrating that far into Georgia stirred already restless waters. Enslaved people began fleeing to the two cavalry divisions almost immediately. Several enslaved men guided McCook during his journey before being forced back at Newnan, and one historian has estimated that by the time Stoneman's cavalry approached Macon, as many as five thousand enslaved people were following along. Tragically, many of those men—and possibly women and children, too—met a brutal fate once the raid went bad. One soldier urged them to "escape while they could, as their fate would be severe if captured" but admitted that "Some followed this advice" while "many others chose to remain" with the soldiers "at the risk of any fate."[10]

The army hadn't experienced anything quite like that as it had moved down from the mountains around Chattanooga at the start of the campaign. One reason was the terrain. There, the land is rockier, full of hills and hollows, and is generally less suited for growing cotton. That was less true of the areas closer to Atlanta and the state's Piedmont, but on the whole, north Georgia, especially northwest Georgia, wasn't quite the cotton kingdom that middle and south Georgia were. As a result, Georgia's northern counties possessed a much smaller population of enslaved people, though the region's heavy industries sometimes employed large numbers of enslaved people in coal and ironworks facilities. Of course, another reason was simply that the area north of Atlanta had already been deserted ahead of the invasion. Before Sherman began marching on Atlanta, the region's white residents had taken flight for safety farther south and forced the people they enslaved to go with them. In some cases, those families fled for their own protection, but they also fled to keep their enslaved people from escaping to the army.[11]

Yet as the raid clearly demonstrated, hundreds if not thousands of enslaved people would eventually make the journey over to the army, which sparked fears among slave owners of an uprising from within. The idea that enslaved people were potential enemies among them had long been a fear of white Southerners, and the war had chipped away at whatever illusions of loyalty they had left. Kate Stone, a well-known Louisiana diarist, likened the whispered rumors of a slave insurrection to living on a land mine. Charles Colcock Jones, a slave owner from the Georgia coast, worried about the same thing. "They are traitors who may pilot an enemy into your *bedchamber!*" he wrote after a man he enslaved had slipped off in the night. Sherman's forays into middle Georgia preyed on those fears, stoking a tinderbox primed and ready to explode. In response, Georgia's governor, Joseph E. Brown, began releasing one man from militia duty per every eight hundred enslaved people in a given county. The released men were to patrol the countryside, catch runaways, and quell any signs of unrest. The governor had actually initiated the policy earlier in the year but accelerated it after the raids, once petitions from worried local whites started flooding in. The message: Georgia was at war on two fronts.[12]

The men and women who fled to Sherman's cavalry units or escorted escaped horseman back to federal lines represent part of a much larger whole. In all, historians estimate that at least half a million enslaved people fled to US Army lines during the Civil War. Any number of others may have run to the army but never made it; many more may have fled to the army but were turned away. In any case, the point is that amid all the fighting and dying, one of the mainstays of the war was that enslaved people consistently and inexorably ran to the US Army. Like death, it was one of the war's few certainties: wherever the army moved, enslaved people followed its movements until they caught up and joined the ranks. It happened first in 1861, when three enslaved men in Virginia rowed over to Fort Monroe in Chesapeake Bay and asked for refuge, but it happened in every theater from the beginning of the war up until the very end.[13]

The army had no choice but to respond. Benjamin Butler, the

dour-faced New Englander who commanded Fort Monroe when the three men arrived, set the army's first policy by declaring the men "contraband of war." As he saw it, the men had been forced to work on Confederate defenses, or so they claimed, so to return them would be equivalent to helping the Confederacy. Had the three men not claimed that they had been forced to work on Confederate defenses, it is unclear how Butler would have acted. Nonetheless, when a Virginia slave owner insisted that the three men be returned, Butler refused, arguing that as a form of Confederate property, the enslaved men could be legally confiscated by the US Army according to the laws of war. That was not exactly an emancipation decree. Butler's reasoning said nothing about freedom. But that was never the point. The importance of the contraband policy was that it established a legal framework that allowed the US Army to "confiscate" enslaved people who arrived at army lines with similar stories. The path to wartime emancipation began with that basic premise.[14]

Congress codified the policy a month later in August 1861 when it passed an Act to Confiscate Property Used for Insurrectionary Purposes, otherwise known as the First Confiscation Act. As its name implies, the bill allowed for the seizure of Confederate property used in the Confederate war effort, and it included wording that applied directly to persons "held to labor or service," which everyone knew meant enslaved people. Yet from the moment Lincoln's signature dried, the bill's complications became apparent: Who, for instance, would determine if an enslaved person had been forced to aid the Confederate Army? According to the US government, that was a decision for the court system, not necessarily the army, to make, which raised questions about how and when a court would make that decision and what the army should do in the meantime. Moreover, because the bill mirrored the contraband policy, it said nothing about freedom, which locked enslaved people into an in-between status as neither free nor enslaved. What did that mean for the freed people who arrived at army lines? What did it mean for the army? All those lingering questions made the First Confiscation Act difficult to enforce and easy to ignore.[15]

Meanwhile, enslaved people continued escaping to the army. By the spring of 1862, large camps of freedom seekers began forming around Washington, DC, and Fort Monroe; other camps formed along the coast of Georgia and the Carolinas on islands occupied by the US Army. Those camps have traditionally been known as "contraband camps," but historians have recently renamed them "slave refugee camps" because that's what they were: makeshift encampments and tent cities attached to the army and housing hundreds, sometimes thousands, of refugees from slavery, many of whom arrived with nothing while others carried all they had in a cart or wagon. Some refugees would eventually find work with the army. Men worked as teamsters or laborers; women often served as cooks or laundresses for a particular regiment. But not everyone found work. Others, especially women, children, and the elderly, lived as bona fide refugees, eking out an existence in the shadow of the army however they could.[16]

Out in the west, where the army moved deeper and deeper into the Mississippi Valley as 1862 wore on, the situation was the same except that the camps there tended to be larger and more numerous. Large numbers of enslaved people fled to Nashville after it fell in February 1862. The same was true for New Orleans when it fell in May, and even larger numbers of enslaved people began arriving in the area around Memphis once the army occupied the city later in June. By then, a pattern had clearly emerged: all along the army's path and especially in places where it had established firm control over a given area, enslaved people arrived in search of refuge. The experience was enough for some within the army to throw up their hands and ask for help from the government in deciding what to do. Ambrose Burnside, a US general known more for his characteristic facial hair than his generalship, captured the exasperation some felt when he wrote from New Bern, North Carolina, describing an attempt to deter the refugees as "utterly impossible."[17]

The collective movement of so many enslaved people into army lines during the first year of the war eventually forced Congress into a policy change. In July 1862, just over a year after the first refugees had arrived at Fort Monroe, Congress passed a second, far more comprehensive Confiscation Act that read like a virtual emancipation decree. It dispensed with the messy distinction that only enslaved people who had been forced to work for the Confederacy could attain refuge and instead declared that any enslaved person with a rebellious master who escaped to federal lines would now be "forever free of their servitude, and not again held as slaves." The new wording made achieving refuge more accessible. But it was the last bit that mattered most of all. The bill specifically mentioned freedom, which moved away from the language of confiscation and announced Congress's official endorsement of wartime emancipation. Enslaved people within occupied parts of the South could now escape to the army and expect freedom upon arrival.[18]

Few people knew, however, that as Congress debated the merits of emancipation on Capitol Hill, just a few blocks away in the White House, President Abraham Lincoln was planning an emancipation order of his own. He presented a prepared draft of an emancipation proclamation to his cabinet for the first time in late July 1862. The document, which he read aloud to his cabinet officials, was mostly modest and constrained. It built upon the precedents set by the two Confiscation Acts and described emancipation as a military measure backed by the legal authority he held as commander in chief. But whereas the Second Confiscation Act applied only to occupied parts of the South, Lincoln's proclamation went further by targeting the parts of the South still in rebellion—essentially, the rest of the Confederacy. But even that distinction carried an important caveat in that it didn't apply to the slaveholding states of Missouri, Maryland, Kentucky, and Delaware, none of which had ever left the Union. It also gave the targeted states until January 1, 1863, to surrender peacefully before Lincoln signed the new emancipation order into law.[19]

Lincoln's preliminary Emancipation Proclamation, which he

announced to the nation on September 22, 1862, following the bloody Battle of Antietam, featured the same sense of measured caution. As he had done in his meeting with his cabinet, he introduced the document by stating within the text that his principal goal was to restore the Union and that emancipation followed as a means of prosecuting the war. He held out an olive branch to any slave state willing to voluntarily end slavery by keeping open the possibility that the US government might compensate slave owners for their financial losses. By retaining his January 1 deadline for the targeted states to lay down their arms, he also gave them a hundred-day window to decide how they wanted to respond. But alongside those carrots, he included a couple of sticks, for instead of simply stating his intention to emancipate enslaved people, he ordered the army and navy to recognize the freedom of enslaved people and prohibited the military from returning freedom seekers who came into their lines. In doing so, he gave the army the authority to enact emancipation by military intervention. That gave the document teeth while still signaling to the American people that he was pursuing emancipation as a war measure and a war measure only.[20]

Yet no matter how careful Lincoln may have been in crafting the document, when he formally signed the Emancipation Proclamation on the afternoon of New Year's Day 1863, the signing immediately transformed the nature of the war. Not only did it change the war's meaning and purpose, turning a war for the preservation of the Union into a war to end slavery, it officially recognized the revolution that enslaved people had been unleashing all across the South. Indeed, like a clarion call throughout the region, the Emancipation Proclamation announced that freedom was now an official war aim. As such, it all but invited enslaved people to continue running to the US Army on the assumption that freedom was a federal promise guaranteed by the power of the US government. It also signaled to enslaved people that those massive federal armies—or, in the case of James Wells, even the smallest band of Union cavalry—were now armies of liberation, whether those armies perceived themselves as such or not. Perhaps only enslaved people themselves could have imagined that that was how the war would evolve.[21]

William Tecumseh Sherman—his middle name coming from his father's admiration of the famous Shawnee warrior—was among the many Americans who were never quite comfortable with the war's evolution. As many of his biographers have suggested, the general's racial views weren't all that different from those of the many Southerners he had befriended while serving in military posts across the South as a younger man. "I think it would be folly to liberate or materially alter the condition of the Slaves," he wrote his brother John, a soon-to-be US senator, before the war. He believed that the South had "inherited" the institution and felt that American slavery was the "mildest and best regulated slave system in the world, now or heretofore." His only problem with slavery, in fact, was that it drove people into their wildest passions: Southerners clung to it and abolitionists railed against it, an impasse that had hurled the country into what he believed was an avoidable war. To him, secession represented the more pressing issue. "On the necessity of maintaining a government, and that government the old Constitutional one, I have never wavered," he wrote, "but I do recoil from a war, when the negro is the only question."[22]

In his midforties when he rode into Atlanta, and with a hard, unshaven face, Sherman owed his life to the war. A native of eastern Ohio, his father, Charles Sherman, a lawyer and local judge, had died of typhoid fever in 1829 when Sherman was only nine years old. His mother, unable to provide for the family, had had no choice but send young "Cump," as he was known, to live with Thomas Ewing, a close friend of his father, who would soon rise in the world of national politics. As a result, Sherman grew up enjoying all the privileges of a prominent eastern Ohio family. He was well educated. He fell in love with the fine

arts, especially Shakespeare, and his foster father's connections opened
the door to West Point, where he excelled and soon found his chosen
career, despite Thomas Ewing urging him to find something better. Living with the Ewings all those years also introduced him to Ellen, Thomas
Ewing's daughter, whom he would later marry, which put him into the
sometimes awkward position of having his foster family as in-laws.[23]

It didn't help that nothing ever seemed to work out for him. After
leaving the army so he could make a better life for his family, he bounced
from one failed venture to the next. He unsuccessfully tried banking
in California on the heels of the Gold Rush; he tried banking in New
York before that ultimately failed, too; he worked as a glorified paralegal
in the law offices of his foster brothers turned brothers-in-law, which
relocated him and his family to Leavenworth, Kansas. He was desperate
and on the verge of accepting professional failure when an offer came to
head up a new military college in Alexandria, Louisiana, the precursor
of today's Louisiana State University. He eagerly accepted, both because
he needed a job and because the position would have him back working
among soldiers. When he arrived in the fall of 1859, everything was
to his liking. He was happy, solvent, and determined to make a go of
it. Then came the war. Louisiana seceded less than two years into his
tenure, and before he knew it, he was back staring failure in the face.[24]

The war would save him but not before giving him his share of heart-
ache and distress. Not only would he lose two sons from sickness during
the war, he suffered a bout of depression that brought him to the brink of
suicide. It happened in Louisville, Kentucky, in late 1861 when the *New-
York Daily Tribune* published an ill-intentioned report describing him
as "gloomy" and implying that he overestimated the enemy's strength.
The public affront to his military character triggered something in his
tired and anxious mind. He began crying wolf about an all-out Confederate assault on targets in the Midwest, including Louisville, which
was improbable at best and began speaking of "absolutely sacrificing"
untrained soldiers. The situation grew so worrying that an aide wrote

to Ellen, who found him in such rough shape that she wrote his brother John, asking him to help her snap Sherman out of his delusions. But it was no use. A military report declared him to be overstressed by the rigors of command, which led to a swift demotion.[25]

His rehabilitation tour began in Memphis, where, in the summer of 1862, he assumed command as the city's military governor. In some ways, governing, or *trying* to govern, Memphis may have been the most formative experience of his career, as it was there in that old cotton town where his distinctive "hard-war" policies were born. Ongoing guerrilla attacks and obstinate, thoroughly rebellious local residents prompted him to start expelling white families as a form of punishment. He also became infamous for responding to those attacks by launching reprisals against nearby towns and villages he suspected of harboring Confederate guerrillas: "the entire South, man, woman and child are all against us, armed and determined," he told his brother, adding "It will call for a million men for several years to put them down." His time there anticipated actions he would later take in Atlanta and elsewhere as he rose in rank, and his musings about the intensity of the war effort would also reappear in various forms later in his career.[26]

Yet Memphis was perhaps most formative for him because it was where he confronted the issue of emancipation for the first time. As his views about slavery might suggest, he believed in neither the necessity nor the reality of wartime emancipation, arguing that it created nothing but needless trouble for him and his men. His chief complaint was that freedom was an abstraction and that the burdens of dealing with it fell to underequipped men already engaged in fighting a war. "The President declares negroes free, but makes no machinery by which such freedom is assured," he wrote John from Memphis just after Lincoln released his preliminary Emancipation Proclamation. John, a sensible and shrewd Republican aware of the shifting political winds in Washington, did his best to bring his brother around on the issue, but the elder Sherman dug in, complaining that emancipation only complicated the war effort.

"We cannot now give tents to our soldiers and our wagon trains are a horrible impediment, and if we are to take along and feed the negroes who flee to us for refuge, it will be an impossible task," he carped. "You cannot solve this negro question in a day."[27]

Despite his tough talk about the folly of emancipation and its impact on the army, Sherman's record while commanding Memphis is mixed. On the one hand, he abided by the terms of the Second Confiscation Act, which went into effect as he began his governorship. When enslaved people came into the city seeking refuge, he refused to send them away or return them to their masters, as the law prescribed, despite countless numbers of local slave owners writing him for help. To his credit, he remained resolute on that score and relished writing back to planters, rebuking them for having the nerve to ask such a thing in a time of war. Yet on the other hand, his instinct was always to do little more than the law required. He wasn't shy about telling his brother, who had spoken up in support of the bill in the Senate, that he disapproved of the policy and wouldn't actually declare enslaved people free. To him, that was something only judges could do, and he wouldn't let John or any other politician convince him otherwise. He also refused to provide refuge to enslaved people unless they agreed to work for the army, a policy that privileged men over women because of the labor they could provide and incidentally left a whole host of women and children without access to the refuge of US Army lines.[28]

As the army began its descent into Georgia in the spring of 1864, another issue arose that revealed the full extent of Sherman's discomfort with the war's evolution. It had to do with the prospect of Black soldiers. Along with declaring enslaved people in the rebellious states free, the Emancipation Proclamation permitted Black men to enlist in the army for the first time. That had been a demand levied on the Lincoln administration by prominent African American abolitionists such as Frederick Douglass and other free Black leaders, most of whom saw African American military service as a means of claiming a right to US citizenship.

Congress had also been debating the policy since the start of the war and provided its consent in the Second Confiscation Act. Its enactment marked a decisive moment in the history of the war, as the formation of the United States Colored Troops (USCT) provided a major manpower advantage to the US Army. In total, close to 180,000 men, some born free and from the North and others formerly enslaved and from the South, would enlist, making up about a tenth of the entire US Army.[29]

Though Black enlistment would go down as one of the most important policy changes in the history of the war, Sherman resisted it at every turn. "I think the negro question is run into the ground," he griped to John from Chattanooga, echoing complaints he had made a year earlier when recruitment had begun in earnest. "I prefer to keep this a white man's war," he wrote to his wife in April 1863, adding "With my opinion of negroes and my experience, yea prejudice, I cannot trust them yet." Except that he had no intention of ever trusting them. Along the siege lines at Vicksburg, for instance, he did everything in his power to countermand the order. He stalled recruiting efforts, told troops that the policy would be revised, and assured his men that African American enlistees would be kept at "some side purpose" and not placed in combat roles. Writing to John, who criticized his brother's handling of the issue, he hit back, saying "I won't trust niggers to fight yet."[30]

Sherman's resistance to Black soldiers eventually forced a reckoning with Lincoln and the War Department on the road to Atlanta over who would have the final say on the implementation of emancipation policy: generals in the field or politicians in DC? The issue hinged on Sherman's preference for using freedmen as laborers rather than as soldiers. North of Atlanta, in Georgia's upper Piedmont, when the army began encountering refugees from slavery as it fought its way south during the campaign, he insisted on converting enslaved men who sought refuge within his lines into military laborers and sending the women, children, and elderly back to Chattanooga—or away from his lines completely. If he was to have freed people in his army at all, he wanted them kept in so-called pioneer roles, where they would perform the hard, menial tasks of fighting a war, drudgery such as building trenches, digging latrines, and burying the dead.[31]

Some of his objections to Black soldiers touched on his personal preference for slow, moderate action. "My preference is to make this radical change with natural slowness," he told a recruiter, referring to the policy of Black enlistment. He would even admit that the policy should be "fairly and honestly tested," but he always came back to the idea that the army should proceed with caution, especially at such a critical time in the war. With Atlanta within reach and the end of the war coming into view, he held that now wasn't the time to insert new soldiers into the mix. He also couldn't let go of the idea that enslaved people would serve the army best by serving as laborers. His obsession with military labor began in Memphis and grew in leaps and bounds the closer he got to Atlanta—in part because he knew that the Confederate Army used enslaved people in a similar fashion. "I believe that negroes better serve the Army as teamsters, pioneers, and servants, and have no objections to the surplus, if any, being enlisted as soldiers, but I must have labor and a large quantity of it," he told that same recruiter.[32]

Word of his immovability on the issue eventually climbed all the way up the chain of command and over to the White House. In August 1864, Lincoln wrote to Sherman, politely asking for his cooperation, but none came. Sherman stood firm. He told his commander in chief that while he had the "highest veneration of the law" and would "respect it always," that particular law conflicted with his own "opinion of its propriety." He then brushed off Lincoln's concerns by promising to address the issue in greater detail after Atlanta had been won. In response, Lincoln, desperate for a major victory and concerned about his own reelection chances that November, decided to let the issue rest. As a result, Sherman won a tacit political concession, suggesting that he could handle emancipation however he wished. It was a precedent he well remembered when he sat down to plan his next campaign.[33]

But after telling Lincoln that he would address the issue at a later date, Sherman wrote to another recruiting agent, explaining himself further. He claimed, in part, that freed people were "in a transition state" and thus not on a par with white soldiers, and that the army couldn't yet trust freed people to win the war. Then he wrote, "No one shall infer from this that I am not the Friend of the negro. . . . I and the armies I have commanded have conducted to safe points more negroes than those of any General officer in the army, but I prefer some negroes as pioneers, teamsters, servants, and cooks, others gradually to experiment in the art of the Soldier." That was him actually being somewhat tempered, but before he knew it, his letter fell into the hands of the press and began circulating in Northern newspapers. For the first time, the American people learned of his apparent insubordination as well as his hostility to the USCT, which wounded him deeply. "As to the negro letter I never would have dreamed it would be printed and made public," he told his brother not long after riding into Atlanta. To a friend, he was less conciliatory, blaming the scandal on the antislavery spirit of the war.[34]

As Sherman defended himself following the release of his "negro letter" in the fall of 1864, he began thinking about the road ahead. On the whole, the view from Atlanta as the army moved in and began its occupation was a far more promising picture than what he had seen as he had surveyed the field from Chattanooga earlier in the spring. The tide had clearly turned. In the east, General Ulysses S. Grant, Sherman's friend and superior and the head of the entire US Army, had engaged the Confederate Army repeatedly, with serious fights totaling massive casualties over a number of days. Though the Overland Campaign, as Grant's Virginia campaign is known, had produced brutal headlines in Northern papers, even earning Grant the nickname "the Butcher, " the strategy had clearly worked. By the early summer of 1864, Grant had successfully pushed General Robert E. Lee's Army of Northern Virginia across the James River, past Richmond, and now had it pinned down at Petersburg, a railroad junction just south of the Confederate capital. In early fall, as Sherman began his occupation of Atlanta, Grant made a few final attempts to break the siege at Petersburg before winter, but Lee's defensive positions held firm. Nevertheless, Grant had the enemy in front of him and victory within reach. He just had to wait through the cold.[35]

Sherman's position in Atlanta was less clear cut. Though Sherman controlled the city, Hood was gone. After evacuating Atlanta, Hood marched his beleaguered army back into Alabama, where he threatened Sherman's supply lines and prepared a move into Tennessee. Sherman could have followed him. He knew, however, that following Hood would mean abandoning hard-fought ground. "If I turn back now the whole effect of my campaign will be lost," he wrote to Grant in early November. He also knew that should he follow Hood, the Confederate general would likely keep retreating, forcing him and his army into a game of cat and mouse. The answer was thus to take decisive action. "Instead of being on the defensive I would be on the offensive, instead of guessing at what he intends to do he would have to guess at my plans," he wrote to Grant. With that, the decision was made: he would leave Atlanta and "strike out into the heart of Georgia." All that was left for him to do was to sort out the details and sell his strategy to his superiors.[36]

On the surface, Sherman's plan was simple: he planned to dispatch a wing of his army to deal with Hood, and he intended to march the rest, some sixty thousand men, deep into Georgia, through Macon and Milledgeville and on to Savannah. He wanted his final destination kept secret, even from his own men, so that Hood and Confederate president Jefferson Davis wouldn't know where he might turn up. Giving him the freedom to move was the fact that his chosen route lay virtually undefended. With Hood gone, the only Confederate forces left in Georgia were a smattering of militia and General Joseph Wheeler's

Confederate cavalry, in all maybe thirteen thousand soldiers. It was as if all Georgia—in effect, the Confederate heartland—sat ready for the taking. Moreover, a move through Georgia would give Sherman greater flexibility as to where he might go next. From Savannah, he could then move on to Columbia or Charleston—or mount a march through the Carolinas and into Virginia, all the while tightening the vise around Lee's position in Petersburg. Strategically, a campaign through Georgia had the potential to topple the Confederacy's entire house of cards.[37]

Yet Sherman's proposal was more than just a strategic end-around; it was an attempt to pummel the South into submission by breaking its people's will to fight. "I propose to demonstrate the vulnerability of the South and make its inhabitants feel that war & individual Ruin are synonimous [sic] terms," he wrote while still pondering his potential routes. Later, in another missive, he repeated himself, but added, "They [Southerners] don't know what war means, but when the rich planters . . . see their fences and corn and hogs and sheep vanish before their eyes they will have something more than a mean opinion of the 'Yanks.'" In other words, it would be no ordinary campaign. Sherman intended to target the South's material ability to withstand the war as much as any Confederate army, all but rending the Confederacy apart by devastating and demoralizing its citizenry. "Until we can repopulate Georgia it is useless to occupy it, but the utter destruction of its roads, houses, and people will cripple their military resources," he explained to the skeptical Grant, telling him "I can make the march and make Georgia howl."[38]

Though historians have long speculated about Sherman's intentions and whether his tactics birthed the idea of "total war," the truth is that he saw his plan as little more than a raw form of nineteenth-century statecraft. "If we can march a well-appointed Army right through his territory, it is a demonstration to the World, foreign and domestic, that we have a power which [Jefferson] Davis cannot resist," he told Grant in November. "This may not be war," he went on, "but rather Statesmanship, nevertheless, it is overwhelming to my mind that there are thousands of people abroad and in the South who will reason thus—'If the North can march an army right through the South, it is proof positive that the North can prevail in this contest,' leaving only open the question of the North's willingness to use that power." War in that case was in fact politics conducted by other means. The March would be more than a matter of military expediency; it would be a means of asserting the legitimate power of the United States by claiming a monopoly on violence and discrediting a belligerent nation to the point of complete capitulation—a show of modern state power stripped down to its starkest form.[39]

Sherman's plans for the March also reflected a new military strategy, which he and Grant had hashed out earlier in the year. Previously, the fighting had revolved around capturing capital cities and transportation hubs, so-called strategic points. The duo's experience in the west, marked by the bloody victory at Shiloh and the long siege of Vicksburg, had convinced them that capturing such points deflected resources away from what they recognized as the fundamental reality of the war: defeating the Confederacy meant defeating Confederate armies. What the two envisioned instead was a strategy that would place greater pressure on the Confederacy by pursuing the enemy, not just capturing key cities, and mobilizing the full force of the Union Army until the Confederate armies in the field had nowhere to go. That had been the strategy behind the Atlanta Campaign, a bruising, unrelenting campaign of near-constant combat, and though Sherman would ultimately eschew chasing Hood and target Savannah, that general strategy animated the March to the Sea: "To stop war we must defeat the Rebel Armies," Sherman would write from Atlanta, adding that "To defeat those armies we must prepare the way to reach them in their recesses."[40]

At the same time, the underlying strategy of Sherman's March embodied a much larger evolution in how the war was fought. Though it had begun as a limited or contained war, it had grown increasingly harsher and more all-encompassing as the conflict wore on. Lincoln's embrace of military emancipation signaled a shift toward that more unrestrained mode of war. So had the federal government's use of a military draft, the first in US history, as had the sheer ferocity of the fighting. Sherman, his resistance to military emancipation notwithstanding, had been one of the great proselytizers of this harder, less restrained turn in the war from the very beginning. His March through the state of Georgia was thus in some ways him unleashing his basic instincts about the unsparing nature of the war. As he told the mayor of Atlanta, "You cannot qualify war in harsher terms than I will. War is cruelty, and you cannot refine it: and those who brought war into our Country deserve all the curses and maledictions a people can pour out."[41]

Still, despite Sherman's confidence in his ability to make the March, Grant had serious reservations. The issue was not necessarily strategy. While Grant preferred a much stronger movement to push Hood away from Tennessee, he trusted Sherman's judgment. The issue was logistics. Marching through Georgia would require relinquishing the army's supply lines in Atlanta, which would mean practically detaching the army from any base of support. The soldiers, all sixty thousand of them, would have to move across the state foraging whatever they could find. It was a risk Grant was not sure was worth taking, especially after corralling Lee at Petersburg, taking Atlanta, and sending Hood fleeing into Alabama. It involved too many unnecessary risks: What if Georgia wasn't as bountiful as Sherman imagined? What if Wheeler's cavalry pestered Sherman to the point of slowing the army down? What if the rivers and roads proved too difficult for a marching army to navigate? Potential pitfalls presented themselves at every stage, though Grant eventually gave in. "Great good fortune attend you," he wrote, telling his friend "I believe you will be eminently successful." It was the green light Sherman needed to start "smashing things to the sea."[42]

Preparations began in earnest on November 9, when Sherman issued his official campaign orders. His first order pertained to military structure. He reorganized the army into two wings. He gave General

Oliver Otis Howard, a native of Maine, command of the right wing and General Henry W. Slocum, a dapper New Yorker, command of the left. Sherman then provided orders for how he wanted the foraging done. He instructed his men to "forage liberally," giving them license to appropriate enough food for ten days at a time. Soldiers were never to enter homes or threaten civilians; only corps commanders had the authority to burn cotton gins, cotton mills, and plantation homes. If local whites obstructed the campaign, sheltered guerrillas, or attacked any of his men, his officers could enforce "a devastation more or less relentless according to the measure of such hostility." Furthermore, any of his mounted men could appropriate pack animals as they wished, though he urged restraint in taking animals from the poor, who he presumed could hardly afford such a loss and were generally apathetic about the war; but he encouraged force in the case of the rich, who he felt could afford to lose a horse or two and were, he believed, still keeping up the fight.[43]

His last order, attached at the end almost like an afterthought, detailed his plans for the enslaved men and women the army would meet as it moved deeper into Georgia's rich plantation belt. It read: "Negroes who are able-bodied and can be of service to the army may be taken along, but each army commander will bear in mind that the question of supplies is a very important one and that his first duty is to see to them who bear arms." The order was all Sherman would allow by way of a "refugee policy," and its cursory nature deserves consideration. In some respects, its interest in only those who could work, its subtle urging to remember the problem of supplies and provisions, its insistence on provisioning soldiers first, and its implied endorsement of military impressment—of ambiguously suggesting that enslaved men and women might be "taken along"—all align with how Sherman had approached enslaved people. From Memphis to Atlanta and at stops in between, emancipation had never been one of his stated objectives. He had either resisted it, qualified it, or manipulated it to meet his own needs or opinions. He was a cautious, if reluctant, liberator, and the working of his supposed "refugee policy" crystallized his reluctance into place.[44]

Yet the order is also baffling in a way. Sherman may have been reluctant to fully embrace emancipation, but he had also been stationed in Memphis. He had spent many months fighting in Mississippi. As a young man, he had even lived in the South and had once traveled through the same Georgia countryside he was on the verge of invading. In other words, he knew slavery. He knew the size of the plantations between Atlanta and Savannah. He must also have known from the raids and other movements that enslaved people would flock to the army and persist even in the face of death or recapture. Though he might have had no idea just how large an emancipation event the March would become, how many men and women might follow his army, or how many more might join him in Savannah, he had to have known that his "refugee policy" was hardly suitable. Surely he knew, too, that at that point in the war, with victory within reach and the Emancipation Proclamation now two years old, emancipation was no longer something he could ignore.

The order's principal shortcoming was that it was written with a certain conceit, as if the army alone would determine the course of emancipation. That had never been the case, and the March would reveal the ways in which emancipation evolved according to the *pull* of the army and the *push* of enslaved people. Sherman could plan one vision for the campaign, but enslaved people would respond according to their own vision of what the March meant. At every stop along those dusty Georgia roads, these two competing visions of the war, emancipation, and the army's role in inaugurating the new birth of freedom came into contact, turning the March into a month-and-a-half-long collision course exposing the highs, the lows, the hopes and failures, and all the beauty and horror of how emancipation actually happened. Sherman's March has been remembered mostly as the campaign that conquered the South, but the underlying battle between soldiers and enslaved people was what gave the March its most profound meaning.

The campaign started, perhaps appropriately so, with a fire. For several days, from November 12 through 16, Atlanta burned once more. Tall billows of smoke rose high overhead. "FIRE! FIRE!! FIRE!!! In every corner of the city," wrote one soldier. Another compared the flames to "ocean waves" roiling the city before "struggling upward like a thousand banners in the sky." Contrary to local lore and Civil War legend, Sherman never intended to burn Atlanta completely to the ground, at least not officially. Instead, he ordered a selective destruction of all the city's military assets—"all depots, car-houses, shops, factories, foundries, &c.," as he told his chief engineer, adding that "fire will do most of the work." By that time, Atlanta was the last industrial center left in the South besides Richmond, and Sherman's goal was to neutralize whatever arms-producing capacity it still had. Notably, there was no mention of burning residential buildings, though Sherman may have expected that soldiers would take matters into their own hands and was willing to look the other way as stray fires engulfed the city.[45]

Indeed, as early as November 6, with the plans for the coming campaign still up in the air, Sherman informed Grant that he planned to leave Atlanta "utterly destroyed." He had perhaps already set his plans into motion as early as September, mere days after the occupation had begun, when he issued expulsion orders, forcing local civilians to either flee or face arrest. In response, Atlanta's locals raised a ruckus. Even Hood, Sherman's Confederate rival, wrote to him, protesting the policy, but Sherman held firm. "If the people raise a howl against my barbarity & cruelty, I will answer that War is War & not popularity seeking. If they want peace, they & their relations must stop war," he explained to his old friend General Henry Halleck, the army chief of staff.[46]

Yet even if Sherman planned to torch Atlanta without quarter, the now-famous inferno likely spread beyond anything he could have imagined. Exploding buildings sparked raging fires that spread from structure to structure, and rowdy, uncontrollable men were let loose upon the town, torching shops and stores and even a few homes while singing the patriotic tune "John Brown's Body." As had happened when Hood had destroyed his own arsenals before evacuating the city in September, fires lit stores of unused munitions, causing shells to burst all through the night. Sherman even remembered an explosion erupting not far from his own official headquarters—a startling signal that the blaze had gone beyond anyone's control. By the morning of the fourteenth, the devastation was enough for the reporter David Conyngham to describe Atlanta as "a thing of the past." Whole city blocks—the "heart of the city," as Sherman later remembered—had been set aflame and reduced to rubble. The next morning, November 15, with the city still smoldering and a pall of smoke lingering in the air, the army rose to begin its next campaign. Sherman's great March to the Sea began.[47]

Sherman and his generals circa 1865. From left to right: Seated: John Alexander Logan, William Tecumseh Sherman, Henry Warner Slocum. Standing: Oliver Otis Howard, William Babcock Hazen, Jefferson Columbus Davis, Joseph Anthony Mower. All but Logan took part in the Savannah Campaign.

Chapter Two

THE POLITICS OF THE PLANTATION

O n November 13, as the city of Atlanta burned and the army readied itself for the march through Georgia, Henry Hitchcock, an adjutant general, paced across a livestock stable in Marietta, Georgia. With horses moving around him, he probably checked his watch. He may have even cursed a time or two. It was his first assignment, and he was already late. Worse, if he dawdled any longer, he would miss what was sure to be the grandest campaign of the war and his chance to witness it while riding with Sherman and his staff. His duties serving in the state government of his native Missouri had already kept him from much of the war, and if it had not been for a well-connected uncle who had pulled some strings and gotten him assigned as one of Sherman's staff officers, he might have missed the war completely. Instead, he now found himself serving, in effect, as Sherman's personal scribe. "Pray don't think me likely to turn Boswell to any man's Johnson," he wrote to his wife, referencing the famed English writer and his distinguished biographer. As he saw it, it was his last chance to claim a piece of the war, and if he couldn't shoulder a musket or raise a saber, he could at least wield the one weapon he knew he could use with expert proficiency: his pen.[1]

He was getting angry now. He had been up before dawn and had to leave by a quarter to seven, but Aleck was nowhere to be found. Like many officers of his rank and position, Hitchcock had hired a personal manservant before leaving Atlanta. Typically male and mostly formerly enslaved, manservants—or valets—were commonplace among the traveling caravan that was the US Army. They helped dress their bosses, carried their personal belongings, built fires, and cared for horses—all the tasks that made camp life less of a burden. Hitchcock had hired Aleck the night before and had given him time to arrange safe passage for his family—"wife, Laura, mother, Amy, and three children"—out of town. He had also promised to help Aleck and his family afterward if he served faithfully, but that morning, a future relationship did not seem likely. Then, to Hitchcock's great surprise, Aleck arrived "running, breathless," and with "traces of tears." He had been at the depot to see off his wife and family before they left for Chattanooga. "Disarmed" but also relieved, Hitchcock told him to "hurry up now." The army wouldn't wait.[2]

Over the next six months, Hitchcock got exactly what he wanted. He got his taste of the war while marching into history. He saw it all—Georgia, the Carolinas, even the Grand Review in Washington, DC—and he recorded his experiences in a campaign diary that has become an indispensable record of the March. And Aleck? Aside from the occasional compliment or complaint, Aleck remains mostly invisible throughout. Hitchcock often commented on the enslaved people he met while serving on the general's staff, but he never stopped to write more than a line or two about Aleck or muse about what Aleck thought of it all. Yet the basic fact of the diary is that Hitchcock wrote himself into history while riding first class on the back of Aleck's labor, which gave him the comfort to collect his thoughts and the time to write, thus preserving the March for all posterity. Not only does Aleck deserve appreciation for his services, it is worth noting that innumerable freed people just like him toiled away for those documenting the war. In fact, Hitchcock once even described his conversations with George Ward Nichols, a fellow staff officer and diarist of the March, about the relative strengths of their two servants, Aleck and Sam. Any history of the March owes as much to them and their labor as to those who wrote it all down.[3]

Yet the better question about Aleck is not "Where?" but "Why?" Why would he, presumably a freed person, leave his wife and children to serve at the behest of a white officer embarking on a dangerous military journey through the heart of the slave South? Money was likely a factor. The allure of military service probably was, too. But considering that a stray bullet could end the payments and that in this case, service meant shouldering a saddlebag instead of a gun, neither of these factors alone explains why Aleck left his wife and family. We don't know why he did so and probably never will, but we do know this: for Aleck to take such a drastic and unknown step, he must have felt as if he were on the verge of something momentous, as if some great opportunity knocked. In that sense, he and Hitchcock, his new employer, shared one thing in common: they both knew that they couldn't miss the next campaign.

In the early days of the campaign, Sherman's great March seemed destined to live up to expectations. Signs of the campaign's progress rose high over the treetops: "Dense volumes of smoke can already be seen looming up in massive billows to the skies," wrote a private from Illinois, explaining that smoke was often "a most truthful indication" of the army's whereabouts. "At times the whole circle of the horizon is dark with smoke that arises from fires," wrote another, casting blame on the Georgia pines, which caught fire and sent "writhing flames" up to their "topmost branches." Some of the smoke was probably a spillover from the blaze that seared Atlanta. On the first days out, thick wisps of smoke rolled by as the army marched from the once bustling railroad hub. But as the long blue columns moved further into Georgia, signs of fire telegraphed the army's movements, alerting one column to the movements of the other due to the amount of cotton being burned. For Georgia's enslaved communities, who anxiously monitored the army's movements, those same thick clouds signaled that the army was slowly circling in and would soon swarm all around, which made pillars of smoke signs of freedom and terror all at once.[4]

The first enslaved communities to see smoke on the horizon were those to the south and east of Atlanta. Coming out of the city, the army's two wings split into two corps each, moving like four legs along corresponding paths. Henry Slocum's left wing, made up of the Fourteenth and Twentieth Corps, took the more easterly route. The plan was for Slocum's two columns—the Fourteenth Corps, commanded by General Jefferson C. Davis, and the Twentieth, led by General Alpheus Williams—to converge on Decatur, just east of Atlanta, before gently sloping south toward Conyers, Madison, and Eatonton, small Piedmont towns to the southeast of Atlanta. Somewhere around Milledgeville, the state capital, Slocum was to start angling his lines down toward Savannah and the thick, swamplike channels of the Savannah River, where the landscape would become as much of an impediment as any stated enemy. That was especially true for Davis's Fourteenth Corps, whose lines came the closest to the Savannah River and made up the army's far left flank.

Oliver Otis Howard's right wing—the Fifteenth and Seventeenth Corps, commanded by General Peter Osterhaus and General Francis Preston Blair, Jr., respectively—took the other route, marching due south from Atlanta before eventually turning to the southeast. That route took Howard's two columns through Jonesboro and Jackson. The idea was to make a feint on Macon, the largest city in middle Georgia, which sits in the dead center of the state, before turning east toward Savannah and Georgia's coastal plain. Osterhaus's Fifteenth Corps took up the farthest right flank, which meant that his lines swept the farthest to the south for the entirety of the March. In either case, once through Macon and Milledgeville, both wings began heading east for Savannah. Each column's path ran it headlong into Georgia's "Black Belt," an immensely fertile region named for its abundant layers of airy black topsoil, which is to say that all the forces marched down into the heart of Georgia's slave system.[5]

But the army didn't need to march that far to witness slavery, for enslaved people constantly moved toward the army. Sherman and his staff had no sooner left Atlanta's burnt-out shadow before that reality set in. On the first day's march, on a roadside just past Decatur, Sherman and his team of traveling officers, riding first with Slocum's left wing alongside a cavalry escort, met an enslaved man, who explained that two of his peers had already run to the army. Hitchcock wrote that the man was now *"in possession,"* which meant that he had either been impressed into service or allowed to join the army on his own accord. But perhaps the most salient part of the encounter was less that the man had *come* to the army or that he had *joined* the army, "in possession" or otherwise, and more that he told Sherman and the staff that he thought himself worth "$100,000," a vast exaggeration. The actual average price of an enslaved person was somewhere in the range of $800. The man was likely inflating his worth in an attempt to convince Sherman to let him come along, but the point is that he did so by leveraging the value that he knew hung over his head. It was an example of the chattel principle—the idea that the enslaved were "living property" or a "people with a price"—in action and an example of exactly what was at stake in the army's seeing emancipation through.[6]

Indeed, the man's self-appraisal serves as a stark reminder that emancipation is a story about how slavery died as much as about how people became free. Admittedly, this is a fine distinction. Hitchcock certainly didn't understand it, at least not at first. But he began to do so when he spoke with the enslaved people he met along the way. When doing that became a regular occurrence, the institution's barbarity became hard to ignore. Most shocking in those early days was what he heard at a plantation near the Alcovy River just outside Covington. It was a place owned by a man named Judge Harris, who possessed "sixty or more slaves," according to Hitchcock. At first, the visit was a pleasant surprise. Several enslaved men had escaped from a nearby plantation and arrived willing to share their stories, which Hitchcock—a lawyer with a knack for deposing witnesses—took full advantage of, using the occasion to hold what amounted to an unofficial inquiry into how enslaved people viewed the war.[7]

Hitchcock immediately pressed one of the men on whether he believed all the rumors of what the army had done to enslaved people in Atlanta: "No sir!!" the man replied. "We didn't believe it—we has faith in you!" He then asked another why he had run away, given the risk involved. "I was bound to come," the man said, telling Hitchcock that the "[local whites] don't think nothing 'bout here of tying a feller up and givin' him 200 or 300 *with the strap*." Another enslaved man explained that he had caught word of his master and his family preparing to "run off all their negroes down to Macon and thence to Florida." When told to saddle up the horse that morning, the man saddled the horse and then "rode over to the Yankees himself." Yet what a man named Uncle Stephen said impressed Hitchcock the most. Enslaved by Judge Harris, Uncle Stephen was reluctant to talk at first but then explained to the staff exactly what he thought of the war, saying that it was "mighty distressin'" but that "*the right thing couldn't be done* without it." To Hitchcock, a war booster at heart, that was what he wanted to hear, and he ate it up, writing "the old fellow hit it, exactly."[8]

Then, as Hitchcock and the others were preparing to leave, the mood among the staff grew darker and more indignant. George Ward Nichols, one of Hitchcock's colleagues, had a long talk with the plantation driver. Drivers were typically enslaved men charged with the task of regulating the work of their peers and reporting back to the master or overseer, which sometimes placed them in a leadership position within a slave community and sometimes alienated them from the community, depending on how they handled their role. In this case, the man was trusted enough to speak for the enslaved women on the plantation. He told Nichols, who told the rest of the staff, that despite being elderly and having a family, Judge Harris "obliges" the enslaved women to "submit to him, and *straps* them if they refuse," an admission that shocked the staff.

On top of learning that Judge Harris was a serial rapist, Hitchcock and others discovered why one of the older men on the place had but one leg. Apparently, Harris's wife, the plantation mistress, had "deliberately" shot him over an issue with how the man planted potatoes—and for that, he had lost a leg. From then on, Hitchcock remained troubled by acts of wanton foraging while on the March, but he became less bothered by the misery the army inflicted on the white population. The war needed winning, but more specifically, slavery had to die.[9]

Elsewhere in those early days, enslaved communities greeted Sherman's columns as if slavery was already dead. In McDonough, just south of Atlanta, one Ohioan recorded that as the army passed through the town, enslaved people went "wild with joy." Another wrote, "So far as the negroes were concerned, they seemed overjoyed to see us." While enslaved people tended to err on the side of caution, on street corners and in town squares their excitement spilled over, often showing itself in the form of raucous street performances and collective celebrations. Adding the fact that so many of the encounters happened alongside military bands and raised flags, along with horses and lines of marching soldiers, the March must have seemed like one grand emancipatory parade. "The bands played as the column marched through the town, attracting crowds of negroes, who often joined the marching column, sure that their day of freedom had arrived," remembered a soldier with the 55th Ohio Volunteer Infantry Regiment. Another remembered seeing enslaved people crowding around the edges of the road, looking up and down the lines of soldiers, marveling at the numbers of men passing through. A Pennsylvania veteran painted a similar picture, writing that "The [enslaved] men doffed their hats" amid "Shouts of 'Glory to God!' and 'Bless the Lord!'"[10]

The shouts, prayers, and praise brought a spirit of revival to the affair. The catharsis—the feeling of release, not just the physical and emotional release of one's own enslavement but of history, of escaping four hundred years of human bondage—was real, and religion was a medium powerful enough to hold the kind of profound meaning that enslaved people ascribed to the moment. It tapped deep roots. For centuries, enslaved people in the United States and other parts of the Americas had been fashioning and refashioning elements of Christianity in accordance with their own needs, beliefs, and worldview. For some, religion was a form of resistance. For others, it was a pillar of hope and a promise of some future reckoning. Just as God had done with the Israelites of the Old Testament, leading them out of bondage and away from Egypt, so, too, he would do for the enslaved people of America. And as the God of the Old Testament promised, he would one day return and right the world according to his pledge to his people.[11]

It makes sense, then, that as the March unleashed the joys of emancipation, it evolved into a profound religious experience. "The whole land seemed to be inhabited by negroes," wrote John Richards Boyle, a Pennsylvania soldier, "and the appearance of the army inspired them with a profound religious sentiment and awakened in them the most extraordinary religious emotion." "They [enslaved people] were frantic with joy," remembered Adin B. Underwood, a Massachusetts soldier, writing that it was as if they had "long heard about it [the March], and yearned for it, and were warned by some under-ground telegraph that the day of the Lord had come." With that religious feeling permeating the lines, Sherman marched into what was practically his own deification. "Wherever Sherman rode, they [enslaved people] crowded about him shouting and praying with a touching eloquence," wrote Underwood. Sherman even wrote to his wife from Savannah, "It would amuse you to see the negroes; they flock to me, old and young, they pray and shout and mix up my name with Moses, and Simon, and other scriptural ones as well as 'Abram Linkom,' the Great Messiah of 'Dis Jubilee.'"[12]

There is a mocking tone in Sherman's description of how enslaved people regarded him, and there's more than a little white saviorism at work in the self-significant way soldiers remembered the religious enthusiasm of enslaved people. But that religious feeling, even if mocked and contorted by white soldiers, is important because it shows that enslaved people experienced emancipation as a fulfillment of biblical prophecy: "The majority [of enslaved people] accept the advent of the Yankees as the fulfillment of the millennial prophecies," remembered George Ward Nichols. That religious millennialism, it turns out, was more than a recurring theme; it was the keynote of the entire March, and the idea of "Jubilee" represented the central cord—the central metaphor, if you will—tying the experience together. The idea appears everywhere: a foreign correspondent reported that enslaved people welcomed the soldiers while proclaiming that "de day of jubilee hab arribed!"; another soldier wrote, "While the whites are in perfect consternation, the blacks hail our approach as a day of jubilee"; and perhaps most evocatively, another soldier reported that in Eatonton, as the "calaboose [jail] and whipping stocks were burned," enslaved men and women "danced to see them in flames" all while "under the impression that the year of jubilee had come."[13]

Within the first week of the campaign, it seemed as if the day of Jubilee had indeed arrived. Not only were enslaved men and women escaping bondage, the start of the March went off without a hitch. "Certainly *this* is the 'perfection of campaigning,'" wrote Hitchcock, describing those first few weeks. An Illinois soldier marching with Howard's right wing put it in more extravagant terms, calling the campaign "probably the most gigantic pleasure excursion ever planned." The soldiers were all happy, triumphant, and parading around like conquerors. But that was on the road and on the March, where the army's movement obscured the work that made its pace and relative peace possible. Out on the farms and plantations of central Georgia, where Sherman's foragers descended and did the work of crushing the Confederacy in mind, body, and spirit, there was a different version of the March breaking out at stops all along the route toward Savannah. In that space soldiers and enslaved people met on a much different footing and on a field of battle unlike any other in the history of the war, which casts the story of emancipation in a far more unstable and perilous light. Christ, you might remember, promised a return, but he also promised a struggle.[14]

They had different names. Officially, Sherman and the War Department called them foragers. They were troops organized into small foraging parties that would fan out from the main column to do what their name implies: they would forage for food and goods from nearby plantations and farms, which made them the foot soldiers in Sherman's plan to destroy the material base of the South. Unofficially, however, soldiers often referred to them using the more colloquial term "bummers," except that more informal moniker is itself somewhat confusing. To some, the term *bummer* was simply a stand-in for *forager*. To others, *bummer* was a slight pejorative, describing foragers who had gone rogue. They were men or groups of men who broke protocol, cut away from the army or larger parties, and took the task of debilitating the Confederate home front into their own unrestrained hands. Complicating matters even further was that sometimes the so-called bummers were "stragglers" or "hangers-on"—men who traveled behind the army. Perhaps most telling was that oftentimes the soldiers couldn't distinguish one from the other, which speaks to the chaos that broke out during the campaign.[15]

Foraging fueled the army. Early each morning groups of soldiers as large as a hundred or more detached from the main column and roamed into the countryside, typically splitting into smaller groups as they went. They moved fast and with authority—"jest lak thunder," one enslaved woman remembered—before returning to the roadside with their bounty. "When the treasure-trove of grain, and poultry, and vegetables has been secured, one man was detailed to guard it until the proper wagon came along," wrote one soldier, remembering how the foragers sat "upon some crossroad, surrounded with their spoils—chickens, turkeys, geese, ducks, pigs, hogs, sheep, calves, nicely dressed hams, buckets full of honey and pots of fresh lard." Nearly all found central Georgia particularly lush. One soldier described it as the "granary of the South." The men consumed an abundance of corn and sweet potatoes. They burned copious amounts of cotton, sometimes lighting gins and cotton houses on fire, and they requisitioned livestock such as horses, mules, and cows. Foraging had occurred elsewhere in the war, but rarely in such deliberate fashion and on such a large scale for such an extended period of time.[16]

To be fair, Sherman had never intended for the March to be the kind of spasm of wanton plundering that popular Civil War mythmaking sometimes makes it out to be. He maintained that foraging should be done "by the book." As he outlined in his campaign orders, soldiers were not supposed to enter houses or commit trespass, only officers could order the burning of property, and theoretically there was a limit to how much foraging parties could take; they were supposed to only take what was needed to maintain ten days' worth of food. The soldiers understood that they were to never assail noncombatants—unless, of course, something was done that merited swift vengeance, such as firing upon foraging parties or actively resisting the army. Also, as mentioned earlier, soldiers were to make distinctions between poor farmers, who seemed defeated by the war and ready to switch loyalties, and the rich planters, who, on the whole, owned lots of slaves and property and continued to prop up the war effort. Those were the rules, and for the most part, the army tried to enforce them—at least at first.[17]

But the orders failed to keep the foraging parties from slipping out of hand. For one thing, Sherman's language was vague and contradictory. Despite laying out the rules for the March, he also, in the same orders, instructed his men to "forage liberally," which the soldiers understood as a subtle nod to do as they pleased. In one instance, Sherman himself came upon a soldier with his face buried in a bottle of molasses. When he became aware of Sherman's presence, the man looked up and cried out, "Forage liberally!" to excuse his behavior. Moreover, while Sherman ordered leniency in the case of poor or small farmers, that distinction was never all that clear or closely followed. Though the soldiers reserved a special kind of vengeance for large planters, small farmers were never protected or immune. It is also worth pointing out that every homestead, large or small, represented a potential place of battle as scores of Confederate officials, including the state governor, called on citizens to rise up and harass the army as it moved.[18]

Inevitably, too, there were moments along the March when the chaos of such a large body of men moving at such a rapid pace simply consumed the countryside, breaking down any semblance of order. Times like those were when some of the worst excesses and abuses occurred. "It is becoming apparent that unprincipled men are taking advantage of the license given them to forage, and are pillaging," wrote S. F. Fleharty of the 102nd Illinois Infantry Volunteers in late November after being on the road with the army's left wing for more than two weeks. Similarly, Harvey Reid of the 22nd Wisconsin Infantry Regiment documented how hard it had been to keep the plundering at bay, especially once official foraging parties left and the stragglers began playing by their own rules. "A guard is placed at every house we pass with order to admit no soldier, but he only remains while his division is passing," he explained, adding "then come the trains accompanied by a thousand 'bummers,'" who "ransack the house, taking every knife and fork, spoon, or anything else they take a fancy to, break open trunks and bureaus, taking women['s] or children's clothing, or tearing them to pieces, trampling upon them and so forth besides taking everything eatable that can be found."[19]

Enslaved people had more than a few reasons to fear the foraging parties. The sight of armed white men alone was reason enough for caution. In addition, though enslaved people had their own sense of the war and what it was about, nothing was certain. Even if enslaved people trusted the soldiers, they had no idea what would transpire when foragers arrived and started rifling through the plantation—or if a fight broke out on their doorstep. There was also an issue of food scarcity. By 1864, after nearly four long years of war and a debilitating blockade, some plantations, particularly those in the swampy, less fertile pine barrens to the southeast, suffered serious food insufficiencies, and it was enslaved people who bore the brunt of the shortages. There was thus a cruel irony at play: an approaching army could bring freedom, but scavenging soldiers could just as easily pick the place clean and leave an enslaved community destitute. All that was why for every celebration that began in towns and on roadsides across Georgia, equal numbers of enslaved people preferred exercising caution by keeping the soldiers at arm's length.[20]

Compounding the complexity of the situation was that as enslaved people watched, waited, and did their best to determine the soldiers' intentions, a rumor war raged between them and their masters. It was a conflict that had been raging across the South for most of the war. In the face of an approaching army, enslavers typically spread erroneous stories about how the US Army treated enslaved people. One common tale in Georgia held that during the Battle of Atlanta, Sherman had used enslaved people as cannon fodder and shot those who had dared run away; another conspiracy theory was that as the troops had left Atlanta, they had rounded up enslaved people and locked them inside burning buildings. There were additional stories of forced drownings and a constant vilifying of all things Yankee. "The negroes were told that, as soon as we got them into our clutches, they were put into the front of battle, and were killed if they did not fight; that we threw women and children into the Chattahoochee, and when the buildings were burned in Atlanta we filled them with negroes to be roasted and devoured by the flames," wrote George Ward Nichols, describing the wide gamut of tales about Sherman and his men.[21]

What white slaveholders were too conceited to realize, however, was that the informational war was never as one-sided as they imagined. Enslaved people tended to know much more about the war than they let on and were often one step ahead of those who enslaved them. Fenwick Hedley, an adjutant from Illinois, wrote that "in countless instances" enslaved people had possessed news of the war in advance of the troops as well as the local whites. Their knowledge so amazed the soldiers that common folklore held that enslaved people had some underground circuit of information relaying information across the South. Hitchcock reported the same. At a stop near Millen on the army's left flank, he met a group of enslaved men whose spokesman was "perfectly aware of Lincoln's Proclamation." When asked about recent Confederate discussions about arming slaves, the man replied that he knew about that, too. Asked if he would fight for the Confederacy, the man bluntly shot back, "No sir—de day dey gives us arms, *dat day de war ends!*"[22]

Given all that enslaved people knew, the absurd stories about Yankee depredations typically fell on deaf ears. Some enslaved men and women believed them, but on the whole, most ignored them for what they were: desperate attempts at control. John Van Duser, one of the army's chief telegraph officers, reported that a group of enslaved people from Conyers had been told that the army had locked enslaved people inside burning buildings in Atlanta, but he concluded that "not one of them believe [*sic*] such stories." For many, the logic was as simple as a kind of "enemy of my enemy" rationale. "What for de Yankees want to hurt black men?" one enslaved man asked George Ward Nichols as the March moved along. "Massa hates de Yankees, and he's no fren' ter we; so we am de Yankee bi's fren's." Others held a much more intuitive position, knowing full well that if slavery had been the cause of the war, emancipation was its clear consequence. It is also likely that local whites had already lost what little credibility they had left by the time the army marched through. One enslaved man told Hitchcock that his master had insisted that he would "wade in blood knee deep before Yankees come here" but had then run off like a scalded dog once word had come that the army was roaming about nearby. Another joked that all the slaveholding families were "very brave" and then just "*git up and dust*" once the army drew near. When local planters fled like that, it was clear that the charade was up.[23]

Moreover, knowledge transformed enslaved people into active wartime agents. Take what happened whenever the army descended on a plantation and began foraging as an example. As was common across the South, slaveholding families along the March prepared for the army's arrival by hiding their valuables and foodstuffs. Men and women stored family heirlooms and food under floorboards. They ordered horses, cows, mules, and other farm animals out to corrals hidden deep in adjoining woods or swamps. The most common move was to pile personal possessions in large trunks and bury them in either a field or a family graveyard. Foraging parties were wise to the practice, so when soldiers arrived at a plantation, the scene devolved into a glorified scavenger hunt. Soldiers checked corner closets and storehouses, interrogated white families, and even went about looking for signs of uprooted dirt. "It was amusing to see the foragers going around prodding the ground with their ramrods or bayonets, seeking for soft spots," wrote one Ohio soldier, who once had the surprise of his life when the foragers found a "live citizen" buried with a cache of goods and only his nose sticking up from the earth.[24]

Yet few white families ever hid the items themselves. Instead, they forced their bondsmen and women to do it for them, which armed enslaved people with knowledge of where most everything had been hidden and made them third-party brokers in the ongoing standoff between foragers and local whites. If the soldiers appeared unfriendly or too intrusive, enslaved people could withhold what they knew, calculating that it was best to avoid men brandishing bayonets. Or, if they had a mind to, enslaved people could tip the scales in favor of the army, which they overwhelmingly did at stops all along the March. "We would have seen harder times but for the colored people," remembered a soldier in the 105th Ohio Volunteer Infantry. "They hailed our arrival with pleasure and were ever willing to disclose hidden supplies and pilot us to distant swamps that concealed horses, mules, and forage." "They [the enslaved] very readily tell us where anything is concealed, and seem well pleased when we find various articles," echoed George S. Bradley, a chaplain marching with a Wisconsin regiment, just two nights after "some twenty negroes got together, took 40 of their masters mules and horses, and come over to us."[25]

The effort on the part of enslaved people to reveal those hidden stores carried real significance. Oftentimes handing over concealed goods provided them with a chance to escape the plantation and possibly join the army. One Indiana soldier caught a glimpse of that when he discovered a lone enslaved man sitting on a roadside at the head of a wagon loaded down with fresh hams. The man had been told to take the meat out into the woods, away from the army, but instead he had ridden off to the main road, hidden in a ditch, and waited to fall in with the army. At other times, revealing the whereabouts of hidden treasures was less about making a break for freedom than it was joining in the material devastation of their enslavers. That was possibly a strategic move in the sense that aiding the foragers weakened the Confederate home front and thus hastened the end of the war, but it must have also been a little cathartic—a moment to either celebrate or enact vengeance. That was perhaps why enslaved people also tended to disclose the location of gold, valuables, and even, in John Van Duser's experience, a cellar storing "five large demijohns, one of no 1 whiskey, and the rest Madeira wine."[26]

Enslaved people sharing their knowledge could also save a soldier's life. H. H. Tarr, a captain from Connecticut who marched along with the army's left wing, discovered that on two different raids. Much to his exhaustion, both raids turned into wild multiday affairs that carried him deep into the Georgia countryside, and in each case, enslaved men and women shepherded him from place to place, often shielding him from potential threats. On the first, which he began four days into the campaign, he slipped stealthily behind enemy lines with the help of "negro guides" who led him and his men down what he coarsely called "nigger paths." Those were hidden trails cut out of the dense Georgia underbrush that enslaved people relied on to move between plantations without being spotted by patrollers, overseers, or, in this case, Confederate cavalry. His first day out was a great success. He and his men alighted on multiple plantations, where they burned "$150,000 or $200,000" worth of cotton, destroyed several gins, and feasted on roast chicken. Early the next morning, however, a group of enslaved people roused Tarr to let him know that a "large Rebel force" had been spotted only a mile or so from where they slept. "These negroes had, on their own hook, gone out beyond my pickets and stood watch for our additional safety," he wrote, astonished at how the enslaved men and women had acted as his guardians and perhaps saved his life.[27]

As Tarr rushed to leave, the same group told him where to find "a large corral of horses and mules" hidden well out in the woods, which he and his men went to immediately. They took the livestock and set off, but the soldiers didn't travel alone. The enslaved people mounted the horses—Tarr said two to each horse—and headed out with the soldiers, turning the foraging party into what the Connecticut captain referred to as a "cavalcade." It was a good thing, too, for such a large number of mounted men riding alongside Tarr gave the appearance of a much larger force, as if a larger detachment of US cavalry were riding through the countryside instead of a small group of mounted infantrymen and a posse of enslaved people. Tarr realized that when they rode into Eatonton. Though they were "in the face of the enemy," the troop burst into the town and "made enough noise for an army corps," which Tarr implied scared off the Confederates still lurking in town without them having to fire a shot. From there, the group rode on to Milledgeville, the capital, where they rejoined the main column and celebrated their success.[28]

Tarr's second wild ride, only a day or so out of Milledgeville, proved to be as harried as the first and began just as the earlier one had, with the helping hand of enslaved guides. After being repelled back to the main column by a force of Confederate cavalry, Tarr and his twenty-five men followed the guides into the woods, no doubt following a similar network of footpaths worn by generations of enslaved people traveling with hushed steps between plantations. The company's first stop was at a plantation where a group of enslaved men emerged from the woods with "fifteen head of stock" including "four of the best bred racers." "I was advised by the negroes to get out quickly," wrote Tarr, for a group of enslaved people told him that the plantation's owner had dispatched a message to the nearest Confederate force. So Tarr, his team, and the enslaved people with him ducked back into the woods, with the enslaved guides leading the way. The next day, following a brief run-in with mounted Confederate cavalry, Tarr's band stopped at a plantation, and on two separate occasions, enslaved people pulled him aside to reveal where undisclosed items had been hidden. One search produced only a buried trunk full of trinkets and dresses; the other recovered a neighborhood's worth of livestock hidden in a swamp. Tarr's troop returned the next day and ran a small stockyard back to the army.[29]

Tarr's adventures on the backroads and plantations of middle Georgia demonstrate two important points. The first is that as agents in the war effort, enslaved people did way more than reveal hidden plantation treasures; they partnered with the soldiers, offered their assistance, and fought their own version of the war. The most obvious way they did so was by providing knowledge in the form of military intelligence. It was a phenomenon that happened at all stages of the March. The army's high brass, even Sherman on occasion, routinely relied on intelligence gathered and passed on by enslaved people, and for some, the information came unsolicited and in the nick of time. The second point is that so much of the knowledge enslaved people shared came from their intimate understanding of the landscape. That makes perfect sense given the long history of slave politics. As the historian Stephanie Camp's pathbreaking work on slavery and resistance has shown us, slave owners sought to control their space as a way of controlling enslaved people—hence, the presence of things such as pass systems and patrols. Enslaved people, in turn, subverted that "geography of containment" by constructing "alternative ways of knowing and using plantation and southern space"—or a "rival geography," as she termed it.[30]

During the Civil War, enslaved people once again turned to those spaces, except this time they did so to bridge the gap between slavery and freedom. As Camp demonstrated in her work, the rival geographies that sustained enslaved people during slavery opened new avenues for them to escape the plantation as the war raged on. A similar story unfolded along Sherman's March but with a slight amendment: enslaved people not only used those spaces to chart their own paths to freedom, they also used them to partner with the army and ensure its success. In doing so, they mobilized an entire infrastructure of knowledge and thrust it right into the center of the war. And make no mistake: access to those rival geographies was a real strategic advantage for Sherman's army. It was like having a map that revealed a separate plan of battle or a compass that led deep into the politics of the plantation, which, in a way, was always Sherman's intended target.[31]

Perhaps nothing demonstrates the value of this knowledge more than the reports of how enslaved people escorted escaped prisoners back to the safety of US Army lines. Indeed, soldiers tended to sit wide eyed, open mouthed, and in a state of awe as they listened to their bedraggled friends tell of their escapes and attribute them to enslaved people. "The colored race here as elsewhere had been the truest friends of those who were unfortunate enough to taste the woes of captivity," wrote one soldier, recalling the time two escapees had arrived at the army accompanied by an older enslaved man and his mule. The man had apparently "hidden them in the swamps and fed them for weeks" before ushering them back to the army, avoiding what must have been a labyrinth of patrolled roads and the ever-present threat of Confederate cavalry. Another soldier remembered one particular prisoner, a captain, who, after spending almost a full year bouncing from one prison to the next, escaped from a camp in Columbia, South Carolina, and with the help of two enslaved men traveled ten nights and some 180 miles to Sherman's line of march.[32]

Thus the praise: "So it was through three States," wrote John Richards Boyle, reflecting on the March from North Carolina. "Every black face was the face of a friend, every black hand was wide open . . . every black man's poor cabin was a city of refuge to a hunted or imperiled Union soldier." Another soldier spoke for his regiment when he wrote that enslaved people were "always our faithful allies and friends." Those kind words make for a feel-good story of racial reconciliation, but they can also deflect attention away from the story of how the underground world of enslaved politics—a politics forged in the history of slavery—burst forth alongside the army and became a force of its own, pushing and guiding Sherman's columns on toward Savannah, the end of the war, and the death of slavery. It happened on the ransacked farms of Georgia with a particular vigor and significance, but mobilizations such as that had taken place throughout the war, which reaffirms Stephanie Camp's conclusion: "The rival geography created by the enslaved over generations offered, in wartime, the literal roads to freedom."[33]

In those first few days, with the four columns all marching into middle Georgia, the fires never ceased. Clouds of smoke blanketed the horizon, and the army continued its work. "The whole country is clouded with smoke," wrote one soldier near Milledgeville, adding "This mighty army is making a terrible sweep." "The country through which we pass is terribly scourged," wrote another, noting that "everything combustible is in a blaze." Some homes were burning, but the bulk of the smoke came from cotton houses and other farm buildings: "Our men burned all cotton gins and presses that have cotton in them, day after day as the column moves along," wrote a soldier with the 34th Regiment of Illinois

Volunteer Infantry. "Many of the people say the Confederacy is played out," the man noted, though elsewhere it was clear that Southerners could still fight back. Civilians sometimes fired on approaching soldiers, and at one stop, soldiers found comrades dead, their throats cut, with cards pinned on them that read "Death to all foragers."[34]

Ira Berlin, one of our nation's foremost scholars of slavery, once wrote, "Born of violent usurpation, slavery would—and perhaps only could— die in the same bloody warfare." The March was a reflection of this idea gone haywire. The violence of the March was ever present and wielded in a variety of forms. Soldiers carried rifles, revolvers, and bayonets. They lit fires, requisitioned food under the force of arms, and stormed plantations. What, after all, was an army—in this case some sixty thousand souls and an ungodly number of horses, wagons, ambulances, engineers, and artillery brigades wheeling around screeching cannons and live ammunition—if not a moving monopoly of violence? There were also a smattering of Confederate militia and Joseph Wheeler's phantomlike band of Confederate cavalry to contend with. Wheeler's men hovered around the army and struck fast—sometimes sweeping up soldiers or escaped slaves in short, pell-mell raids, where sabers and sidearms were the usual weapons of choice. Add into this mix the presence of slave catchers, stragglers, and the vengeful glare of Southern whites, and it is easy to see why enslaved people tended to act with caution. Threats lurked all around and could come from any direction at any time.[35]

Even the dogs weren't safe. One of the most frequently recorded and oft-talked-about acts all along the March was the ritual killing of canines on plantations along Sherman's path. It was a widespread, even celebrated, phenomenon. Escaped prisoners reported that Confederate patrols tracked fugitives with hounds and hunting dogs; enslaved people reported much the same, informing the soldiers that those plantation animals haunted the dreams of anyone who dared run away. So the soldiers killed them. "The foragers never spared any of them [the dogs], but killed them on sight," wrote one soldier. "Permission was given in orders to kill them, wherever found," wrote another. One Ohioan remembered a plantation where, after several of the buildings had been burned out, "in the door-yard lay the dead bodies of several blood-hounds that had been used to track and pull down negroes and our escaped prisoners . . . wherever our army has passed, everything in the shape of a dog has been killed." Hitchcock remembered several of these instances as well, revealing that of all the cotton burned and food stolen, of all the miles marched, one of the most distinctive features of Sherman's campaign through Georgia was that it left about a 250-mile stretch of road littered with the lifeless bodies of dogs.[36]

The mournful yelps of dying dogs aside, the violence of the March could also just as easily present itself in ways more subtle and subdued, though no less traumatic. One example of that more understated form of violence was that freedom occasioned reflection. Because Sherman's men asked questions and had a penchant for conversing with enslaved people, the enslaved people relived past traumas while thinking ahead to freedom. Inquiries about a particular master or mistress brought back recollections of whippings, beatings, and slave sales; other questions about why certain enslaved men and women looked as white as the soldiers meant recalling long-repressed histories of serial rape. Painful memories also came up in conversation unsolicited like some long-awaited expurgation of withheld pain and suffering, a moment to vent and voice one's traumas as the March moved along. The sense of standing on the verge of freedom likely had something to do with those reflections, but regardless, enslaved people throughout the March often experienced emancipation while also remembering slavery.

Slavery was a violent institution. As both a social and legal system, chattel slavery permitted an enslaver's use of force over enslaved people. Southern whites, therefore, often responded to seeing slavery crack and crumble exactly the way one might expect: with more violence. But they didn't always have to. History sat heavily on the mind of the living. Instances of past violence carried a profound weight, which meant that the mere threat of violence, backed up by a history of violence, was often as politically expedient for Southern whites as an actual show of force. Colonel Tarr once glimpsed the power of the past during one of his wild rides when he asked an enslaved man to reveal the location of a family's hidden livestock. The man refused, telling Tarr "I am too old to go with you's, for good, and I am too young to stay here an' be murdered."[37]

Yet the power of the past cut both ways, and enslaved people could sometimes harness it to wreak a kind of vengeance. For example, Hitchcock once met an enslaved woman near Eatonton who had had a child by her master, a horrid and all-too-common occurrence in the plantation South. White masters forced themselves upon enslaved women and had enslaved children grow up alongside their free children—except in this particular case the woman's mistress had never had any children of her own, resulting in what Hitchcock described as a "*Sarah and Hagar case only worse.*" As a consequence, the enslaved woman reported receiving cruel treatment from the plantation mistress—which likely meant suffering years of repeated predations while also living under the gaze of a jealous tormentor turned serial abuser.[38]

Hitchcock never said so explicitly, but his diary implied that with that information in hand, the men "foraged liberally," even taking all the peanuts the mistress had drying on the roof of her shed. Later, he reported that the barn was ablaze; he noted that the fire could have been the result of fires lit to warm the men, but in any event, no one put it out and the whole building burned down. Are we to believe that the enslaved woman had that outcome in mind when she told Hitchcock her story? Maybe. In any case, the point is that her story fit a pattern shared by her peers: all along the March enslaved people leveraged the past to influence the present. They relived past cruelties, disclosed their masters' true sympathies, and revealed plantation goods in an effort to control the difficulties of emancipation and reverse the politics of the moment to their own benefit. Sometimes they did so to curry favor with the soldiers; other times they did so to enact their own form of justice.[39]

While enslaved people used the army as a buffer between themselves and their masters, the army was also a threat, especially the foraging parties, who routinely appropriated the property of enslaved people. It was actually quite common for enslaved people to own pieces of property. Many planters also allowed enslaved people to grow their own vegetables or have their own personal provision grounds in a corner lot somewhere near the slave quarters. In some cases, access to a garden or a chicken coop was a way of supplementing the meager provisions provided by a slave owner. Property ownership on a larger scale—the owning of livestock, carts, wagons, and such—was particularly prevalent farther to the south, nearer the coast, where the slave system's history of rice production influenced the labor system and created more opportunities for the enslaved to own property. But even in the cotton-growing regions of central Georgia, where there were fewer opportunities to do so, enslaved people still had important possessions of their own, whether food, supplies, personal items such as clothes and blankets, or family heirlooms passed down from parents to children.[40]

Nevertheless, soldiers showed little compunction about taking what they wanted. Foragers rifled through slave quarters, ransacked the houses of enslaved men and women, and walked off carrying goods and valuables belonging to enslaved people. "We have soldiers so degraded and low born as to plunder the houses of the blacks of the last mouthful of food and every valuable," complained a colonel from Ohio. Hitchcock once witnessed the destruction firsthand when an enslaved woman came begging for his help, crying "Please, Sir, soldiers robbing me of all I got, clothes and everything." Sure enough, he found "four or five soldiers" in her cabin "turning things over" and had to order them out. In Liberty County, on the coast, where enslaved people tended to own a greater amount of property, an enslaved nurse put it this way: "Dey've took ebry ting I had," she told an interviewer, adding "What kin you spec fum a hog but a grunt."[41]

Also, knowing where plantation goods had been hidden gave enslaved people a valuable card to play, but the soldiers eventually caught on. Soon foraging parties on all lines of march developed a new strategy: "Should they [the soldiers] not succeed, after a thorough search through every nook and cranny of the house," wrote George Sharland, an Illinois soldier, ". . . they then threaten violence to the half affrighted negroes if they do not make known the place of its concealment." Rice C. Bull, a New Yorker, said as much when he wrote that "the Negroes were used, or I might say forced, to reveal the hiding places" of concealed items. In one instance, John Potter, the man who had witnessed Sally's reunion with Nan, wrote about once having pulled his revolver on a group of enslaved men who had balked at helping him haul away a cart of stolen corn. When the threat of the gun hadn't gotten the men moving fast enough, he had gone a step further and threatened to take one of them away, which was soldier speak for impressing him into the army.[42]

Potter's threat to seize the man exposes another of the March's darker characteristics. Impressment—the forced seizure of men and women for the purpose of military labor—ran rampant. One enslaved woman recalled that when the soldiers had arrived, they had entered the plantation home, stolen all the sweet milk, helped themselves to the contents of the smokehouse, and then seized two enslaved men. Dolly Sumner Lunt, a white widow from Covington, who kept an extensive diary, wrote that soldiers who had arrived at her home had forced the issue of impressment by flashing their bayonets, which had created a moment of delirium. One enslaved man named Newton had run for his cabin; a young boy had hidden in a crawl space; another named James had hidden in the house and later been captured while escaping through a window; and Jack had tried to run but had soon found himself staring down the barrel of a gun with a man threatening to shoot him if he refused to come along. In addition to those men, the soldiers had seized Mid, another enslaved man, and Bob had simply disappeared in the fracas, though Lunt was sure that the soldiers had seized him as well.[43]

Bear in mind that understanding impressment along the March is challenging. Mainly, the passivity of the language—enslaved people being "taken off" or "carried away"—sometimes leaves a lot unclear. Even so, impressment certainly occurred, and, moreover, the army had a significant interest in seizing enslaved people and incorporating them into the army as military laborers—chiefly as pioneers, teamsters, or road builders. Along those same lines, individual soldiers used impressment as a means of acquiring their own personal valets or porters, and regiments likewise impressed men and women into service because they wanted their own laundresses and cooks. There is also this: to some (but not all) of the soldiers, enslaved people were seen as yet another resource to requisition. The more enslaved people they seized, the more damage was done to the South. From that perspective, impressment operated as a function of the foraging process writ large, making it more feature than flaw within the wider workings of the March.[44]

Indeed, military impressment was a symptom of a larger reality: violence defined the March. The potential for violence underlay the campaign, and enslaved people were never immune from violence on the March, sometimes dying simply by being caught in cross fire. In one instance, Hitchcock remembered walking down a railroad track when a hidden Confederate battery fired off a cannon blast. The ball rattled down the track and struck an enslaved man, killing him instantly. Another tragic event happened in Milledgeville. One of Sherman's soldiers fired off two shots at two enslaved women who were celebrating the army's arrival from a balcony overhanging the street, killing them both. The man was held in prison for a time, but an investigation reportedly concluded that the shooting had been "purely accidental," which strains belief. Nonetheless, the point remains: violence hung over the March like those thick wisps of smoke and could come from anywhere at any time.[45]

Exactly a week after pushing out of Atlanta, Sherman's right wing locked horns with a militia force in the first and only serious engagement until the army reached the coast. In the days leading up to the battle, Georgia's governor and members of the Georgia state legislature launched their final, desperate attempt to stave off Sherman's advance. They passed an emergency conscription bill forcing all able-bodied men (excepting themselves, of course) into the militia in the hope of rallying for one last defense of the state of Georgia. It didn't work. Not only did the conscription order not circulate in time to create any real defense, all the state could feasibly muster was about three brigades of Georgia militia, which in truth was little more than a sad assemblage of old men and young boys. In any case, the inexperienced and ill-trained men took to arms. They were on their way to Augusta, Sherman's presumed target, but turned back when word of the army's movements reached them. They made their stand near a stop along the Central Georgia Railroad, a small speck of a place northeast of Macon called Griswoldville.[46]

The Battle of Griswoldville was a fierce fight, if only for a moment. The militia charged and charged and then charged again. About twenty-three hundred militiamen threw themselves against a single Union brigade of about three thousand troops, but the veterans of Sherman's right wing held firm. They repulsed the attacks and finally forced the ragtag band of militia men into making their retreat. The result was about five hundred Confederate casualties to a little less than a hundred Union casualties. Of all the epic battles fought by Sherman's men, that, it was clear, was not one of them. The sights following the battle told the soldiers all that needed telling. "I was never so affected at the sight of wounded and dead before," wrote a soldier from Illinois. "Old grey haired and weakly looking men and little boys, not over 15 years old, lay dead or writhing in pain." Theodore Upson, another well-known documenter of the March, called it a "harvest of death," noting that fathers and sons, young and old, lay dead and mangled together. The bodies told two sides of the same story, reflecting at once the sorry state of the Confederate war effort and the irresistible force of Sherman's federal army. The dead were also signs of something more material and more important to the soldiers: with the Georgia militia vanquished, Sherman's forces could now march on to Savannah practically unopposed.[47]

That very same morning, within hours of the opening shots at the Battle of Griswoldville, members of Sherman's left wing strode into Milledgeville. Henry Hitchcock and the staff had been warned by several enslaved people that Confederate officials planned to put up a fight, but the members of Georgia's state legislature had all fled the city days before the army arrived. Sherman's men moved in with little opposition and all the fanfare of a military parade. The regimental bands struck up songs, and the soldiers waved flags and marched through the city from end to end. "The day was cloudless," remembered a Wisconsin veteran, ". . . The troops came in well closed up, marching in perfect step to martial music." Another soldier remembered the men marching "through the city by the music of our bands." "The Star-Spangled Banner" and "Yankee Doodle Dandy" played throughout the day, and at some point, someone hoisted a regimental flag of the US Army high over the roof of the statehouse. Confederate Georgia had finally fallen.[48]

It wasn't long before crowds of enslaved people joined in the procession. Though many enslaved people had been forcibly removed during successive evacuations, freed men and women filled the city's streets as the army marched past. "The colored people hailed with demonstrative delight the advent of the Union army," wrote the Wisconsin veteran, recalling that enslaved people had showered the soldiers with blessings and reached out as if to hug the men whenever the columns marched by. Another noted that there had been "general rejoicing" among enslaved people and that in terms of food and forage "all were willing to divide everything with us." The bottleneck leading into Milledgeville was also the point at which many of the soldiers first noticed the refugee crisis of Sherman's march beginning to set in. The numbers of freed refugees following the army had been growing steadily by the day, and their number seemed even larger as they pushed into the town, exacerbating the pandemonium breaking out on the streets of Milledgeville.[49]

Yet if many other soldiers failed to notice the refugees, it was probably because they were busy reveling in the fall of Georgia's Confederate government. Sherman wanted the destruction kept to a minimum, but with so many symbols of the Confederacy strewn about, the soldiers couldn't help themselves. Troops broke into the state arsenal, destroying an assortment of pikes, knives, and other weapons. They requisitioned stacks of now-worthless Confederate money, burned the railroad depot, and ransacked the state library. Most memorably, a group of soldiers broke into the statehouse and convened their own special legislative session. Rollicking with laughter, they announced themselves as speakers of the House, passed motions, and issued their own ordinances of secession; the session ended only after someone stood up in the back and yelled "The Yankees are coming," at which the entire body howled in laughter and ran out of the chamber in mock hysteria. Insult was clearly being added to injury, but there was also more to it than that. The fall of Milledgeville was the political counterpart of the rout at Griswoldville. Together, the two events toppled some of the last state institutions still standing and thus some of the last vestiges of Confederate Georgia, fulfilling, in a sense, one of Sherman's predictions. "Pierce the *shell* of the C.S.A.," he told Hitchcock, "and it's all hollow inside."[50]

Except Hitchcock didn't need Sherman or the fall of Georgia's government to tell him that the Confederacy was hollow inside. The confirmation had come a day or so earlier, just before he and the staff had joined the main body in Milledgeville. It was bitter cold that day—so cold that Sherman intruded into a "negro hut" to warm himself by a fire. An enslaved woman, presumably the cabin's owner, told him that if the general and his staff went further up the road, they would find a larger, more comfortable dwelling. That more comfortable dwelling turned out to be an abandoned plantation owned by none other than Howell Cobb. A scion of one of the state's most powerful families, Cobb was a powerful politician. He had served as the Speaker of the US House of Representatives from 1849 to 1851 and later as governor of Georgia before returning for a second stint in the House of Representatives. In 1860, he served as secretary of the Treasury before resigning and becoming a fierce champion of secession. He was a delegate to the first secession convention in Montgomery, Alabama, the president of the first provisional Congress of the Confederacy, and a colonel in the Confederate Army. Sherman rightfully called him "one of the leading rebels of the South"; Hitchcock described him differently, calling Cobb "one of the *head devils*."[51]

Head devil, indeed. What Hitchcock, Sherman, and the rest of the staff discovered on his plantation appalled them to no end. Cobb had apparently ordered the plantation abandoned only days before. The place was empty—or so Hitchcock and the others thought. When they explored the place, they discovered that Cobb had left behind forty enslaved women, children, and old men. They were starving, poorly clothed, and cold. The wind whistled through their cabins. The more Hitchcock and others poked around, the more they believed that Cobb had left the men and women there to die. On top of that, they were all terribly frightened of Sherman and his men. Earlier a gang of Confederate horsemen had ridden through disguised as Union officers and coaxed them into leaving the plantation, which had been only a vile trick. When a number of them had agreed to leave the plantation, the horsemen had nearly flogged them to death. In response, Sherman and his staff ordered the place destroyed. They ordered food turned over to the enslaved people and instructed their cavalry escort to spare them nothing. That night they lit a huge bonfire, and everyone—enslaved people and all—warmed themselves while enjoying what was left of the Cobb plantation.[52]

Hitchcock later learned that that was not *the* Cobb plantation but one of many owned by Cobb. According to information gathered on the scene, Cobb was said to possess an additional four to five plantations (the total number was actually thirteen) and enslave as many as five to six hundred men and women across his estates. This one—a 600-acre estate worked by a hundred enslaved people—was just his wife's place, an inheritance gained by Cobb by his marriage. For Hitchcock, that discovery about the extent of Cobb's power seemed to put the entire Confederate project into perspective, revealing in the starkest of terms the moral emptiness in the idea of a slaveholder's republic. It also rein-forced what for Hitchcock had been an ongoing realization: the war, he knew, needed winning, but to really defeat the Confederacy, slavery would have to die, two things that were not necessarily the same. One would simply put down a rebellion; the other would cut the rebellion off at its root. One could potentially retain the status quo; the other would remake American society by removing its most malignant tumor. As Hitchcock sat, stared into the fire, and listened to the stories of the men and women Cobb had enslaved, it was a distinction that had never been so clear to him.[53]

Nevertheless, the fall of Milledgeville completed what Hitchcock described as the campaign's "first act." He was perhaps more right than he realized. After leaving Milledgeville, the army not only crossed the midpoint of the March, it passed over the state's fall line. From that point southeastward, the landscape slopes softly, flattening out into a sandy plain, and most of the region's rivers flow to the southeast, their mouths opening into the warm waters of the Atlantic Ocean. The roads there were ruttier and the fields leaner, and the plush pastures of central Georgia eventually gave way to murky swamps. As Georgia's terrain changed, so did the process of emancipation. Movement became as important as ever. Faced with a daunting landscape and new impediments to the army's progress, soldiers began turning enslaved people away from the army lines, which transformed their pursuit of freedom into a disorienting odyssey of surviving at the tail end of Sherman's army. Even worse, not only was there as yet no clear destination or endpoint in sight, the threats never ceased, clarity never came, and there were still many rivers to cross.

Freed refugees from Virginia in the summer of 1862, typical of the self-emancipated people who fled to Sherman's army in Georgia.

Chapter Three

ON THE MARCH

While the movement of refugees toward the army had begun almost
as soon as Sherman's columns pulled out of Atlanta, Henry Hitchcock didn't realize the extent of the situation until the fifth day out,
two days before arriving at Howell Cobb's plantation. It happened at
a place called Shady Dale, which Hitchcock accurately described as
being not quite "a town or village but the farm of one man, containing
7,600 acres—250 negroes." The proprietor was one Mr. Whitfield, who
was said to be worth a million dollars, though Hitchcock specified in
his diary that that had been before the war. Now Whitfield was on the
run, his plantation swarming with federal soldiers. "We are told he left
yesterday or this morning, having collected his horses and mules and
ordering the negroes to bring them along," Hitchcock wrote, noting that
none of the enslaved people had obeyed the order. Instead, they had
"remained with the stock and joined with the Yanks in high glee." "So
it is everywhere," he added, realizing that he was witnessing the start of
a much larger phenomenon.[1]

And a phenomenon it most certainly was. "Negroes by the hundred
are coming into our line and we are keeping them with us," wrote an
Indiana soldier, adding that the freedmen were able foragers and "not

bad fellows to have along." "They [the enslaved] were overjoyed at the coming of our army," wrote an Ohio soldier, describing a time near Madison, only a few days out from Atlanta, during which "hundreds from this one neighborhood seized the opportunity to escape to freedom." It was like that all across the upper reaches of middle Georgia. Enslaved men and women were meeting and joining the army in large numbers—groups, according to the soldiers, as large as a hundred at a time. For the soldiers, many of whom had never seen slavery or experienced the war in such a way, seeing enslaved men and women flee to the army like that made for a dumbfounding experience. One Indiana soldier perhaps captured the experience best when he wrote, "Men, women, and children poured in from every direction."[2]

Yet it wasn't just enslaved people's running to the army that shocked and astounded the soldiers; it was the way they did it. They came on foot, of course, but they also came on top of horses and mules, in carriages, and in the backs of wagons, with bags packed, food stored away, and in their best clothes. "Whole families are frequently seen coming in on the cross roads, with some old mule team and wagon, having on board what few household matters they could get together," wrote George S. Bradley, the chaplain from Wisconsin, noting that the wagons had lined the roadways, waiting to fall in. "Some [rode] in buggies of the most costly and glittery manufacture; some on horseback," was how another soldier remembered it. The resounding message was that the freed men and women were prepared to go wherever the March might take them. One woman who marched alongside the stampede of livestock and rolling wagons, a child in her arms, said as much when she responded to an officer's query. "Where are you going, Aunty?" the soldier asked, invoking a common racial epithet. With a "beseeching look," the woman replied simply, "I'se gwine whar you'se gwine, Massa," as if the question needn't have been asked.[3]

The decision was never an easy one. Whether to follow the army or stay behind was a decision that was made based on countless considerations. First and foremost was risk versus reward, what could be gained against what could be lost. Then came the practicalities: freed people had to consider their overall health and ability to make the March. Did they have access to a horse or buggy to ease the burden? Did they have enough food? They had to think about their family and community. Would they go alone or in a larger group? Would following the army mean leaving a parent, sibling, or loved one behind? And ironically, they had to think about white slaveholders and consider the prospect of future retribution for leaving. What might happen, for instance, if people had to return to a home plantation? Would they be banished or beaten—or kept from seeing their family? Finally, leaving meant wrestling with a set of unknowns such as where the army was going and what life would look like when they got there. For thousands of freed people in Georgia, those were risks worth taking, but for many others, either the risk was too great or their circumstances wouldn't allow it, making it best to stay behind.

Moreover, if making the decision was hard, following through could be just as difficult. On the one hand, there was no guarantee that the army would accept them. Even if a freed person weighed all the risks, took all the necessary steps, and struck out with bags packed, ready to march, an unsympathetic soldier could always try to turn him or her back. On the other hand, plantation attachments did not just melt away. Leaving meant saying tearful goodbyes to family, friends, community, and a sense of place. Conversely, leaving also meant saying goodbye to, or escaping from, slaveholders, something one Illinois private witnessed while stopped near Madison. After a freed couple announced their decision to leave, the soldier wrote that their former master had done his best to keep them from leaving. He had tried playing up his paternal benevolence. He had tried guilt. Nothing had worked. In tears but also unwavering, the couple had still left. "We must go," the man had said before leaving, telling his former master bluntly, "freedom is as sweet to us as it is to you."[4]

In short, leaving was a complicated experience that required navigating the social world of the plantation—of saying goodbye to peers and parsing one's way out of a master-slave relationship burdened by prior history. Add in the sometimes unencouraging hand of the army, and leaving could also mean getting caught in a tangled web of interpersonal interactions, some of which proved too complex to escape. Unfortunately, that was what happened to Liza, an enslaved woman with whom Hitchcock spoke in early December. Liza made it clear to him that she wanted to leave with the army, but he discouraged her. He told her that the army didn't want women following them, that the marching would be too strenuous, and he repeated the often told lie that the soldiers would soon return. In response, Liza said that she would "like mightily to go wid you now" but then let slip that she felt some responsibility for her master's children, who had been left with their sick mother. It was the opening Hitchcock needed. "Don't leave 'em—stay where you are," he commanded before hectoring on about how freedom wouldn't mean freedom from work. "Two words of encouragement would have brought her along," he later acknowledged, but he never said those two words. Instead, he turned Liza away by exploiting her perceived obligations as a caretaker.[5]

Liza's example is a case in point for why those who stayed behind shouldn't be forgotten or ignored. Her voice—her asking Hitchcock to go along—reveals that while leaving carried a message, it was a message that told only half the story and featured only half of those who made it. The other half are forgotten voices such as Liza's as well as, for instance, a group of five or six "older negro men" whom Sherman and his staff met just hours after Hitchcock discouraged Liza from joining the March. Their spokesman was a man whom Hitchcock described as being "really dignified" and about fifty years old. He spoke with Sherman for a nearly an hour and explained all the reasons the men weren't going to follow the army, saying that "with the age of them all, and the rheumatics of this one and the lameness of that one, and the families they all must leave, it was really better for them to stay where they were." Sherman agreed, perhaps with a wry smile because it was exactly the outcome he wanted. Nonetheless, the men had a larger point to make. They likely knew what Sherman would say, but they held their court and made their point anyway, implying with all the decorum of a diplomatic colloquy that they *would* go if not for their various impediments. Why would the men go to such trouble? Because leaving did indeed make a statement about freedom. But it wasn't the only way to make a statement, and the men made sure that Sherman and his staff knew exactly where they stood.[6]

Still, statement or not, Sherman probably wasn't moved all that much. As the commanding general, he had one overriding goal: to make sure that his army faced as few impediments as possible, which, to him, meant keeping as many freed people away from his lines as he could. Hence his response: he told the men that they were "perfectly right," that they "ought to stay," and that the army would permit only the "able-bodied, who wished it," to go along, which in Sherman speak meant freedmen who were willing and able to work. The exchange fit a familiar pattern. According to Hitchcock, Sherman always spoke to freed people in a frank, disarming style and always heard them out; but he held firm when it came to their wanting to join the March. He often repeated the same white lie that Hitchcock told—that the army would someday return—and he always hoped that those he spoke with would go on to discourage others, spreading through word of mouth his own clear message to stay behind and not overburden his army.[7]

The soldiers were a different story. Though many shared Sherman's apprehensions and many of his subordinates followed his command, others, especially the common foot soldiers, never toed the same line. So long as things were good—that is, so long as the men lived comfortably, trawling the breadbasket of north central Georgia while facing few impediments—freed men and women amassing at the end of their lines was of no consequence to them. As a result, the soldiers would sometimes invite freed men and women to come along or enlist (or impress) a freed person as a valet, cook, or washerwoman. Others simply looked the other way. In their minds, it was all part of the romp—a mere function of being wrapped up in the fever of foraging and moving with wavelike force through the state of Georgia. Things would soon change. The closer the army came to Savannah, the longer the line of refugees extending behind it grew, and the more difficult it became for the men to cross rivers and find adequate food, the more the soldiers caught on to Sherman's message and began turning more freed people away. But even then, there was no hard-and-fast rule, and there was no unifying armywide consensus outside Sherman's original refugee policy, which the soldiers didn't necessarily follow anyway.

That dissonance between policy and practice, between Sherman's aims and what actually happened, created even more opportunity for freed people to join the army's lines. So they kept doing so. They kept leaving plantations and following the army, and they arrived in such large numbers that by the time the army's left wing reached Milledgeville, the full scope of the crisis began to be apparent. "There was a great caravan of negroes hanging on the rear of our column when it arrived in Milledgeville," wrote one Illinois soldier, likening the refugees to a cloud attached to a "thunder storm or tornado." "The negroes continued to flock to the army," recorded another. "Some of them were utilized as servants, but the great mass was becoming an alarming incubus," wrote a soldier who noted that "threats did not deter them" and "their number increased with each succeeding day." Those were the words of someone alarmed about the potential problems of so many refugees following the army. That soldier alluded specifically to supply problems, but there was also a deeper anxiety starting to spread through the soldiery: the March was no longer only theirs, and they no longer had total control.[8]

That, in a sense, was the bottom line of the entire campaign. Sherman conducted the March and orchestrated the army's movements, but he couldn't control it. No one could. The collective force of an army that size moving at that speed made it impossible to police or contain. That was why at some point the March ceased to be a standard military campaign and took on all the attributes of a social convulsion. The army swept through the state, and in response, freed people followed the army's movements. But focusing only on the movement and the large, looming dust clouds arising from the March misses what the movement meant. Socially, the state was coming undone. White families had either fled, creating a power vacuum, or watched as slavery disintegrated before their eyes. Meanwhile, soldiers marched from plantation to plantation, stomping out the embers of the dying Confederacy, and freed people responded accordingly. Their world was changing as well, and they moved to finish the work already under way.

Ironically, as wild and disorienting as such convulsions can be, they can also be strangely, almost quietly, clarifying. The March had that kind of quality. Amid all the threats and shouts, the fear and uncertainty, as if standing in the eye of a storm, freed men and women retained a focused, clear-eyed view of what freedom meant to them. Certainly, what they understood as freedom was never what the soldiers recognized as such, and, moreover, their vision of freedom centered on things we might take for granted today. Yet in their actions and in the many reasons they gave for either making or not making the March, the freed people couldn't have been more adamant that those were real freedoms nonetheless.

Freedom, in a word, was family. It was Ben and Sally escaping to Atlanta and then making the March in the hope that they might reconnect with Nan, their long-lost daughter. It was the woman who begged the soldiers to let her follow them to Savannah so that she could find her husband and children, whom she had been sold away from many years before. And it was the woman who, a soldier wrote, had been "gone with grief going on four years" after seeing her son sold away and wanted to follow the army to Macon so that she might see him again. Family was a major part of how freed people envisioned freedom, and because of the March, reunions now suddenly seemed possible.[9]

The efforts to locate lost loved ones rested on another, even more basic freedom that tended to unlock all the rest: the freedom to move. If slavery rested on a "geography of containment," as Stephanie Camp has argued, the ability to move was thus a building block of freedom. Freed people knew that and made it the overwhelming message of the March. Indeed, if the basic fact of the March gave life to any idea, it was that freedom was found in motion: the ability to migrate and determine one's way in the world, to reconnect with people or a place, and, just as important, to *feel* free, to feel as if no longer constrained by either a master or a plantation.[10]

Generally speaking, that, too, was something that the soldiers rarely understood. Mocking the refugees for the way they moved was a favored pastime. The soldiers laughed at the way refugees ran to the army, with bundles packed, dressed in their best, and with carts or livestock likely taken from their masters. They taunted freed men and women over the idea that the March was for them. And they especially howled at the freed people's presumed naiveté over where they were going and what it meant. In one instance, James A. Connolly, an Indiana private and an otherwise sympathetic diarist, reflected on the refugees in a way that put the refugees' movement into perspective. He wrote that whenever the army passed a plantation, freed men and women generally "pack up their bundles and march along, going, they know not whither, but apparently satisfied they are going somewhere toward freedom." The punch line was that in his mind "a majority of them, don't know what freedom is." "Ask any of them where they are going," he went on, "and the almost invariable reply is: 'Don't know Massa; gwine along wid you all.'"[11]

Connolly clearly saw the refugee experience as the butt of a running joke. What he did not see was that the joke was actually on him. Freed people knew exactly where they were going and said what they meant. They recognized that in that particular moment freedom was precisely as Connolly described it. It depended on their proximity to the army. Scholars sometimes see this attachment to the army as a form of "social citizenship" in action—the idea that individuals build citizenship from the ground up by placing demands on a state or state institution—and maybe it was, but it also boiled down to the fact that following the army provided them with a basic sense of protection. So long as freed people moved with the army, its power provided a safeguard that protected them as they moved. It didn't always work out that way. The army failed the refugees time and again. But following the army was generally seen as a step toward security, perhaps the most fundamental freedom of all.[12]

Those differing iterations of freedom, however basic and fundamental, matter because they paint a new picture of what the March truly was. Traditionally, we've only ever seen the March as a military campaign. What we've missed is that Sherman's army cut a path through the state of Georgia wide enough for freed people to begin putting the pieces of freedom together. They found freedom in movement, sought out lost family members, and asserted claims to bedrock notions of security and independence. The freed people of Georgia thus tell us something about the nature of freedom and what it meant to those navigating the uncertainties of emancipation: it's that freedom was never any one thing; rather, it was an "open-ended process," as the historian Eric Foner wrote, of attaining the things slavery had long denied them. To place the campaign into this context is to finally understand the March for what it was: one of the most active, concentrated, and robust reimaginings of freedom in all of American history.[13]

Late November is hog-killing time in Georgia. The days are temperate and mild, but the nights are cool and crisp—just cold enough to keep a butchered pig from spoiling before being salted, smoked, and preserved. Late fall can also bring bouts of heavy winds and wet weather, and as the army moved on from Macon and Milledgeville, the soldiers complained bitterly of the rain. "It rains incessantly," wrote an Illinois soldier from just east of Macon. "A storm sets in and we get wet as rats," he wrote again a day later. "Mud in places, knee deep; wagons getting mired every few moments," diarized another soldier, noting that the "tramp, tramp of so many feet make deep ruts in the roadside." "Dismal sky and steady rain" was how Hitchcock put it as the general's staff plowed through thick layers of mud, with wagon ruts he tells us in places were "fully 18 to 24 inches deep." "It was bad enough riding through it on a good horse," he wrote, questioning how anyone had made it marching on foot or while driving "heavy teams."[14]

Cold, wet, and miserable as the soldiers might have been, they all had shoes, socks, and jackets. Moreover, their bellies were full. They stuffed themselves with hot hams, coal-roasted sweet potatoes, and roasted corn. And when the day's forage wasn't enough, they had plenty of coffee and cigars—two things that keep bones warm and bodies moving. Some even had freed people doing their washing and cooking, which meant that clean clothes and hot meals were at the ready whenever the army slowed and the weather broke. The freed people who marched behind Sherman's lines had few, if any, of those comforts. True, some of the refugees traveled in carriages and on top of wagons with wardrobes packed and food stored away on board, but those were the select few. Most simply marched along on foot—perhaps shoeless, hungry, and with nothing to counteract the cold but the clothes on their backs. Yet their numbers only grew. Freed men and women continued to follow the army, trudging through the muck and the mire to join the ranks.

By the end of November, with both wings beginning to enter Georgia's coastal plain, marching had been broken down into a science. The army rose at dawn and was down at dusk. Fifteen miles per day was the average distance marched, which meant that on most days the columns moved all day. The men stopped only in spells—long enough to repair a road or remove an obstruction. Otherwise, they kept marching. The foragers kept at it, too. The foraging parties rose early in the morning, trekked off into the countryside during the day, and then met the army late in the evening, often by lining the roads with wagons loaded, sacks

full, and arms overflowing with whatever harvest they had found. For
his part, Sherman and his staff, which had previously ridden with Slocum's left wing, switched over to Howard's right wing around Millen
as the approach to Savannah drew near and the Ogeechee River came
into sight.

Another thing to remember about armies is that, like bodies, they
have a certain anatomy. Though they disguise themselves as one homo-
geneous unit, the reality is that varying parts and pieces make up the
whole. Sherman's army was little different. Each of his four corps had
about fifteen thousand troops, and each of those corps had a legion of
auxiliary support. There were the medical staff, with their ambulances
and medical carts; there were cavalry, who hovered around the army
and escorted generals; there were artillery brigades, with their heavy
guns and wheeled carts full of shot and shell; and there were teams of
engineers, who traveled with the army helping to construct roads and
bridges. On top of that, the livestock foraged from the farms and plantations of central Georgia had to go somewhere, and that somewhere
was usually alongside or behind the marching men, turning the March
into something like one long cattle drive.[15]

Despite the ill-fitting nature of some of the component parts, each
piece of Sherman's army had a proper place that supported the whole,
allowing the body to move. It all started with the supply trains, the cir-
culatory system of the entire campaign. As a testament to how central
the supply trains were to the inner workings of the army, the soldiers
actually allocated much of the road to the wagons. The infantry aligned
themselves to one side, ordering themselves in slender columns, while
the wagons took up the rest. The idea was that by flanking the supplies,
the soldiers could defend the wagons against stray cavalry attacks. Plus,
traveling in formation like that had the added benefit of keeping the lines
tight instead of extending sections of the army out into parts unknown.
The result was effectively three separate lines: one of marching soldiers,
one of rolling wagons, and a third of ranging livestock, which the soldiers

herded together on the opposite side of the wagons as another buffer shielding the supplies from attack. The refugees, meanwhile, carved out a space for themselves somewhere toward the rear, where they had company in the form of delinquent wagons and straggling soldiers.[16]

Yet to look for freed people only at the end of the army's lines is to miss one of the underlying realities of the March: freed people could be found throughout the army and played a vital part in the day-to-day operations of the campaign. As has been mentioned, countless numbers of freed people served in the army as cooks, laundresses, valets, and teamsters. In those roles they put up tents, stoked fires, and stirred boiling vats of louse-ridden clothes. They also prepared the horses, and while the soldiers foraged for food, ham doesn't cook on its own and corn doesn't shuck itself, which meant that the gargantuan task of keeping the army fed often fell to freed cooks. Many of those men and women had, like Ben and Sally, joined the army from as far back as Atlanta; many others had joined somewhere along the way. Some may have even been impressed into service. In all such cases, those men and women didn't follow the army—that is, they were never peripheral to the main column. On the contrary, they *were* the main column. They marched right along and did the work that got the army where it needed going.

One example is the army's pioneer corps. The pioneers were a subsection of the engineering corps, except that the pioneers did all the grunt work that turned design into action—menial duties such as digging trenches, constructing earthworks, and felling trees. Along the March, hundreds of freedmen either joined the army as pioneers or were impressed into service by soldiers who couldn't stomach doing the work themselves. One soldier estimated that for every one hundred soldiers serving in the pioneer corps, there were at least seventy freedmen serving in the same capacity, and Sherman's goal was to increase that number so that fewer white soldiers had to moonlight as workmen. In fact, in his campaign orders, Sherman ordered each of his corps to organize a pioneer battalion "composed, if possible, of negroes," and he charged them with

86

the important task of serving as the army's chief road builders. They were to follow the advance guard and fill in ruts, repair broken embankments, and clear obstructions so that the army could continue at its rapid pace. Imagine, then, what the March must have looked like as out in front scores of freed pioneers literally paved the army's path to Savannah.[17]

The work that the pioneers did was something the army expected to extract from freed people in exchange for access to Union lines. The capacity to work was thus often the factor that distinguished those who marched with the army from those who marched at the rear among the growing crowd of refugees. Yet work didn't apply equally to everyone. Men had opportunities that women didn't, mostly because Sherman held firm: he stipulated that only the "able-bodied" and those "of service to the several columns" could join the army, which, of course, was his euphemism for men of working age. He didn't want anyone who couldn't serve as a surplus laborer to come along, and he especially didn't want any potential impediments milling about his lines. As a result, a gender divide opened up in which men gained access to the army as common laborers while a disproportionate number of women were either turned back or forced to the rear. That distinction meant that freedwomen likely made up the majority of the refugees at the rear of the army.[18]

The distinction based on labor was also devastating in the sense that it had the potential to separate freed families. As toilsome and mean as the work was, many freedmen likely relished the opportunity to work for the army—not only for the reasons outlined above but because military service was a mark of distinction. In a world in which slavery was crumbling and enslaved people were imagining lives outside of slavery, shoveling dirt for Sherman's army was an opportunity to press one's claims for inclusion and prove one's worth as a deserving member of the new America that would emerge from the war. Some men might have felt duty bound or drawn to working for the army on their own accord. Of course, many of the men were likely impressed into service, which makes this a moot point. But the bottom line is that because of the army's preoccupation with military labor, families frayed along the road. Husbands left wives and sons left mothers, leaving freedwomen to pick up the pieces and keep marching.

Picking up the pieces looked a lot like what enslaved women had always done. The women were mothers and providers, and as much as Sherman and the army discounted the labor of freedwomen, it was their labor as caregivers that kept families together while on the March. "Women came with large bundles on their heads, children also carried large packages on their heads, and some of the larger ones carried the little ones," wrote George Bradley, remembering a stop near Milledgeville. Only a day or so later he witnessed another instance in which a family of refugees rode past him. Two children sat on top of "a poor old horse," he tells us, with "the mother leading it, and the father pushing on ahead." "And here comes another woman on horseback," he continued, "with a little boy riding behind her and a small child in her arms." The woman had apparently been with the army from as far back as Marietta and was riding along at the rear while her husband served in the main body of the marching army as a military teamster. In another instance, Samuel Storrow, one of the rare New Englanders in Sherman's army, recalled watching two women march along with as many as twenty-one children all under the age of twelve, a sight that he suggested wasn't that uncommon. "How they [freedwomen] managed to keep up with us I can't imagine," he wrote, adding, "but they did, somehow or other."[19]

Scenes such as these show the importance of freedwomen in Sherman's March. Their experience shaped a message about the March, and even more important, it was a message that the soldiers clearly recognized. As Bradley put it, "All seemed bent on having their freedom." An Illinois diarist even suggested that the "slave women appear more anxious to be free than the men." The man reasoned his way to that conclusion because, in his words, "many a slave mother has carried her little child in her arms, endured hunger and hardships of the march, to be free." What these comments suggest is that it was freedwomen who

88

spoke the loudest to the soldiers; they delivered the most important message of the March: that the campaign was a march toward freedom and that freed people would get there one way or the other.[20]

Yet the soldiers still turned freedwomen away. Freedwomen came to the lines, and the soldiers ordered them back. It didn't matter where the women went. All that mattered was that they get out of the army's way, which turned forcing freedwomen away into a daily routine. "The most pathetic scenes occur upon our line of march daily and hourly," wrote George Ward Nichols, Sherman's aide, adding "Thousands of negro women join the column, some carrying household goods, and many of them carrying children in their arms" before being turned away. Another soldier wrote that most of the refugees "expected to be taken right along to freedom" and expressed a "deep disappointment when told that . . . only such young hearty men as could be made serviceable would be allowed to follow the army." "Day after day he [Sherman] had to explain to them that he could not have his march delayed," the man noted, persuading himself that there must have been some reason or rationale for what he sensed had been a stain on the army's honor.[21]

The man wasn't alone. Turning freedwomen and children away was something most soldiers did with distaste. It was something that had to be done given the circumstances of the March, or so the soldiers told themselves. It would be disingenuous to suggest that the refugee crisis of the March was born of that policy or was of the army's own making. Similarly, not all blame should be placed on Sherman, despite his obsession with military labor. But because of the army's choices, thousands of freed refugees were left with few options beside marching along at the end of those long blue columns.

As late November turned into early December, with Sherman's army inching closer to the coast, the number of refugees following the army continued to grow. "Contraband negroes, both male and female, are now along with the different columns in great numbers," reported an Illinois private from a camp with the left wing just south of Waynesboro, about ninety miles from Savannah. An Ohioan marching with the right wing, then in the vicinity of Swainsboro, summed up the situation like this: "The march by day—winding columns, glittering muskets, glowing flags, General's cavalcades, wagon trains, stragglers, and thousands of negroes in the rear, stretching over miles." Samuel Storrow spared nothing when he wrote similarly, noting that "the number of negroes that flock to our columns is enormous."[22]

One of the basic challenges the refugees faced while marching along behind the army was simply trying to keep up. The columns moved fast and didn't wait. The soldiers charged ahead and left the refugees to their own devices. Remaining together as a family was a problem as well, especially when men and beasts crowded the roads while wagons rumbled along in between. It was easy to get separated, and it was especially easy for young children to lose their way and get caught in the stampede. One soldier remembered a time just past Milledgeville, near the Oconee River, when "all was crowded and in confusion" and a stranded child of about seven or eight years old was "dodging this wagon and that horse" and crying out for his mother. The men driving the teams screamed for him to get out of the way, but the child kept running and crying until out of the soldier's earshot. The man couldn't help but wonder whether the child had ever found his mother, admitting "I've often wondered about it all these years."[23]

When it came to staying together, the refugees who traveled with the help of a horse or carriage had an obvious advantage. For one thing, wagons, carts, and horses mitigated the problem of sore feet. They also kept freed families high and dry and out of the mud, though wheels could always become mired up and a horse's hooves could kick up sludge nearly head high. Important as well was that carriages and wagons provided extra storage, giving families room to stow away trunks of clothes and blankets and baskets of food. David P. Conyngham, the Irish journalist, wrote that he had often seen families piloting "buggies and wagons" loaded down with supplies. Unquestionably, though, the biggest benefit of having some kind of vehicle—be it a horse or a full carriage—was that it provided families a home base, a place to retreat to when things became frantic and to pitch camp when the army stopped and the night grew dark and dangerous. As simple as these things sound, they made all the difference.[24]

The most constant threat was always the most obvious: a chance encounter with Confederate cavalry. Wheeler's mounted cavalry, a force of about thirteen thousand men, hovered around the army and didn't think twice about attacking freed people. In a way, the refugees were easy targets. After all, they were right on the road, and their lines stretched out behind the army. Charles D. Kerr, an Illinois soldier, wrote that "marauding bands" of Wheeler's men "followed our column like an avenging Nemesis, scourging and killing all negroes who were suspected of giving comfort to the enemy." Hence reports such as the one from a Texas cavalry officer who claimed to have "whipped about 1,000 negroes, who were on their way to the enemy." Or this official report by Wheeler himself describing how his cavalry would attack the army's lines at night: "By breaking up the camp during the extreme darkness a great many negroes were left in our hands, whom we sent back to their owners," he wrote, estimating that the "whole number of negroes captured from the enemy during the movement was nearly 2,000."[25]

The task for the refugees was thus to stay in the army's shadow, which sometimes meant evading Confederate cavalry and moving away from the road. "Larger caravans of negroes than before followed our war-path," wrote an Illinois soldier from south of Louisville (pronounced "Lewisville"), noting that the refugees were frequently "cut off by the enemy's cavalry, but by circuitous routes and much hard marching, would make their appearance again." The lines of soldiers and refugees would become extended during the day, but toward dusk, as the army slowed and prepped to camp, the refugees would close the gap. They marched and marched and pressed into the army as close as they could. "Compelled to march in the rear," wrote a soldier with the 104th Regiment Illinois Volunteer Infantry, "they [the refugees] were frequently all night in catching up, not daring to sleep outside of our pickets." He explained that some would even "attach themselves to certain brigades," being sure to "learn the names and numbers of the regiments" so that they could "reach the commands during the night."[26]

It is important to recognize what that kind of persistent movement accomplished. The army denied the freed refugees blanket protection, but by marching in step with the columns and remaining in such close proximity to Sherman's men, the freed people at the end of the lines created a form of refuge for themselves. It was a refuge that was never completely solidified. Nor was it always effective in shielding freed people from danger. It may even be completely inappropriate to think of it as a refuge at all since it was never secure to begin with. Nonetheless, the freed refugees possessed a keen sense of the army's reach and knew that if they pressed into the army, they could avail themselves of its power and protection. That never guaranteed their safety, much less their freedom, but it did make those things more secure. It also reinforced the ideas that the refugees had a *right* to refuge and a *right* to claim the army's power as their own. Both were powerful ideas about what freedom meant to them.

At the same time, the movement into the army's lines was about attaining practical necessities, too. Oftentimes once the refugees came into the lines, the army felt compelled to offer whatever forage could be spared. That general attitude probably applied to forms of shelter and other provisions as well. Pressing into the lines would have also been an occasion for freed people to find work within the regiments as valets, teamsters, or cooks, so there was a baseline level of practical sustenance at stake in following the army so closely. And given that the army's overall posture was to ignore the refugees, pressing deep into the army's lines on a nightly basis was a means of being heard and seen. Doing so forced the soldiers into recognizing the March as something that both the refugees and the soldiers had a stake in.

Of course, the refugees still had to work. And sometimes the soldiers expected a different kind of labor. Night after night they called the refugees into the evening glow of a thousand campfires and made them entertain. They obliged the refugees to dance and sing and strum banjos while the soldiers slapped their knees and cackled into the cool night air. Rice C. Bull, a New Yorker, described the evening festivities as a "new and constant source of fun."

> After the Negros began to follow our army these "contrabands" swarmed our camp at night; they could sing and dance and the boys kept them busy. They sang the plantation hymns and songs and it was as natural for them to dance as to breathe. They often had banjos which they strummed for music; when they had no banjos our boys would beat time on their knees with their hands.

James A. Connolly, the Indiana private, recalled similar scenes, writing about one stop near Louisville during which the "refugee negroes" had performed a "regular plantation dance." Those not dancing "stand in a ring around the dancers" and sing as "loud and as fast and as furious as they can," he noted. He also couldn't help but acknowledge the oddity that here he was, fighting a war deep in enemy territory, and he had spent the evening laughing so hard for so long that his "head and sides" ached.[27]

The laughter was the point. Granted, it's possible to find some genuine goodwill in these moments. John R. McBride spoke for himself as well as others when he wrote that the refugees' "plaintive songs . . . touched the kindly nature of the great body of soldiers," which, in his telling, induced the men to treat the refugees "as humanely as the circumstances would permit." But the jeering laughter and gut-crunching hysterics of the onlooking soldiers overshadowed much of the goodwill being shared.

Moreover, the power dynamics were such that the refugees couldn't refuse. For every gathering that might have started spontaneously, there were equal numbers if not more that happened because the soldiers demanded them. The soldiers "got the contrabands" together, a phrasing that understates the power dynamics in play but still demonstrates that it was the soldiers who initiated those late-evening hootenannies for their own amusement, as if they were the perfect nightcap to a long day's march. It was thus incumbent upon freed people to dance for their place in the lines or risk being blocked from camp. Inclusion came with a cost.[28]

Once south of Louisville, the soldiers rose from their camps each morning to face a new reality. Georgia's landscape was changing and becoming more of an obstacle with each passing day. Confirmation hung on the trees. One soldier wrote from near Millen, not far from Louisville, that for the first time in his life he had seen Spanish moss, the stringy, shaggy epiphyte that hangs on trees in the coastal regions of Georgia and South Carolina. Another wrote similarly about coming upon a cypress swamp, which was "so full of cypress trees that they seem almost impenetrable." To an army of midwesterners, those strange features of the South's coastal landscape were signs that they were close to Savannah and the gentle, rolling hills of middle Georgia were a thing of the past. From there on, marching meant driving headlong into the Lowcountry, a labyrinthlike landscape that saw the shine of the March recede into the swamp.[29]

In addition to the swamps, what made the Lowcountry so difficult to cross was that it was transected by rivers. Even if easily fordable, rivers impede an army's operations. The men had to slow down, stop, build bridges, then start again, all while waiting like targets for a possible Confederate cavalry charge. The soldiers knew how difficult things had become. "As the army advanced more impediments were met," complained one Illinois soldier. "Streams became more numerous, deeper and broader, and swamps more difficult to pass." In some cases, he wrote, the men "were forced to wade for long distances in water sometimes waist-deep." The same soldier who had seen his first bit of Spanish moss described how every major channel had an abundance of streams that ran alongside it, making it terribly hard to move with any speed at all. Even worse, Confederate cavalry had taken to felling trees across the road, which added to the frustration of having to stop and start only to stop and start again. As those impediments became more frequent, the March slowed to a crawl.[30]

Another issue was that Georgia's natural abundance was no more. The once pregnant earth grew barren. The plush fields of middle Georgia, with its seemingly endless stores of food, had slowly given way to a landscape dominated by imposing tracts of tall pine barrens before shading into swampier terrain nearer the coast. For the first time, a sense set in that Sherman's foragers might return empty-handed. It didn't help that Wheeler's cavalry had grown more dogged. In addition to felling trees over the roadways, they had begun to lay waste to whatever might aid Sherman's advance. They drove off cattle, slaughtered pigs, and destroyed whatever rice or corn they couldn't carry in their saddlebags. They also had a penchant for flooding fields, which ruined crops and caused swampy bottomlands to swell up over roadways. All those things made it difficult for the army to move and sustain itself, which seemed to validate the lingering fears that it might stall out before it reached Savannah.

As a result, the calculation changed. Earlier in the campaign, when there had been few swamps to wade through and an abundance of forage to go around, the army had contented itself with letting freed refugees congregate in the rear. Now there was a greater effort to turn freed people away. No official order came down, yet there was nevertheless an attempt to turn back the clock on the past month's worth of marching and renege on what had otherwise been a tacit policy. "Negroes swarmed to us to-day," wrote an Illinois private from the banks of the Ogeechee River. "Saw 30 or 40 turned back," he continued, insisting that it had been "Sherman's order not to let anymore go with us than we can feed." An Illinois officer expressed the resignation that would gradually become the army's default position when he wrote from the near side of Ebenezer Creek, "The negroes come into our lines by hundreds, but we cannot do anything for them."[31]

There wasn't always an armywide consensus on how turning freed people away should be done. In fact, sometimes the speed and severity with which the columns turned back freed refugees depended on who outranked whom and the decisions made by Sherman's lieutenants. There were a number of officers in charge of deciding what should be done about the refugees. Some were more restrained than others. Fortunate refugees might have come into the camp of someone such as General Absalom Baird, a division commander of the Fourteenth Army Corps, whom Connolly described as being "quite an abolitionist." But for every Absalom Baird there was a Jefferson C. Davis, an "ardent pro-slavery man," in the words of one soldier, whose orders would prove tragic on the banks of Ebenezer Creek.[32]

He had a traitorous name. Jefferson Columbus Davis, the head of Sherman's Fourteenth Army Corps, shared first and last names with Jefferson Finis Davis, the angular-faced Confederate president and commander in chief. By the time Sherman's army embarked on its now-famous march, infamy followed General Davis wherever he went, and not just because of the misfortune of his name. Something had happened in Louisville, Kentucky, back in 1862. Davis was there after convalescing at his home in southern Indiana, but things got out of hand when a conflict arose between him and General William "Bull" Nelson, the commanding officer in charge of the city. It was a matter of personal offense. Nelson had insulted Davis during their first meeting by questioning Davis's competence. Weeks later, on a return trip to Louisville, Davis approached

Nelson and demanded an apology, but the hulking three-hundred-pound general just scoffed at the rather diminutive Davis. "Go away, you damned puppy," is what Nelson is reported to have said, which sparked Davis's temper. In a rage, he crumpled up a resignation letter he had in his pocket and flipped the wad of paper into Nelson's face, an insult Nelson responded to by backhanding Davis across the cheek.[33]

What happened next should have had Davis hung. He immediately left Nelson and scoured the city in search of a pistol. When he found one, he returned to Nelson's headquarters at the Galt House Hotel. He marched into the lobby and straight up to the general's office, pulled back the hammer, aimed, and shot Nelson dead. Stunned witnesses later reported that after slaying Nelson, Davis had never tried to run. He had never acted bothered. He had just stood there stoically, stooping over Nelson's rotund body, until the authorities had whisked him away. Though arrested, Davis was ultimately never charged. His friend and fellow general Horatio Wright managed to get him released on account of the army's dire need for good fighting men at the front. As a result, Davis never saw so much as a trial. He returned to the army and worked his way back up the chain of command, though his murdering Nelson wasn't something that anyone ever forgot. Everyone knew that beneath those hollow, sunken eyes lay the heart of a stone-cold killer.[34]

Despite his well-earned reputation for roguery, Davis was one of Sherman's best fighting men. He and his long beard and perpetual frown had been with Sherman since Chattanooga. He had made a name for himself during the monthslong fight for Atlanta and now found himself in charge of the outermost column of Sherman's left wing. Since leaving Milledgeville, he had steered his men through Louisville and Millen while making a slight feint toward Augusta, the city most people had thought would be Sherman's target. He now occupied a path that placed him closest to the Savannah River, which meant that he and his column faced the worst of the rivers and the swampiest ground. The engineers were repeatedly called on to lay out pontoons and get the army from one side of a stream to the next. There were also near-constant reports of Confederate cavalry hovering off the edges of the roads, which placed the men in a precarious position.

Freed people had been following Davis's column for some time. "A large number of negroes, principally women, have been allowed to follow in the wake of the army," wrote one of Davis's men in early December, just south of Louisville. The growing crowd had been grating on Davis since the first few weeks of the campaign. Of all Sherman's subordinate generals, he was the only one to complain of them directly and in writing. "Useless negroes are being accumulated to an extent which would be suicide to a column which must be constantly stripped for battle and prepared for the utmost celerity of movement," he had written earlier in the March. "We cannot expect that the present unobstructed march will continue much longer," he wrote before adding, "Our wagons are too much overladen to allow of their being filled with negro women and children or their baggage, and every additional mouth consumes food, which it requires risk to obtain." He was building his case. In his next line, he imposed new orders. He would no longer allow freed refugees to ride along in wagons, and only "the servants of mounted officers" would be allowed horses or mules. It was an early act of deterrence, and that hard line would get harder still.[35]

Davis first drew the harder line along a stream known as Buckhead Creek, which was fairly shallow and not as imposing as some of the other bodies of water that lay closer to the coast. What happened at Buckhead Creek was a preview of what would happen later at Ebenezer Creek. Colonel John J. Hight, a member of an Indiana regiment in Davis's division, called it a scene "disgraceful to American history." Davis, described by Colonel Hight as a "military tyrant, without one spark of humanity," ordered the bridges up before the refugees had a chance to cross, a decision even more dastardly than it sounds given that Confederate cavalry had been spotted following close at the column's rear. It was also armywide knowledge that should the refugees fall into Wheeler's grasp, his men would either murder or reenslave them, an outcome that meant subjecting them to the terrible punishments reserved for runaway slaves. Those were the clear consequences of leaving the refugees stranded, and to take Hight's word for it, everyone knew it.[36]

Nevertheless, Davis's orders were carried out. Cries of alarm went up with the bridges and grew louder as more refugees realized they were being abandoned. Then panic set in. "The rebels are coming," someone shouted, a false alarm that nonetheless sent groups of refugees plunging into the river while others "ran wildly up and down the bank, shrieking with terror and crying for help." The creek proved to be passable, so most of the freed refugees made it up the opposite bank cold and wet but safe. However, not everyone made it across. Some who went into the water never returned, though exactly how many was never known. One soldier estimated that only a small number had died in the melee. Another soldier expressed amazement that so many had made it, writing that as many as five hundred refugees "were left on the wrong side of the river sure enough, but when we broke camp next morning, they were all there again all the same." "By what means they had crossed," the man admitted, "I do not know."[37]

Pulling up the bridges to block the refugees became Davis's calling card. It would happen later with much more tragic results at Ebenezer Creek, but it seems he used the same ploy on at least one other occasion in the intervening days, likely at the crossing of a stream known as Rocky Comfort Creek. In that particular case, the stream wasn't all that deep, so the refugees waded across without much trouble. Moreover, Hight tells us, the freed people had grown far less trusting of the soldiers and had started finding their own ways to cross without worrying about the army and its bridges, which poses the question: How many more times did Davis pull up the bridges before the tragedy at Ebenezer Creek? The answer isn't clear. What is clear is that it became a pattern. It was premeditated and repeated. Davis kept trying to block the refugees, even after disaster was so narrowly averted at Buckhead Creek.[38]

The terrible tragedy at Ebenezer Creek had thus been in the works before the army arrived at the river's edge. The water was cold, and the creek ran through the heart of what Connolly described as "the most gloomy, dismal cypress swamp I ever saw." The road was also little more than a narrow causeway surrounded by low-lying swamps on each side, a path allowing little room to move and no room for error. The army column sat in that narrow corridor of trees and water for quite some time. Wheeler's men had done a prodigious job of tearing up the roads, and it took some time for Davis's engineering corps to make them passable again. In the meantime, the loud *crack, crack, crack* of rifles went off somewhere toward the army's rear as Wheeler's men skirmished with Davis's stalled column. "It was a mean business to fight in the swamp," admitted one soldier, recalling that the next day, "We krept [*sic*] out of the tangled mas [*sic*] of cypress knees [trunks] and vines toward the road." The army was moving again and finally crossing the creek.[39]

James A. Connolly saw everything coming. Prior to the crossing he had ridden with one of Davis's aides and found another of his aides "turning off the road, into the swamp all of the fugitive negroes that came along," presumably not to let anyone cross the bridge before the army. "When we should cross I knew it was the intention that the bridge should be burned, and I inquired if the negroes were not to be permitted to cross," he wrote. The aide then told him what he already knew: that Davis had ordered them to block the freed refugees from using the bridge. "This I knew, and Genl. Davis knew must result in all these negroes being captured or brutally shot down by the rebel cavalry tomorrow morning," he noted, as he imagined the shouts and screams and the implications of the tragedy. "The idea of five or six hundred black women, children, and old men thus returned to slavery by such an infernal copperhead as Jeff C. Davis was entirely too much for my Democracy," he admitted, saying that he gave the aides a severe tongue-lashing, letting them know just what he "thought of such an inhuman, barbarous proceeding in language which may possibly result in a reprimand." Little good did it do. Connolly could see the tragedy coming, but Davis had his plan set and ready to go.[40]

What happened along the banks of Ebenezer Creek once the bridge went up was nothing short of horrific. Cries rang out as the bridge rose; men, women, and children felt terror as they realized what was unfolding. The true sign of their abandonment came after the army pulled up the bridge and, according to some reports, burned what was left of it, which became a smoldering indication of the army's intention. The quick-thinking got to work building makeshift rafts out of fallen tree limbs; sympathetic soldiers on the other side of the river began felling tall pines across the water to act as bridges or rails to get everyone across. Some refugees, especially the men, went straight into the water, hoping to swim across and hopefully get help on the opposite bank. "It was a really pitiful to see them. They are afraid of the rebels and begged hard to get over," recalled an Indiana soldier who had witnessed it all and remembered that "Some of the men swam the river but the women and children could not get over."[41]

Then came Wheeler and his men. "The rear guard had no sooner crossed the creek than Wheeler's cavalry charged into the crowd of refugees," remembered William Passmore Carlin, one of Sherman's generals. "The Rebels came up and fired into them," recalled a soldier. Whole groups of refugees leapt into the water as bedlam broke out on the near bank; others ran up and down the water's edge trying to escape. Some even tried to crawl under the river bank in a desperate attempt for cover. Screams and shrieks and shouts and shots rose out of the chaos. The water splashed. Bullets ripped into the river, whizzing past those fighting the current. Men and women tried to swim, often with one hand holding on to a loved one and the other treading water in an attempt to reach the far bank. Soldiers standing on the opposite side started throwing logs, sticks, and old planks—*anything*—into the water, so that those splashing and swimming might have some help in getting to the other side. The Irish journalist David Conyngham described it as being like the crossing of the Red Sea absent God's protection. "Wheeler's cavalry charged on them," he wrote, "driving them, pellmell, into" a deep, dark stream whose current swept mothers away from their children and pulled others under, some never to reemerge.[42]

Once the firing ceased and the surface of the water turned still and placid, soldiers watched as men and women reemerged. They dragged themselves up from the water, through the brush, and onto the river's far bank. It was a sad and dismal sight that told the full extent of what had just happened. Most had on very little clothing, recalled an Illinois private, who added that what covering anyone did have was dripping wet. Groups of forlorn survivors huddled by fires lit and set by the soldiers, everyone shivering from the cold and "the poor women and children crying as if their hearts would break." It was clear that not everyone had made it. The same Illinois private noticed that a woman whom he had met only three days before who had declared that "she would go with us or perish" no longer traveled with the small child who had previously accompanied her. The man presumed that the child was dead. Only a short while later the man noticed another broken family trying to gather themselves in the aftermath of the massacre. Both husband and wife had made it across by swimming, but their little boy had drowned. The mother was now crying—likely an inconsolable, weeping cry, the kind that comes from the heart-wrenching pain of a mother who has lost a child. "The sights I this morning witnessed I cannot get out of my mind," wrote the soldier, obviously disturbed by all he had seen.[43]

Exactly how many refugees went into the water and never came out will likely never be known. The same is true for the number of freed people killed or reenslaved by Wheeler's cavalry. All we have are anecdotal reports and personal recollections, but even with such spotty sources, it is clear that the crossing of Ebenezer Creek was both tragic and haunting. Carlin reported that "Many women leaped into the water, some with children in their arms. Some drowned; some were reported to have been killed by the Confederate cavalry. The remainder were held as former prisoners and sent back to their former masters." Another soldier agreed, writing that "some were drowned" and that it was "also certain that many of the old and infirm perished by the way." Charles Kerr later claimed to have seen hundreds of men and women languishing in the "turbid stream." "I speak of what I saw with my own eyes," he wrote. ". . . It is claimed that this was done because rations were becoming scarce; in short, that it was military necessity." "There was no necessity about it," he insisted, adding "It was unjustifiable and perfidious, and across the stretch of twenty years my soul burns with indignation to-night as I recall it."[44]

The soldiers' initial reaction was to condemn Jefferson C. Davis. "I cannot find the words to express my detestation of such cruelty and wickedness," John Hight exclaimed. "May God Almighty save this nation from the responsibility of General Davis's acts!" Hight wasn't alone. Soldiers didn't hold back in damning Davis to Hell. "If I had the power I would have him [hanged] high as Haman," wrote James Comfort Patten, an Indiana medic. "There is great indignation among the troops," he went on, suggesting that outrage had apparently spread so far and wide that Davis ought to fear for his life. For his part, Connolly threatened Davis in a different way. After cursing Davis's aides prior to the bridge being pulled up, he vowed to "expose this act of his publicly" and threatened that, "if he [Davis] undertakes to vent his spleen on me for it, I have the *same rights that he himself exercised in his affair with Nelson*," a reference to Davis's having murdered Nelson. Apparently, Connolly penned a letter about the incident at Ebenezer Creek to his congressman, who forwarded the letter to the *New York Times*, though no such letter of his has ever been found.[45]

The massacre at Ebenezer Creek was a watershed moment in the short history of Sherman's March. For the soldiers, the guilt of having betrayed the refugees combined with the testimonies of how freed people had gone to such great lengths (and lost so much) to cross the river inspired a newfound respect for them. "And what is it all for? Freedom. They are periling their lives for freedom, and it seems to me that any people who run such risks are entitled to freedom," insisted the Illinois private who saw it all. Jacob D. Cox, an early historian of the March, concurred, writing that the incident demonstrated to the soldiers that "it was literally preferable to die freemen than live slaves," a growing sentiment that spanned the army. For the refugees, the crossing of Ebenezer Creek changed everything. People died, people mourned, families had been shattered, and the survivors wore the remnants of the crossing in the threads of their soaking wet clothes. It was also a point of no return. Marching ahead now meant carrying an unerasable trauma, and those who might have wanted to turn back couldn't. They could neither recross the creek nor risk facing Wheeler's men, making continuing onward the only option.[46]

Another reason that the crossing at Ebenezer Creek was such an inflection point for Sherman and his March was that it had political implications far beyond the wagon roads that led to the coast. In pieces and in fragments Northern newsreaders soon learned of the incident. In turn, news of Ebenezer Creek slowly emerged as the central plank of a much larger narrative positing that Sherman and his men had turned their backs on the freed people following the army. Though that general narrative never came close to matching the triumphal reports of how Sherman had subdued Georgia and rode into Savannah a conquering hero, it did undercut his standing among politicians and policymakers back home. So what awaited Sherman when he arrived in Savannah was a tangled political knot, which he eventually dealt with by issuing one of the war's most transformative orders. The legacy of Ebenezer Creek thus shaped the South well after the war.

Yet while news of Ebenezer Creek stirred political winds in Washington after the army arrived on the coast, as of early December, there was still a long way to go. Savannah lay roughly twenty-five miles from Ebenezer Creek, which meant that the long lines of men and women following the army still had days of marching ahead of them. Worse, Davis wasn't done. After leaving the swamp that surrounded Ebenezer Creek, his Fourteenth Corps came upon another creek, Lockner Creek (sometimes spelled Lochner Creek). There, he once again ordered the pulling up of the temporary bridges so that none of the refugees could cross, and as one soldier recalled, "The order was obeyed to the letter." The freed people following Davis's column rushed to the water's edge and begged that they might be let across—to no avail. The rear guard simply marched on and left the refugees to find their own way across the creek, which required wading through another dark stream in the damp Georgia winter. Once again, freed people pushed, and the army pulled back. The March, meanwhile, went on. Savannah lay ahead, and its defensive guns were now louder than ever.[47]

When Sherman's army reached the outskirts of Savannah in mid-December, most, if not all, of the refugees would have been footsore and weary. The March had lasted for more than a month. Some of the refugees had been with the army from as far back as Atlanta and beyond. Most of the others had joined at various points along the way. Many hundreds, if not thousands, more had run to the army and joined the March but then turned back before completing the campaign. "Ten thousand negroes left the plantations of their former masters and accompanied the column when it reached Savannah, without taking note of thousands more who joined the army but from various causes had to leave it at different points," wrote an Iowan who marched in Sherman's ranks as he reflected on the campaign. "There are thousands of negroes with our army," another soldier wrote from just outside Savannah. Yet even with the city coming into view, the refugee experience was still far from over. Savannah would prove to be not the end but only the end of the beginning.[48]

Freed people from Beaufort, South Carolina, circa 1862, not long after the Port Royal Experiment began.

Chapter Four

THE PIVOT TO
PORT ROYAL

I t was a cold mid-December day, and S. Willard Saxton, the second
son of New England abolitionists, could hear guns firing in the distance. Sherman's army was massing around Savannah, and every so often
the low, rumbling echo of war made its way to the South Carolina Sea
Islands, where Willard served as an aide to his older brother, General
Rufus Saxton, the region's military governor. Willard, who wrote letters
and documents for Rufus, recorded the army's movements in the pages
of his diary. "Fort McAllister was taken yesterday morning," he wrote
on December 14, referencing the redoubt on the Ogeechee River. With
Fort McAllister, the guardian of Savannah, in federal hands, the city had
no defense. Just as important, Fort McAllister's fall and the opening of
the Ogeechee meant that Sherman now had access to the Atlantic Ocean
and to the neighboring Sea Islands just up the coast. "These are good
& exciting times in this dept.," Willard wrote, no doubt suspecting that
Sherman's arrival would mean major changes for his brother's command.[1]

Meanwhile, as the Union Army waited on the outskirts of Savannah following the fall of Fort McAllister, the war arrived on Georgia's
coast. "Squads came all day until near dark," reported Mary Mallard, the
daughter of the deceased Charles Colcock Jones, one of coastal Georgia's

wealthiest planters. "Squads of Yankees came all day," she wrote two days later as Union cavalrymen swarmed their plantation. The soldiers fleeced them of all their chickens, drove off their cows, ransacked the kitchen, broke open chests, and rifled through closets. Some assumed a veneer of common courtesy; others went in wildly. "All our pleasant things are laid low," her widowed mother, Mary Jones, moaned after nearly a month of it all. "Every trunk, bureau, box, room, closet . . . and whatever was wanted of provisions, clothing, jewelry, knives, forks, spoons. . . . The whole house turned topsy-turvy."[2]

As wave after wave of roving soldiers arrived on the Jones plantation, the chaos of the war fanned out across the region—to plantations and roadsides, along rivers and creeks, out into the marshes and the piney woods. Sherman's right wing encamped at a place called King's Bridge, a former river crossing of the Ogeechee located just upriver from Fort McAllister and not far from the Joneses' coastal empire in Liberty County. In the coming days, Sherman would turn the old crossing at King's Bridge into a federal depot. With Fort McAllister out of the picture, the US Navy, which had a number of ships in port on the South Carolina Sea Islands up the coast, began sending ships loaded with mail, supplies, and whatever else the army needed. The camp there would serve as a base of operations even after the fall of Savannah with most of the army located in the city, as the Ogeechee remained one of the region's strategic arteries, a coastal waterway that commanded the entire region south of Savannah and beyond.

The situation was a bit different for Sherman's left wing. The two army corps had approached Savannah from the north, with Davis's Fourteenth Corps moving along the Savannah River, and were now inching closer to the city. The situation there was far more hazardous, mostly because it had turned into a slog. The upper neck of the Savannah River nurses interminable swamps and streams and is bisected by a number of marsh-filled river islands that can seem almost impenetrable to the naked eye, much less a moving army. Moreover, whereas the troops encamped at

King's Bridge received an infusion of fresh supplies, those trudging through the swamps north of Savannah didn't. They were too far away to be provisioned and thus had to keep foraging, except that foraging wasn't as productive as it had used to be. Food was now much harder to come by, and many of the soldiers believed that they would've starved if it hadn't been for enslaved people and their knowledge of rice.[3]

To Sherman's army, made up mostly of midwesterners, rice might as well have been a foreign substance. They could find it in abundance, but most had never seen it unhusked, and they didn't know how to handle the mortar and pestle, the tools needed to hull it. "Not being used to the devices for separating the two [the rice from the hull], we made slow work at it," reported a Wisconsin man. Colonel Oscar L. Jackson of Ohio reported likewise, writing "The men tried to get something eatable out of the rice . . . but it was almost impossible to hull it." Fortunately for them, the region's enslaved people had an intimate knowledge of rice. The tiny Old World grain had been a West African import, brought over on some of the earliest slave ships, and enslaved people on the coast of Georgia and South Carolina had been harvesting rice for almost two centuries in some places. It defined how they worked and how they lived, and it carried their history, creating a cultural imprint that had given rise to a plantation world distinct from the rest of the cotton-growing South.[4]

The soldiers survived on rice partly because enslaved people were willing to share it with them—even if sometimes for a small fee. The same Wisconsin man who complained of not knowing how to work the mortar and pestle reported paying enslaved people as much as fifty cents a quart for them to hull the rice. Another Indiana man wrote about employing enslaved people to thresh and hull it—and said that if he and his comrades had only had a little salt to season it, they wouldn't have had reason to complain. In other instances, soldiers learned how to use the mortar and pestle by watching enslaved people and then were able to hull it themselves. The way some soldiers described "keeping them [the enslaved] at work" suggests that some form of coercion may have been used to compel the labor of enslaved people. Even so, the point remains that Sherman's left wing ate and survived because Georgia's enslaved people sustained them.[5]

Of course, if rice was tantamount to a foreign substance, Georgia's coastal rice plantations might well have been foreign lands. It was all strange and new: the sluice gates, canals, and ditches, even the language. What the soldiers would soon learn was that enslaved people there tended to speak in a patois known as Gullah, a creolized pidgin form of English that had grown out of the African majorities of the colonial period and never disappeared. There were also large numbers of enslaved people who spoke not just in differing dialects, such as Gullah, but in actual foreign tongues including French and Spanish. "Many of them used the French language and could not understand a word of English," remembered one soldier in reference to a group of enslaved people who ran a rice mill for the soldiers just north of Savannah. Another remembered happening upon a plantation where "some five or six score of French or Spanish negroes" had been enslaved. Many of those men and women may have been smuggled into the United States via the international slave trade, an institution that had been banned in the United States in 1808 but still existed illicitly.[6]

One of the rice barons with a set of plantations on the Savannah River was a Lowcountry planter named Charles Manigault. He was a member of one of the South's wealthiest families. His ancestors had been some of the original French Huguenots to arrive not in Charleston but in *Charles Town*, back when it had been a colonial venture cut out of the Carolina swamps. His grandfather Peter Manigault had at one point in time been the wealthiest man in North America, with most of his wealth invested in land and slaves. Like his Manigault forebears, Charles was a wealthy man. He had been a successful merchant, with contacts around the globe, and in 1827, he had inherited his first plantation, Silk Hope, in the Berkeley District of Charleston, along with its 126 enslaved people. A decade later, he expanded his holdings by purchasing two rice plantations, Gowrie and East Hermitage, on Argyle Island, a marshy island in the Savannah River, which brought the total number of people he enslaved to about two hundred. His son Louis Manigault managed his father's affairs at Gowrie and East Hermitage, and it was Louis who had last checked in on the place in December 1864, just days before Sherman's Twentieth Corps turned the entire island into a staging ground for the advance on Savannah.[7]

Not long after the army arrived, the Manigault fiefdom on Argyle Island went up in flames. Sherman's soldiers destroyed "Gowrie Mill, then the Gowrie Dwelling, and lastly the entire Gowrie Settlement," wrote a neighboring overseer, who claimed to have seen it "with his own eyes." The barn had also been burned, as had the threshing house, which was first looted and stripped of all its contents. Then, in the days after the army left, the whole place flooded. "A large Freshet"—a flood of water—"came down," wrote J. M. Bandy, the Manigault overseer, and like a busted dam, gushing water swelled over a bank near the house, likely flooding the yard and everything in it. That wasn't all. "The Negroes before I left cut the Canal bank at the red trunk to make their escape in a big flat," remembered Bandy. They had apparently dug out a section of the canal, floated onto the river, and made their escape via the water. When Bandy wrote to Charles months later, he explained that they had all left for "Savannah, Hilton Head, or elsewhere."[8]

None of that surprised either Charles or Louis. A subtle sense of resignation imbued their letters, and unlike the Jones family, who had long believed that some kind of paternal kinship existed between them and the people they enslaved, the Manigaults knew otherwise. The war had disabused them of that idea. "Paid my last visit to the Plantation during the war, and saw my Father's Negroes for the last time," wrote Louis after his last visit in December before the army's arrival, aware that he would never see them again. Charles had the same realization.

"I presume the [enslaved] Men are all gone," he wrote to Louis just after Christmas, guessing that if anyone remained it might be the women and only because Sherman's army would have refused them access. The Manigaults had largely resigned themselves to reality; yet at least some part of them must have agreed with Mary Jones, their Lowcountry neighbor to the south, when she penned her own plantation elegy, writing "Clouds and darkness are round about us; the hand of the Almighty is laid in sore judgement upon us; we are a desolated and smitten people. . . . At present the foundations of society are broken up; what hereafter is to be our social and civil status we cannot see."[9]

William J. Hardee, a former West Point commandant of cadets and the author of a popular field manual used to train soldiers in both the Union and Confederate armies, was an experienced soldier. Following the fall of Fort McAllister, the river fort on the Ogeechee and Savannah's last line of defense, the seasoned Confederate general knew it was only a matter of time until Sherman launched a direct assault his forces in Savannah couldn't possibly withstand. Accordingly, Hardee, a native Georgian, did what Confederate armies in Georgia had grown accustomed to doing: he *fled*. On the night of December 20, around dark, he marshaled his men, marched them across the Savannah River using a temporary bridge, and cut his way north into South Carolina. It was a quick and slippery movement that saved his army but relinquished the ultimate prize. Savannah, Georgia's old colonial birthplace and still the largest city in the state, had no choice but to surrender, and early the next morning, Sherman's army moved in and let out a sigh of relief. The wait was finally over. The campaign was officially complete.[10]

The city had seen better days. Though some of the soldiers recognized the neatness of its parks and squares, its public greenery, and its handsome streets lined with beautiful homes, the war had clearly taken its toll. One soldier likened the city to a "half-dressed old maid, whose clothes had been out of fashion and repair for half a century." Others noted the apparent destitution of the place: the lack of food, the deserted buildings, the people peddling wares on the street. More than a few of the soldiers also felt a sense of national déjà vu, for Savannah was, and still is, a living testament to the American Revolution, with squares named for some of the war's heroes. In fact, right in the center of town on Monterey Square, the soldiers discovered a nearly thirty-foot-high column with a bronze plaque commemorating General Casimir Pulaski, Savannah's Polish-born Revolutionary War hero, who had died defending the city against a British attack. The marble-and-limestone monument with a Lady Liberty figure on top commanded their attention, serving as a solemn reminder that the heirs of independence were retracing the steps of history, fighting a war to finish a struggle that the previous war had left incomplete.[11]

The feeling was hard to ignore—in part because Savannah's African American community wouldn't let the soldiers see it any other way. Exultations went up and celebrations began almost as soon as the army moved in. "When the morning light of the 22d of December, 1864, broke in upon us, the streets of our city were thronged in every part with the victorious army of liberty . . . and the cry went around the city from house to house among our race of people, 'Glory be to God, we are free!'" recalled James M. Simms, a formerly enslaved person born in Savannah and once a pastor of the First African Baptist Church of Savannah, the first black Baptist congregation in North America. On street corners across the city people rejoiced. Freed people praised and blessed the soldiers. They also danced and sang and joined with the soldiers, with the notes of "John Brown's Body" and "Blow Ye the Trumpet, Blow" lifted up into the cool winter air. One soldier remembered an evening celebration at the Second African Baptist Church, where the choir sang in a rapturous chorus:

Blow ye the trumpet, blow!
The gladly solemn sound
let all the nations know,
to earth's remotest bound:
The year of jubilee is come!

Sherman received his share of adulation as well. During the first few days of the occupation, scores of black Savannahians—from formerly enslaved people to members of the city's free Black population—lined up to meet the general and pay him their respects, telling him, as one did, "Been praying for you long time, Sir, prayin' day and night for you, and now, bless god, you is come."[12]

The well-wishers met Sherman at his new headquarters, the beautiful Green House on Madison Square, a nineteenth-century Gothic Revival mansion built from money made in the cotton trade. Its owner, Charles Green, a native of England, had welcomed the general and his staff, as had most of the city's white residents. It was not necessarily a sign of amity; rather, it was an effort to prevent what had happened in Atlanta from happening in Savannah. The sentiment was one that Sherman appreciated, and indeed, he kept destruction to a minimum and was willing to work with the city's leaders to rebuild the place and make it functional again. But he wasn't ready to fully oblige them—at least not yet. In his earliest acts as the de facto head of the city, he requisitioned the last of the city's store of cotton, close to twenty-five thousand bales, and its remaining guns; dismantled the city's defenses; took possession of all the public buildings and warehouses; distributed his men through-out the city, turning those neat little squares into army encampments; and later, on the night of December 22, made a show of the transfer of power, sending a widely publicized letter to Lincoln that read "I beg to present you, as a Christmas gift, the city of Savannah."[13]

Over the next several days, the army made itself at home. Though there was no official word, most all the soldiers knew they would remain in the city at least through the holidays, so they relaxed. They ate, drank, and paid freedwomen to wash their clothes. They feasted on fresh oysters sold by the pail, and when they weren't performing official duties or attending church, they explored their new surroundings as wartime tourists, with some taking leisurely strolls along the river or visiting the city's many parks. "Savannah is all that the Tourists have pictured it in books," wrote a Chicagoan, recalling the beauty of Bonaventura, a plantation turned cemetery full of live oaks that still attracts thousands of visitors a year. Unlike in occupations past, the overall mood remained mostly cordial and calm. The stress of such a large army hadn't yet worn the city thin, and local whites were still trying to charm the soldiers into not burning the place down. It wouldn't stay like that for long. But for the time being, the soldiers enjoyed a quiet and peaceful end to an otherwise long and violent year.[14]

That was not the case for the freed refugees. Most of the many thousands of freed people who had followed the army would never see Savannah. Nor would they have a chance to rest or gather themselves before having to move on again. Just after the fall of Fort McAllister, while the soldiers were still digging in and expecting a siege, Sherman issued orders for an armywide scaling back. He wanted most of the surplus material his men had requisitioned while on the March to be sent away, and his orders included the freed men and women. "Army commanders will forthwith send to General Easton, chief quartermaster, at King's Bridge, all negroes, horses, mules, and wagons rendered surplus by our change in operations, or to such points on the Ogeechee River as General Easton may indicate," the order, dated December 16, read. The freed people who had attached themselves to the army as cooks, valets, or common laborers would remain in their posts, and those men and women most likely followed the army into Savannah; all the rest were forced, likely under arms, over to the Ogeechee River, where they would wait until transports could take them up the coast to Port Royal, a small Union outpost on the coast of South Carolina that had been in the army's hands since November 1861.[15]

Sherman opted for such an elaborate movement because the post-campaign reports confirmed what he had suspected: that the number of freed people attached to the army had grown to an astounding figure. Alpheus Williams, the head of the Twentieth Army Corps, reported that as many as six to eight thousand refugees had followed his army during the March and as many as twenty-five hundred were waiting outside Savannah with his columns. Henry Slocum, Williams's superior and the commander of the left wing, reported an even larger number. He believed that as many as fourteen thousand freed people had joined the March and guessed that more than half that number had arrived in Savannah. Sherman, for his part, believed that the total number of refugees with his army was larger still. He suggested at one point that no fewer than twenty thousand freed people had followed his columns to the coast, a number that almost matched the total population of Savannah in 1860 and was nearly double the prewar population of Atlanta.[16]

At first, there was no special reason for where the refugees were located. Most arrived on the coast with the columns they had traveled with, though some efforts had been made to congregate the freed people in temporary camps—or *colonies*, to use the language of Sherman's men. One such camp was at the Colerain Plantation, a former rice plantation north of Savannah where as many as seventeen hundred refugees worked a rice mill while they waited for the army to move. Another was at King's Bridge, where in the ten days between the army's arrival on the Ogeechee River and the eventual fall of Savannah, close to twelve hundred freed people had pitched camp near the army's temporary headquarters. Charles E. Smith of the 32nd Regiment Ohio Volunteer Infantry was one of seven men charged with overseeing the makeshift encampment. He and his team managed to feed the refugees with a share of the army's rations, but living conditions remained primitive at best. A "few old tents" and what Smith described as "pole and brush shanties"—otherwise known as lean-tos—were all that stood between them and the "uncommonly cold" winter weather.[17]

The unfolding situation at King's Bridge was a piece of what Sherman could see was a much larger problem. Twelve hundred, after all, is only a sliver of twenty thousand, and that twenty thousand didn't include the enslaved population of Savannah, which had been about seven thousand in 1860. It also doesn't include the large numbers of freed people from outside the city, who in the coming weeks would arrive and turn Savannah into an unsettled hub for displaced people from across the region, further swelling the number of refugees within the army's orbit. The situation, while stable for the moment, was close to snowballing, and Sherman knew it. The army was on the brink of having tens of thousands of refugees—upward, perhaps, of twenty-five to thirty thousand—pressing into its camps in need of necessities such as food and shelter, a prospect which, try as it might, the army couldn't possibly ignore. It was time to face up to the crisis at hand. But facing up to the problem was only part of it; even if the army endeavored to help the refugees, provisioning that many people presented a basic problem of supply.[18]

Savannah was also only a temporary resting place. The war hadn't yet been won, which meant that the army would soon be on the move. What then? One thing was certain: Sherman wasn't going to let the refugees follow him any farther. He already thought it a minor miracle that they hadn't impeded the campaign's progress, and he wasn't about to keep what he considered to be an albatross tied around the army's neck. But the situation was also such that he could neither ignore them or send them away. What he needed was a much more suitable solution, because if a message had emerged from that long march through Georgia, it was that the refugees would keep marching. They would follow the army and endure incredible hardships just to get to where the army was going. Collectively, the overwhelming movement of people convinced Sherman that he needed a more permanent place to put the refugees—or else he'd find himself in the same situation, with thousands of freed people following the army into the next campaign.

As it happened, what seemed as good a solution as any sat just up the coast at Port Royal. Located on the Beaufort River alongside the deepest deepwater port on the southern coastline, Port Royal was the key to an island complex that was both a federal military enclave and an expanding freedmen's colony. As of December 1864, close to fifteen thousand freed people were living on the islands alongside teams of Northern white agents—a motley mix of missionaries, educators, capitalists, and would-be plantation managers. The agents had been on the islands since the spring of 1862 and had served, in their own minds, as vanguards of the revolution. They had built freedmen's schools, organized churches, and administered aid, but—and this is a critical *but*—they had also forced the freed people back into the fields, not as slaves but as free laborers working for an unspecified wage. The project had federal backing via the War Department under the auspices of the Port Royal Experiment, and at its head was General Rufus Saxton, an abolitionist and former quartermaster who now presided over Port Royal and the surrounding Sea Islands as the military governor of the Department of the South.[19]

In all likelihood, Sherman had probably made the decision to send the refugees to Port Royal weeks earlier while still on the March. On December 13, just after arriving on the Ogeechee and in one of his earliest letters announcing his presence on the coast, he wrote to General in Chief Henry Halleck, telling his old friend "My first duty will be to clear the army of surplus negroes, horses, and mules" and that he supposed General Saxton could help "relieve me of these." In Sherman's mind, shipping the freed refugees up the coast to Port Royal was an obvious answer, but it wasn't the only option. General Grant, it seemed, wanted the refugees sent all the way to City Point, Virginia, where presumably the freedmen would have been put to work on the siege lines around Petersburg. Halleck, though, convinced Grant otherwise. He explained that not only would the refugees struggle through a winter in Virginia, but to send them North would "create a panic among them" and potentially deter escapees from the interior. "Rebel papers are already harping on this point in order to frighten their slaves," he wrote after recommending that the refugees be kept with Saxton in the Department of the South.[20]

But Saxton had serious reservations. As he noted in his end-of-year report, the project at Port Royal had swollen in size within the past year. New refugees arriving from elsewhere along the coast had increased the overall population of freed people, putting pressure on the project's already meager resources. There were also more military personnel operating on the islands, which had left a dearth of shelter and space. In response, Saxton wrote to Sherman, begging that the refugees might instead be sent to either St. Simons Island, a small island located farther south on the Georgia coast, or Edisto Island, a South Carolina island situated just up the coast from Port Royal. "I greatly fear that if these contrabands are sent to this post there will be much suffering among them," he explained, "as I have neither men nor the means at my command to provide them with shelter." "Every cabin and house on these islands are filled to overflowing," he added, reminding Sherman that he already had "some 15,000" freed people under his command.[21]

Sherman sympathized with Saxton's pleas, but in the end, little changed. Preparations went ahead as planned. Steamers made their way up the Ogeechee. Refugees serving in the army as either personal servants or military laborers stayed put. All other able-bodied men were given the chance to sign on as laborers—or enlist in the army as members of the United States Colored Troops. All the rest—with a preponderance of women, children, and the elderly—were subject to Sherman's orders. They journeyed to General L. C. Easton, the chief quartermaster stationed on the Ogeechee, and were made to wait—likely in the already established refugee camp at King's Bridge—until federal steamers could take them up the coast. That next migration likely began on December 22, 1864, the day Savannah fell. Sometime that morning, amid jeers from soldiers hailing them as the "African Brigade" or the "Ethiopian Corps," the first group of about seven hundred refugees ascended the gangway of an unknown steamer bound for Port Royal, where the refugee experience of Sherman's March entered its second and more complicated stage.[22]

Port Royal's wartime transformation began on November 7, 1861, otherwise known as "the day of the gun-shoot at Bay Point." On that day, Commodore Samuel Du Pont's gunboat *Wabash* sailed into Port Royal Sound and fired heavy rounds at the two Confederate forts sitting on each side of the sound. The assault was a Union success. The forts fell in quick succession, and in response, the remaining Confederate military presence skedaddled—as did most of the region's white inhabitants, which gave the US Navy control of a large natural sound on the Atlantic coast and a base of operations for future attacks. The operation was an early step in the War Department's initial strategy for prosecuting the war, known as the "Anaconda Plan." From Port Royal, the US Navy could sustain its blockade of both Charleston and Savannah, thus suffocating the Confederate war effort by stanching the flow of valuable goods and supplies.

Shortly after the battle, military personnel were shocked to find thousands of enslaved people greeting them onshore. The region's white planters were long gone, the plantations had been evacuated, and enslaved people had been greeting the Union Army occupation by celebrating the sudden change of affairs. For all intents and purposes, the men and women were free. The federal government didn't see it that way, though. Federal emancipation policy at the time still considered them to be "contrabands of war"—not free men and women but requisitioned property. Moreover, as many as ten thousand enslaved men and woman called the islands home, which meant that the army now had about ten thousand so-called contrabands living within its lines, a number that went far beyond anything the army had experienced up to that point in the war. Such a large number of freed people posed a particular problem for the small force that had taken the islands: not only would the plantations need provisioning, but the last thing the army wanted was to have thousands of freed people disrupting its operations, making it evident to most everyone involved that the situation at Port Royal required a new approach toward dealing with freed people who sought refuge within federal lines.[23]

Yet where some may have sensed a problem, Salmon P. Chase, Lincoln's secretary of the Treasury and an abolitionist from Ohio, sensed an opportunity. He called on Edward L. Pierce of Boston, a man who had worked among the first so-called contrabands at Fortress Monroe, and sent him south to report on conditions at Port Royal. Pierce spent about three months on the islands, from December 1861 to February 1862. When he returned, he handed Chase a report that described conditions before proposing a plan for the islands. First, he proposed placing white superintendents in charge of the abandoned plantations. The superintendents would manage the plantations, convince enslaved people to work as paid laborers, and teach them the ways of the wage. The idea was for Port Royal to become a quasi training ground where enslaved people would work as free laborers and develop the thrift and discipline that Pierce believed were essential to preparing them for "all the privileges" of citizenship.[24]

Second, Pierce envisioned teams of missionaries traveling to the islands to teach freed people what the wage couldn't. He imagined regular religious services capable of providing moral instruction while instilling a "religious zeal for faithful labor" and "clean and healthful habits." He also wanted educators to be sprinkled in among the missionaries, so that freed people might enjoy lessons in reading, writing, and arithmetic. Furthermore, aid would be administered while the freed people adapted to a cash economy, and just as important, none of that was imagined as permanent. "As fast as the laborers show themselves fitted for all the privileges of citizens, they should be dismissed from the system and allowed to follow any employment they please . . . [and] have the power to acquire the fee simple of land, either with the proceeds of their labor or as a reward of special merit," Pierce wrote, insisting that "whatever was thought best to be done" needed doing fast. It was the first of the year, and the spring planting season was only a few months away.[25]

With its focus on the wage, the market, merit, and the real bedrock of the proposal, "paternal discipline," Pierce's vision for Port Royal was peak nineteenth-century liberalism put toward an antislavery end. It assumed the all-encompassing power of the market, and it rested on the idea that a healthy wage system could undo all wrongs and reform society for the better by letting the competitive marketplace shape society. By the start of the Civil War, that loose set of ideas had become Republican ortho-doxy under the banner of "free labor" and had become a real weapon in the war against slavery. As a matter of social policy, those ideas would ultimately prove unsuitable for the needs of the freed men and women at Port Royal. Yet it's important to see the plan for what it was. That was still early 1862. At the time, there was no real effort for emancipation within the government, so the proposal was nothing less than an early action plan designed to spearhead a wider, fuller-throated embrace of emancipation at the federal level.[26]

It helped that from where Chase sat the plan made perfect sense. Any plan he endorsed had to have a fundraising feature, which Pierce's did because it kept Port Royal's plantations intact and, in theory, kept cotton production going. The money made from selling the cotton could then fill the coffers of the depleted Treasury (a major political selling point to skeptics and critics alike) and help fund the war, all while, Chase believed, inching the country closer to a general emancipation order. Even better, the underlying rationale for the project laid waste to one of the pillars of pro-slavery thought: if freed people could return cotton to its prewar yields and provide a financial stimulus to the war effort, it would effectively prove that free labor was just as productive as slave labor, essentially scuttling one of the South's oldest defenses of slavery. A solution with such far-reaching potential was ultimately too good to pass up. In February 1862, after receiving approval from President Lincoln, the newly christened Port Royal Experiment was launched. The first wave of Northern agents embarked for the islands in March.[27]

The team of Northern agents served as the project's foot soldiers. Spiteful military personnel already stationed on the islands derisively called them "Gideon's Band"—or "Gideonites," after the prophet from the Book of Judges. The agents wore the name like a badge of honor, seeing it as emblematic of their zeal as well as the divinity of their cause. The first group's members came from New York and Boston and represented a range of interests, occupations, and institutions. "It is a queer farrago we are," wrote the educator William C. Gannett, "clerks, doctors, divinity students; professors and teachers, underground railway agents, and socialists." Pierce bragged that he had recruited the "choicest men of New England . . . men of practical talent and experience," but women were involved as well, most of them serving as the teachers or missionaries who coordinated classes and ran the Sunday schools. There was also a sprinkling of young technocrats and aspiring capitalists in the mix, men such as Edward Philbrick, a Boston engineer, who would soon become the most polarizing figure on the islands.[28]

What united the agents was their opposition to slavery as well as their reformist spirit. They had overwhelmingly come from old antislavery families with deep roots in Northern reform efforts, and they wanted nothing more than to reshape the slaveholding South in the image of the North. But no amount of zeal or common cause could paper over what were real rivalries and divisions: the New Englanders distrusted the New Yorkers and vice versa; the Unitarians had deep theological differences with the Evangelicals; and most of all, those who saw the project's primary mission as providing humanitarian relief ran up against those who were more interested in nurturing the profit motive—in turning the islands into free labor laboratories where formerly enslaved people would remain in the fields working as wage laborers. That last division—aid and instruction versus labor and production—plagued the project from the start, and over time, it would peel everything back to the fundamental paradox of the entire venture: How could a project meant to lift people out of bondage do so while still keeping the plantation system in place?[29]

Port Royal *was* its contradictions. On the one hand, the more social and humanitarian aspects of the project went swimmingly. The white agents retained a paternal lordship of sorts over island affairs, which was always a source of tension, but in certain matters, freed families accepted the agents and their mission. For example, religion bonded them. The Northern agents never understood the intense emotion freed people put into their worship, and the priggish New Englanders disdained the way freed people sang and danced their way through a service. Nevertheless, the holy word became the project's common ground. Church services took place regularly and were often so well attended that crowds spilled out into the churchyards, with services sometimes being held underneath moss-covered trees. And the Northern agents extended the work of the church by performing marriage ceremonies, consecrating previously unrecognized unions with celebrations and marriage certificates.[30]

Schools were another early success. A nearly instantaneous bond formed between the many white educators on the islands and the freed people. Two teachers, Edward E. Hale and William C. Gannett, described the alphabet as a kind of "talisman" in a report on the islands and wrote that after having been forbidden to learn to read or write (made illegal by an 1834 amendment to the South Carolina Slave Code), freed people desired the "power of letters" with what seemed like an insatiable thirst. That spawned a wide-ranging educational program. Teachers held Sabbath schools that promoted literacy by way of religious study; they held mixed classes that instructed adults and children at the same time;

they held night classes two and three times a week; and some teachers led individualized lessons from the comfort of their homes. Most of the formal classes in the early years were held in the Old Brick Church on St. Helena Island, which was always too small for the number of pupils, until 1864, when the Pennsylvania Freedmen's Relief Commission sent down building materials for an institution known as the Penn School, one of the first freestanding freedmen's schools in the country.[31]

Port Royal was also where the United States Colored Troops got its start. In May 1862, General David Hunter, stationed there as commander of the Department of the South, went rogue. He began enlisting freedmen into army regiments and later issued his own general emancipation order, declaring slaves in Georgia, South Carolina, and Florida—the three states under his command—"forever free." It was a bold stroke that shocked his commander in chief. Hunter had acted without Lincoln's knowledge or approval, which drew a swift rebuke from a president whose administration remained intent on keeping the slaveholding border states in the Union. Lincoln rescinded the emancipation order but otherwise looked the other way as Hunter's Black regiments kept drilling into the late summer of 1862, just as Lincoln and the War Department were rethinking their stance on Black enlistment. Most of the enlisted men later formed the 1st South Carolina Volunteer Infantry Regiment, one of the first USCT regiments raised from the South and one of the first to see action, launching successful raids on the Georgia coast in November 1862, more than a month before the Emancipation Proclamation went into full effect.[32]

The Port Royal Experiment was one of the key points at which the social revolution of the Civil War began to turn and one of the early points at which the profound transformations of the war began to take hold. In that sense, Chase and Pierce were basically right, or at least half right: once emancipation was broached and begun at Port Royal, there was no bottling it up again. The changes would only accelerate, not slow down. Its very existence forced Lincoln, his party, and the War

Department to take stock of what was happening and forced the government into seeing emancipation as a natural outcome of the war, which helped prepare the way for a full evolution from a limited, restrained war to a war that would destroy slavery. For all of its inherent limitations, the project at Port Royal helped open doors that enslaved people had been trying to kick in.

On the other hand, Port Royal could never escape its contradictions. Nowhere were these contradictions more evident than when it came to labor. The crux of the matter was that freed people saw wage work as little more than a modified form of slavery. Not only were wages often withheld, delayed, or lower than promised, but the Northern agents initially insisted that the freed people work in gangs and on schedules similar to those used by plantation overseers. Some superintendents were also not opposed to using punishments or other penalties as a way of imposing more regimented work routines. That was never how freed people had imagined freedom. Freedom meant working on their own time and in smaller, self-determined units, and freed people largely rejected the cultivation of cotton (which had mostly market value) in favor of subsistence items such as corn and sweet potatoes, foods that filled gardens and family tables. Freed husbands also didn't want their wives to have to work in the fields; they wanted them, instead, to be wives and mothers and take on the responsibilities that they felt befitted them and their families.[33]

That resistance was a rejection of the market logic the project had been built on. Freedom, to the freed men and women, should be more robust and meaningful than the narrow freedom to work for a wage—a belief that threatened to undo the project's governing rationale. As a result, labor became a festering source of discordant expectations, particularly in those early days. Laura M. Towne, a white teacher from Philadelphia, once wrote of a "little rebellion" breaking out on account of a man refusing to work his time in cotton. She also recalled a time when a freedman had interrupted a church service by saying that "The

Yankees preach nothing but cotton, cotton." The situation remained tense until superintendents made key concessions. Some plantations, for instance, dispensed with the gang system in favor of family tasks. But the structure of the plantation system remained in place, causing disputes to persist through the war and into Reconstruction.[34]

Landownership was another issue that exposed the contradictions at the heart of the project. All along, many of the missionaries and teachers believed the old plantations would eventually be broken into plots and turned over to freed families. That was certainly what most freed families expected as well. They wanted their own homesteads and the independence that would come with owning their own land. Some superintendents believed, however, that turning the land over to them was too much like a handout—that for freed people to make it in freedom, they would need to buy the land and engage in the market economy just like everyone else. Anything less, they argued, would send the wrong message about freedom and set freed people up for a harsh transition into the free labor economy. Complicating matters even more was that in the rush to abandon the islands and secede from the Union, the original plantation owners had stopped paying their federal taxes. Accordingly, most of the land in use at Port Royal had been foreclosed on by the US government and, by law, was to be sold at public auction, which meant that as of March 1863, all the land within the bounds of the project risked being privatized.[35]

Momentum shifted when Rufus Saxton assumed command. By late 1862, a simmering squabble between the Gideonites on one side and a mix of military officials and Treasury agents on the other reached a boiling point. An army colonel had gone as far as punching Edward Pierce in the face. He left the islands shortly thereafter, and the powers that be decided to protect the project better by placing it within the War Department and appointing a military man as its head. They settled on Saxton, a child of Greenfield, Massachusetts, who turned out to be the right man for the job. Saxton's parents had been abolitionists, followers of William Lloyd Garrison. His father, in particular, had been an early feminist and transcendentalist lecturer who had dreamed of having his son live in a utopian socialist community known as Brook Farm. Instead, Rufus had enrolled in West Point while his brother, Willard, his eventual aide at Port Royal, had gone to Brook Farm. But Rufus never strayed from the ideals of his youth. He spoke the Gideonites' language and shared their sense of mission but added a degree of levelheadedness gained from a career in the military. He was also honest and earnest, and in the three years he spent at Port Royal, he won the trust of the freed people by proving himself to be a faithful friend and advocate of their interests.[36]

Saxton's arrival fortified the project by giving it military backing, but as of early 1863, the land sales still loomed. Desperation set in. All the Northern agents could see that if nothing was done to negate the sales, they'd be boarding northbound ships in no time. Indeed, everyone would have been on those ships if it hadn't been for Laura Towne, the white teacher from Philadelphia. Her idea was to throw the army's weight around by getting either Saxton or David Hunter to declare the islands essential to military operations and therefore off limits. In essence, she wanted the government to nationalize the islands for the project's sake—and the tactic worked. One night over dinner, she floated the idea to Saxton, who then took the idea to Hunter, who then halted the sales on the grounds of military necessity. The move wasn't a long-term solution, but it mucked up the works just long enough for Republicans in Congress—many of whom had come to support the venture—to amend the tax law and settle on a compromise: the sales would go on, but a large portion of the land would be set aside and reserved for federal use. That limited but didn't kill the project. It wasn't the out-and-out mandate many had wanted, but most of the agents celebrated the fact that a crisis had been averted and the Port Royal Experiment would be continued.[37]

The emphasis here is on *most* of the agents. A ring of superintendents led by Edward Philbrick, the Boston technocrat, and other industrialist types (all but one from Boston) had come to see privatizing the land as the best solution to the project's problems. Private ownership, they believed, would not only make for a more successful system, producing better yields and better profits, it would solve the ongoing problem of not having any cash for wages or supplies by letting private owners pay and provision freed people directly rather than wait for federal funds. Just as important, if all the privatizing was done by people already associated with the project—i.e., themselves—there would be a nearly seamless transition, giving the project the stability it had lacked. Many among the privatizing wing of the group also thought that working for a private employer would do the freed people some good. It would teach them how to be employees and give them a supposed guardian to look out for their interest. Philbrick, in particular, believed it would be best for him and his peers to hold on to the land and sell it back once freed people had proven themselves "fit" for freedom and could buy it outright.

When the dust settled and all the sales had been finalized, the March 1863 land auction turned the project's divisions into a wide, nearly unnavigable chasm. Saxton retained the land set aside for the project, which turned out to be over three-quarters of all the land up for auction, more than he had expected. Some freed families, meanwhile, managed to pool their money and buy smaller plots. All the rest went to private buyers, including one who was already affiliated with the project: Philbrick and his newly formed joint stock company wound up as the largest landholder on the islands. He became the owner of eleven plantations, some eight thousand acres, and close to a third of St. Helena Island, one of the largest islands within the project's bounds. For roughly a dollar per acre, a bargain price of $7,000 in all, he basically bought his own empire and, in the process, split the Port Royal Experiment in two. He became a lightning-rod character among the Gideonites, with some supporting and some criticizing him, and his landholdings fragmented the project's perceived sense of unity, turning a collective endeavor into a form of private enterprise.[38]

The response from the agents not under Philbrick's sway was to double down. Most of the agents were lukewarm apostles of Philbrick's doctrinaire approach to free labor anyway. So with Philbrick's influence concentrated on his own private affairs, the various Northern agents retreated from the more commercial aspects of the project and refocused on their social agenda. But as the project's head, Saxton knew that he and the other agents were operating on borrowed time. The land sales proved that the end goal of redistributing land to freed families was far from certain, and over the next year or so, Saxton shifted the project's focus to a policy known as preemption. The underlying idea of the policy was that Northern agents would help freed families raise money and preempt the purchase of homesteads before the land could be auctioned off again. It didn't work. Despite some assurances from people in power, there was a second land auction in the spring of 1864. It took place under a shade tree (with freed people watching as old home places and burial grounds were parceled out and sold to the highest bidders) and ended much as the first one had, setting a somber, dispiriting tone for what would be a long year of stalled dreams and dashed hopes.[39]

Sherman's arrival on the Georgia coast capped a long and difficult year on the islands. Morale had sunk—which says a lot considering the unbounded optimism of the Gideonites—and disenchantment had started to set in. Even worse, the Gideonites began losing the trust of the freed men and women. The confidence they had accrued over the last two years dissipated with the 1864 land sales. Protests became more frequent. Freed people demanded to know why white Northerners suddenly had a right to lands that they still claimed as their own. Some refused to work for new employers, reopening old wounds regarding labor and land that had been patched up and managed over the past two years. That led to more work interruptions, a growing independence on the part of freed laborers, and a lack of interest in working in the Port Royal system. Freed people had also started to resent some of the army's heavy-handed recruiting practices, with allegations of impressment, a constant theme, running rampant across the islands.[40]

Rufus Saxton knew that he was overseeing a project on the wane. The land sales had crippled his authority, tied his hands, and spread deep mistrust across every settlement on the islands. But he also knew that all was not lost. As he saw things, the solution for the islands came down to landownership. Helping freed families secure homesteads, he knew, would do more in terms of paving their way to freedom than all of the work in the past two years combined, and as important, land seemed to him to be what the freed people wanted and deserved. He wrote frequently that freed people had already paid for the land through their many years of unrequited toil, and he believed that the best way to lift them out of slavery was to start by repaying the debt that was owed them. The issue was that with preemption failing, he was down to the only hand he had left to play, and that was to start lobbying.

For the better part of 1864, Saxton beat the drum of Black homesteading, becoming perhaps the single most influential white champion of Black landowning in the history of the war. He told anyone who would listen that the surest way to success at Port Royal would be to have freed families settled on land that they could live and work on as theirs. It was the subtext of his reports and all his relevant letters. Preemption may have failed as a policy, but he kept its spirit alive by chastising his superiors for the disastrous and unjust way the land sales had occurred. In one long and biting report from early March, he voiced his frustrations and those of the freed people, writing that "after abandonment and forfeiture of their former possessors" it seemed to him that "the right of the slaves to the land could not be justly denied." "They had been the only cultivators, their labor had given it all its value, [and] the elements of its fertility were the sweat and blood of the negro so long poured out upon it that it [the land] might be taken as composed of his own substance," he wrote, concluding that the Sea Islands around Port Royal might well be considered a "fore-closed mortgage for generations of unpaid wages."[41]

Saxton's increasingly public position on the land issue opened up a quasi cold war between him and Philbrick that had been brewing for some time. Saxton was careful not to impugn Philbrick's character, telling the newly minted member of the planter class that he didn't doubt his sincerity or personal integrity. But he didn't hold back, either. In a long letter written after the two published contradictory accounts in separate newspapers, Saxton told Philbrick, "The immediate possession of the land without purchase is the indefeasible right of the negro, and I am not able to perceive the pertinence of calling that act of justice 'petting' him, than I am the propriety of calling the act of withholding it from him a fraud and a wrong." "Neither do I believe," he maintained, "that a 'purely commercial basis' is the proper starting for an enterprise designed . . . for the benefit & elevation of the negro," something Philbrick had apparently once said.[42]

Saxton then accused Philbrick of viewing freed people as "an agricultural peasantry" and criticized the young technocrat for scrimping on the time he allowed freed people to work for themselves. Next, he hit Philbrick where it hurt the most by eviscerating his position on the land sales:

It is stated as something that "remains to be proved," whether the giving of the land to the negroes—which you call "special privileges to them to the exclusion of whites"—is "best for the future of the community." This again you characterize as "petting" the negro, and relieving him of a portion of his responsibility.

He continued:

There is far more danger in being unjust to the negro, than of petting him—whatever that may mean. I suppose it did not properly and logically come within the purview of an enterprise founded on a purely commercial basis to consider the antecedent claims and paramount rights of the negro to the soil, and the very slight claim which any white man can make to any portion of it.

Moreover, Saxton argued, the "market value" that Philbrick spoke so longingly about was not only irrelevant to the project at hand, it was dependent on landlords such as Philbrick reducing freed people to a permanent class of peasantlike laborers. "With a market condition and the price competition of capitalists depending upon negro labor for the working of the lands," he wrote, "the negroes chances [to own land] will be reduced to a minimum, and land will be attainable by but a very small number." Preemption, he later claimed, wasn't a perfect policy, but it at least recognized the "principle of justice" and charted a path for its future fulfillment—an understanding that he believed could have been the basis of a much more successful project.[43]

But that didn't happen. Instead, as Saxton hammered home at length while drawing his letter to a close, Philbrick had strong-armed his way into taking the project down a different path. He was again cordial and respectful, saying that he didn't doubt Philbrick's personal honor, but he wrote:

What protection do you propose for the negro against white men of another character and unhonorable purposes? What chance has he to get land out of the clutches of the human vultures, who care for him only as they can gorge themselves upon his flesh? If you had seen the hungry swarms gathered here at the land sales in February, I think your views concerning the exclusion of whites would be somewhat modified. . . . What you call "special privileges to the negroes to the exclusion of whites," seems to me to be vital to the safety and hope of advancement of the negro—the plainest justice and the wisest policy.

With that Saxton signed off, perhaps not quite realizing that the issues he had just pointed to would soon balloon out from Port Royal and become one of the defining issues of the war's aftermath.[44]

The cold war between Saxton and Philbrick lingered throughout the year. The two put on a friendly face. They spoke together, they wrote to each other, and they still saw themselves as being on the same side to some degree. But the lines had been clearly drawn. It also didn't help their relationship that the land issue never went away. It remained the central, looming question on the islands, and it became more of an issue as people could begin to see an end to the war. Yet while the land question hung over the islands, there were also other important issues that needed dealing with. Labor remained a constant headache. Saxton didn't believe in the superintendent system as a long-term solution, as evident in his debates with Philbrick, but he also knew that without a preemption policy and with venal private buyers looking to buy their way into the islands, it was best to salvage what he could from the current system. Speculators and Treasury agents hassled him about instituting workhouses in order to tighten the work regime; he always rebuffed them. He also took practical steps to build the trust of the freed people by shielding them from abuse.[45]

Nevertheless, as of Christmas 1864, the project was still on the wane and experiencing a season unlike any other on the islands. The army had increased its personnel. There were now more soldiers on the islands than ever before. Plus, Sherman's movements kept everyone in a state of suspense: Where would he go next? Would his army sweep through Port Royal, and if so, what would that mean for operations there? Christmas also coincided with the start of disease season. The winter before had been particularly severe. Anecdotal reports indicate that a short-lived epidemic might have broken out on the islands, and though it was too soon to tell if the sickness had returned, illness had already gotten to Willard Saxton. On Christmas Eve, he complained of ill health and spent much of Christmas Day in and out of bed while Rufus sailed away for a meeting with Sherman in Savannah regarding the situation at Port Royal. Rufus returned a few days later, unhappy with the message he received. Apparently, the "heads of that army" had told him that they didn't "care that much about humanitarian labors" and planned to "leave the more important and perplexing work to others"—those "others" being a euphemism for *him*.[46]

As Willard spoke with his brother in the last few days of 1864, that "more important work" was already well under way. While Willard lay in his sickbed on Christmas, the first of the many thousands of refugees from Georgia were on their way to Port Royal. They had been forced to the camp at King's Bridge, boarded onto steamers, and sent down the winding routes of the Ogeechee River. They may have stopped downstream at Fort McAllister, which was now operating as another federal depot, but in all likelihood the first ships probably steamed right past the old Confederate fort into the Atlantic Ocean and then turned north, making the wide swing around Tybee, Daufuskie, and Hilton Head before turning into Port Royal Sound. From there, the steamers likely sailed past the docks at Port Royal and landed upriver at Beaufort, where Rufus Saxton had his headquarters. The first seven hundred freed people arrived on Christmas; more arrived soon after that; and by the end of January, just over a month after the first transports had begun, as many as seventeen thousand Georgia refugees would find themselves starting a new life on the Sea Islands of South Carolina.

Fortunately for Willard, he felt better by New Year's, just in time for the planned festivities. It was not only a new year, it was now two years from the day the Emancipation Proclamation had gone into effect. The islanders celebrated the occasion on the second with an Emancipation Day ceremony full of speakers, hymns, and public readings. The affair was fast becoming a New Year's tradition. The Lowcountry morning began with a long procession of freed men and women led by a military band, and in between a carriage team pulled a cart carrying a "Goddess of Liberty." The parade went on throughout the morning and ended at the local library, where three to four thousand people crowded around, listening to the slate of speakers and singing patriotic songs. The next day, later in the evening, well after things had died down, a second procession took place: a segment of Sherman's right wing—some sixteen to eighteen thousand soldiers—marched through the town of Beaufort and began setting up their camp, another clear indication that the little island experiment was on its way to becoming the center of something huge.[47]

The Green House off Madison Square in Savannah. This house served as Sherman's headquarters during the winter of 1864 to 1865.

Chapter Five

THE SAVANNAH WINTER

Charles C. Coffin, a well-known war correspondent, arrived in Savannah sometime in early January 1865. Sherman's army was camped throughout town, and Coffin, who had been on the ground at the bloody battles of Antietam and Gettysburg, had a hard time believing what he was seeing. "Society in the South, and especially in Savannah, had undergone a great change," he wrote in one of his histories of the war. Sherman's arrival had been "a convulsion, an upheaval, a shaking up and a settling down of all the discordant elements," he added, writing that the Army of the West had marched through the city "like a moral earthquake, overturning aristocratic pride, privilege, and power." As hyperbolic as Coffin's claims may sound in hindsight, the evidence was hard to ignore: old colonial homes had been deserted, influential families were penniless, and masters and formerly enslaved people found themselves in a new relationship. "A reversal of the poles of the earth would hardly have produced a greater physical convulsion than this sudden and unexpected change in the social condition of the people of the city," he wrote, describing his experience in Savannah.[1]

Slavery's demise triggered a transformation in Savannah as swift as the one that had swept through Atlanta earlier in the fall. Freed people celebrated, soldiers styled themselves liberators, and the city's old social fabric was coming completely undone. Freed washerwomen simply stopped working, some leaving water in the tub and clothes on the line. Freed laborers demanded wages and sought to reclaim their lost property. Other freed people taunted their old masters and mistresses by noting how drastically the tables had turned: one woman laughingly told her old mistress that the rebels had all gone to Hell now that Sherman was there; a man laughed at the fact that his white master, who "Couldn't git a glass o' water for he'sef" now had to go out and work the pump. Savannah's slave system was disappearing in front of everyone's eyes. "It is a dream, sir, —a dream!" one freedwoman, a servant at the Pulaski House Hotel, said of freedom, telling Coffin that it was almost as if she didn't know where she was.[2]

For the city's white slaveholders, the changes had been swift indeed. Like the slaveholder who now had to pump his own water, nothing said that the old antebellum order had collapsed with greater certainty than the indignity of their having to do basic tasks themselves. In one instance, George Ward Nichols, one of Sherman's adjutants, met one of Savannah's most aristocratic ladies in an utter state of distress. "It is terrible, sir!" she told him, saying that her slaves had all left, her family's plantation had been "broken up," and she feared she might actually have to work. Her pleasant summer vacations in the North and her $20,000-a-year income, Nichols sarcastically noted, had all been "swept away at a single blow." When the woman then told him that she thought she might have to "submit to the disgrace of giving lessons in music" just to get by, Nichols replied with contempt, "Madam, I hope so."[3]

Yet perhaps the surest sign of the tremendous changes sweeping through the city came in the early morning of January 10. Around breakfast time, close to five hundred African American schoolchildren emptied out of the First African Baptist Church on the west side of Franklin Square. The children of varying ages and sizes crossed Montgomery Street, where they entered Savannah's old city market and then ascended the stairway to A. Bryan's Negro Mart, Savannah's premier establishment for the buying and selling of human beings. It was now a school. In just a few short weeks, Savannah's African American leadership had taken over the building, hired teachers, and turned the auction room into a schoolhouse. Shackles and iron bars still hung from the walls, the auction block served as a lectern, and the teachers taught reading and arithmetic as a new Savannah was being built out of the remnants of the old.[4]

As of early January, the most urgent work pertained to the freed refugees and Savannah's status as a de facto hub for refugees from across the region. Despite Sherman's scheme to ship refugees up the coast to Port Royal, the unfolding refugee crisis was still a long way from being solved. Hundreds, if not thousands, of freed people still waited outside the city for ships to take them up the coast. Many had begun to press into the city, where they joined the soldiers in sleeping on the streets in makeshift camps. Moreover, refugees from the city's immediate outskirts had also begun to make their way into Savannah, and another flow of refugees moved in from points farther south, the vast plantation regions along the Georgia coast. The result was a city unsettled and on edge: refugees pressed in from all angles, and without adequate food, water, or shelter, they faced the threat of a long, hungry winter.[5]

Another, more troubling development loomed in the form of sectional reconciliation. On the one hand, it was partly Sherman's doing. While it's true that he had requisitioned all the cotton, destroyed Confederate war materiel, and forced the city's citizens to house his men, he also wanted Savannah to be stable and in good working order. Although he didn't just hand the city back over to Southern whites, his Special Field Order No. 143, issued the day after Christmas, did just that: it ordered that "The Mayor and City Council of Savannah *will* continue to exercise their functions" (italics added). The idea was to keep the possible tinderbox of a city away from any unnecessary explosives (in fact, one goal was to keep the fire department in operation), but what it effectively did was guarantee that freed Black leaders wouldn't be part of any decision-making process. The people who had been most supportive of the army, the people out there and the people leading Savannah's freed population into the postwar period, saw the levers of city government return to the old masters in the name of social stability—a decision that slowed the tremendous changes already happening within the city but also the potential for more.[6]

On the other hand, part of the general spirit of reconciliation had to do with the perceived "Unionism" of white Savannah. The city's mayor, Richard Arnold, surrendered the city willingly, and Charles Green, the owner of the Green House, invited Sherman into his home as an honored guest. They weren't anomalies. Throughout the occupation, Savannah lived up to its now-popular reputation as the "Hostess City of the South," lulling the soldiers into a false sense of security. "There is more Unionism in Savannah, than in any place we have been in yet," observed George Bradley, the chaplain from Wisconsin, noting that the "people seem to be glad that we have come." Charles Coffin agreed, writing that he saw less "sourness" there than in either Memphis or Louisville, two places occupied earlier in the war. George Ward Nichols noted much of the same: "While I have no doubt that most of these people actually sympathize with their relatives and friends in the Rebel army, I am equally sure that they rejoiced that the city was in the hands of our army and under the government of the old Union."[7]

The truth was probably somewhere in between. Despite the army's relatively warm welcome, as Bradley noted, much of the supposed "Unionism" stemmed from the calculation "that so long as the rebels held the city, trade would remain dead." The federal blockade would remain in place, preventing all traffic in and out of Savannah's port. People such as Mayor Arnold invariably acquiesced to Sherman out of fear that the general might pulverize the city into a pile of rubble, which was why he and several others had reportedly written to General Hardee begging him to evacuate the city rather than defend it. The fiery inferno of Atlanta hung in everyone's mind. There was also a realization setting in among many that after four years of fighting, after four years of a debilitating blockade, and after a year in which losses had seemed to pile up and defeat had seemed more and more inevitable, it was best to acquiesce while suitable terms were still on the table. In other words, what Sherman and the Northern soldiers took for surrender or submission or even Unionism, white Savannahians recognized quite clearly as their own self-interest.[8]

The allure of Savannah's perceived Unionism went beyond Sherman and the soldiers. The idea that Savannah deserved a return to normalcy soon spread throughout the nation's newspapers and the well-heeled parlors of the Northern elite. War-weary readers convinced themselves that it was true. Thus the seemingly inexplicable: in early January, Sherman and Arnold organized a relief commission designed to procure vast sums of Northern relief—which in an early act of reunion, the commission received. Northern relief organizations, located primarily in New York, Boston, and Philadelphia, raised enough money to send three steamers loaded with goods and supplies to the city; one of the ships couldn't even fit all the cargo on board and had to leave a substantial amount behind. Sectional reconciliation was already stirring. Though the idea was for the aid to go to the poor and suffering of Savannah regardless of race, and though some was meant for the refugees, it didn't work out that way. When asked about the food and supplies by Charles Coffin, the freedwoman from the Pulaski House Hotel complained, telling him bluntly, "Not a mouthful have I had."[9]

For those reasons, Savannah in the winter of 1865 sat on a razor's edge. The social revolution of the war was already under way. The city was experiencing tremendous changes, and the antebellum order of things had started shifting, giving way to a new spirit of possibility among the city's free people of color and the many thousands of refugees who now joined them. But there were headwinds from unlikely sources beating back against the many changes that slowed the city's transformation and, for the moment at least, narrowed the scope of the politically possible. Which way would things ultimately turn? That was the question as of early January 1865.

An answer arrived on January 11, when Secretary of War Edwin Stanton and a group of War Department administrators arrived in Savannah. Stanton's mission, at least ostensibly, was to oversee the requisition of Savannah's unsold cotton stores. Yet once that was done, he remained in the city longer than expected and had Sherman show him around. As it happened, Stanton lived next door to and was quite close with Sherman's brother John, which added a personal element to their professional relationship. So over several days, the two strode Savannah's streets. They visited sections of town where the soldiers had pitched their tents and made their camps. Stanton, an administrator with a long, graying beard and round glasses, found the camps surprisingly neat and impressive. He was particularly amazed at how the soldiers had managed to jerry rig supplies and scrap parts for use as camp accommodations. But Sherman also sensed that Stanton's small talk about tents and troops masked his primary concern. "He talked to me a great deal about the negroes," Sherman remembered.[10]

It was the start of an ongoing investigation. At one point, Stanton point-blank asked Sherman about his subordinate Jeff. C. Davis and pulled out a newspaper article alleging crimes along Ebenezer Creek. In response, Sherman skated around the issue and played it down. He assured Stanton that Davis was an "excellent soldier" and that he didn't believe that Davis had "any hostility to the negro." He told Stanton that much of what had been reported was only rumors. He then sent for Davis to let him speak for himself. Talking with Davis seemed to satisfy Stanton for the time being. Still, in bringing up the refugees and asking about Ebenezer Creek, Stanton had touched a nerve. Sherman went out of his way to defend what had happened, suggesting that any general in Davis's position would have done the same. Later, in his memoirs, he would turn against Stanton, writing pointedly that whereas most everyone in the army had felt a sympathy for the freed people, it was a form of sympathy different from that of Stanton, whose feeling, he wrote, was "not of pure humanity, but of *politics*."[11]

In truth, Sherman probably saw everything coming. On January 1, Sherman's old friend Henry Halleck, stationed in DC as the army's chief of staff, gave his fellow West Point graduate an important piece of advice. "While almost everyone is praising your great march through Georgia and the capture of Savannah, there is a certain class," he wrote, "who are decidedly disposed to make a point against you . . . in regard to the 'Inevitable Sambo.'" According to Halleck, rumors in Washington held that Sherman "manifested an almost *criminal* dislike of the negro" and instead of complying with the government's orders on emancipation, had repulsed freed people from his lines "with contempt." The whisper campaign also alleged that the army could have brought close to fifty thousand freed people with it to Savannah, "thus stripping Georgia of that many laborers and opening a door by which many more could have escaped from their masters," but that instead "you drove them from your ranks, prevented them from following you by cutting the bridges in your rear, and thus caused the massacre of large numbers by Wheeler's cavalry."[12]

Halleck assured Sherman that the accusations would soon pass "as the idle winds" and that people understood the position he was in, but the situation was serious enough for him to restate his case. He wrote:

> Some here think that, in view of the scarcity of labor in the South, and the probability that a part, at least, of the able-bodied slaves will be called into the military service of the rebels, it is of the greatest importance to open outlets by which the slaves can escape into our lines, and, they say, that the route you have passed over

should be made the route of escape and Savannah the great place of refuge. These I know are the views of some of the leading men in the administration, and they now express dissatisfaction that you did not carry them out in your great raid.[13]

Halleck then nudged his friend along by asking some important questions: Would it not be possible to reopen the lines of escape, especially now that there were no more difficulties about supplies? Could escaped slaves find at least partial refuge on the abandoned plantations around Savannah? What about the cotton and rice plantations on the islands along the coast? Halleck assured Sherman that whatever course he chose would get government approval and that such a course "will do much to silence your opponents." In effect, he was telling his friend to wise up and face the facts—that the March was over and, politically speaking, he needed to protect his flanks.[14]

Halleck wasn't wrong. From his perch in DC, he had heard the whispers and read the newspapers. It is unclear exactly how, but word of what had happened along the banks of Ebenezer Creek had clearly gotten out. Soldiers must have written home to their families, their congressmen, or local journalists. Either way, the government had caught wind of things as well, which was why Stanton had been down there asking questions. No one had a good story to tell. What had actually happened at Ebenezer Creek and who was to blame differed from one story to the next; but then again, the truth didn't matter all that much. What mattered was that the news was spreading and a troubling narrative was on the rise that Sherman and the army had acted maliciously toward the refugees, that they had shirked their responsibility to enact emancipation, and that because of that, disaster had struck along a dark stream somewhere in Georgia.

The army's response followed a pattern. Most responses tended to deflect blame away from Sherman while indicting Davis, a move that kept responsibility on a single rogue actor instead of the army as a whole or its venerated leader. But even with all his apparent villainy, Davis had his defenders. "On several occasions on the march from Atlanta we had been compelled to drive thousands of colored people back, not from lack of sympathy with them, but simply as a matter of safety to our army," wrote Henry Slocum, Davis's immediate superior during the March. Henry Hitchcock wrote similarly. "His [Davis's] first duty was to see [to the safety] of his own corps, and whatever that duty reasonably required he was bound to do, regardless of any incidental consequences," as he put it, which was his way of saying that along the March military necessity had reigned supreme and was all that generals such as Davis had been responsible for. It was also a clear example of an army starting to circle its wagons in order to protect one of its own.[15]

No one closed ranks quite as hard or as fast as Sherman himself. Around the time that Stanton landed in Savannah, for instance, former secretary of the Treasury Salmon P. Chase wrote to Sherman about what the general described as the "Negro question." In response, Sherman offered a full-throated defense of himself and all his men. He assured Chase that everything he had done had been out of necessity. "If you can understand the nature of a military column in an enemys [sic] country, with its long train of wagons you will see at once that a crowd of negroes, men women children, old & young, are a dangerous impediment," he told Chase, saying that a similar number of white refugees would have been just as much of a problem. He went on to reiterate his best line of defense, boasting that he and his army had led "hundreds of thousands" to "freedom & asylum" and that the "negro constituents of Georgia would resent the idea" of him being "inimical to them." "They regard me as a second Moses or Aaron," he proudly told the esteemed member of the Lincoln cabinet, as if that closed the case.[16]

No matter what was said or done, Sherman never understood the criticism. In his mind, he was a general, not a politician. His object was to win the war as fast and with as little risk as possible, and as odious or as unpopular as it was, such a result necessitated that his lines remain free of refugees. He also felt that he had been respectful to the freed people he had met along the way—and indeed, their support for him was unequivocal. Further, he believed he had acted in the freed refugees' best interest by discouraging them from following the army and enduring what was sure to be a long and fretful march. To him, sending the refugees to Port Royal had been the best-case scenario for both them and the army, as the islands were a place where they could find safety and security away from the ravages of the war. Just as important, Sherman proudly considered himself and all his men to be liberators. Never mind his personal views or past comments; his March through Georgia had freed more enslaved people than any other force in US history and had done so at a great risk to him and his men. Why couldn't anyone see that?[17]

It was mostly because Sherman didn't do himself any favors. His past clung to him. He also never moderated. Nor did he relent. When it came to something like Ebenezer Creek, there was no remorse and no apology. Also, it didn't help matters that as he settled into Savannah, he embroiled himself in controversy by continuing to block the recruitment of Black troops. Sherman, it should be said, always maintained that the real story was those "avaricious recruiting agents from New England" impressing men into service. But he still preferred that freedmen join the army as laborers or pioneers and not as soldiers, saying to Chase, "If the president prefers to minister to the one idea of negro Equality [i.e., Black soldiers], rather than military success . . . he should remove me, for I am so constituted that I cannot honestly sacrifice the safety and Success of my army to any minor cause." Or, as he told his wife, "I want soldiers made of the best bone and muscle in the land, and I won't attempt military feats with doubtful materials." "I am right," he told her, "and won't change."[18]

The irony is that Sherman *had* changed. His thinking on those issues had evolved from earlier in the war—and would continue evolving through the war's end and into its aftermath. For instance, whereas he had begun the war denying that slavery had any place in the conflict, he now accepted emancipation as being a central part of the war effort; whereas he had once refused to declare enslaved people free, he now fully recognized that slavery was dead and that formerly enslaved people were bound to become free men and women; whereas he had once recoiled at the idea that freed people would have a place in a postwar America, he now saw that as inevitable, though he firmly believed that that was an issue best left to politicians such as his brother, not to fighting men like himself. He just never changed as *much* or as *fast* as others wanted him to. As he would later tell Stanton, he considered himself "unable to offer a complete solution" to what he thought of as the "negro question," but even if he had been able to, he preferred leaving it "to the slower operations of time."[19]

Sherman was also immensely stubborn, and even worse, when backed into a corner, he compounded his stubbornness by doubling down. Hence his eventual reply to Halleck's letter from January 1. Upon learning that "a certain class" of men had been whispering about his conduct in DC, he unloaded: "Don't [*sic*] military success imply the safety of Sambo and *vice versa*?" He then turned to what he called that "cock-and-bull story" about Ebenezer Creek, saying "I didn't turn anyone back." Jefferson C. Davis had prohibited some freed people from following him, he was willing to admit, but he insisted that Davis hadn't blocked anyone at Ebenezer Creek on purpose. Instead, he claimed, Davis had simply wanted to preserve his bridge and pulled it up to do so, a story that contradicts the reports that Davis's men had burned the bridge gratuitously. He then informed Halleck that neither Davis nor Slocum believed that Wheeler's men had actually killed anyone in the melee, another contradictory claim.[20]

After writing in rage for a moment, Sherman sobered himself and became somewhat reflective. He wrote to Halleck not just about the rumors or what had happened along the March but about his stance on emancipation in general. As always, he stressed restraint: "The South deserves all she has got for her injustice to the negro but that is no reason why we should go to the other extreme." He then offered to Halleck perhaps the most precise summation of how he saw his role in enacting military emancipation: "I do and will do the best I can for the negroes, and feel sure the problem is solving itself slowly and naturally . . . but, not being dependent on votes, I can afford to act, as far as my influence goes, as a flywheel instead of a mainspring"—as something, in other words, that stores or maintains energy instead of propelling it directly.[21]

Yet the story of the March is that while Sherman may have seen himself as a flywheel and nothing more, enslaved people intervened. Tens of thousands of enslaved people ran to his army, followed his army, and in due course turned his March though Georgia into a march of liberation, placing him and his campaign in the center of America's most revolutionary moment. Even more, the ground hadn't yet stopped shaking and the March's enormous impact hadn't yet waned when Stanton arrived in Savannah and started asking questions, which meant that Sherman had to come up with answers—or at least pacify the secretary into ending the inquiry. Thus, when Stanton asked for a conference with a group of local Black leaders, Sherman could only comply. He opened his headquarters, prepped his staff, and sent invitations. He was confident that the freed people of Georgia considered him a great friend and deliverer, yet he must also have entered the evening knowing he was walking into his own tribunal, a meeting in which both he and his campaign would have to stand scrutiny and await a verdict.

On the evening of January 12, 1865, Garrison Frazier, a formerly enslaved person and retired pastor, ascended the spiral staircase of the beautiful Green House, Sherman's Savannah headquarters. As he entered the master bedroom, which Sherman had converted into a working office, the room became crowded and warm. Nineteen of Frazier's peers—leading

African American ministers from churches across the city—gathered around him as their chosen spokesperson for that monumental meeting with two of the most powerful men in the country. Sherman and the bespectacled Edwin Stanton likely took their places at a small table in the center of the room. A fire flickered under the mantle. The room's sleek wood furnishings glimmered under the gaslight, and a hush filled the air as the mood turned stiff and formal. There was important business to discuss, and for the next hour or more, Frazier held court, sharing all he knew about slavery, the war, and the present situation in and around Savannah.

Though Frazier served as the group's spokesperson, the biographies of the twenty ministers revealed why they were there. Some were presently in charge of congregations; others were retired; still others, such as James Hill and Abraham Burke, were lay ministers or deacons. Some, such as Alexander Harris, had been born free; others had purchased their freedom; and remarkably, Jacob Godfrey, John Johnson, Arthur Wardell, and several more had all been enslaved until Sherman's army had arrived in Savannah. There were three different denominations represented: Baptists, Methodists, and a single Episcopalian. Collectively, the ministers had well over two hundred years of ministerial experience. Frazier and a man named Glasgon Taylor were the longest serving at thirty-five years apiece; and while most of the ministers tended to be older, the two youngest attendees were still in their twenties and several were in their thirties. Three generations of Black Savannah, both enslaved and free, sat in a single room.[22]

One of the attendees deserves singling out as an exception. James Lynch, age twenty-six, was the only one of the twenty guests not from Savannah or the surrounding area. Born in Baltimore to a free father and an enslaved mother, he had had formal religious training and arrived in the South sometime in 1863, landing first at Port Royal, where he had served as a minister and missionary, before moving to Savannah, where he had worked to build churches and schools. That was what he was doing at the time of the colloquy with Stanton and Sherman, but it is what he did afterward that made him famous. Following the war, he remained on the coast for a spell, but he eventually relocated to Mississippi, got involved in politics, and in 1869, was elected secretary of state for Mississippi, becoming the first Black elected official in Mississippi's history. He would go on to become one of the most important Black politicians of his generation, and his time spent in Savannah among the ministers and missionaries served as his training ground.[23]

Yet on that January 1865 evening in Savannah, Lynch, a budding political star, deferred to his elders—and to Garrison Frazier in particular. Frazier and his wife, Diana, had been brought to Georgia by their master fifteen years earlier. In 1852, he had purchased his and Diana's freedom for about $1,000 and he had spent the next eight years pastoring Savannah's Bryan Baptist Church. Though aging and apparently in poor health when Sherman's army arrived, a contemporary described him as a man "of fair natural ability and good delivery." He had little in the way of theological training, but he could explain the Bible, and he had a knack for speaking in plain words but impressive tones. Once the proceedings began, the meeting became a stage. Stanton, the presiding officer, was lawyerly and formal. His questions—thorough, exact, and prepared—read like a deposition. But Frazier was cool, calm, and precise. He took command of the room as a pastor would a pulpit and never wavered. He not only answered Stanton's questions, he did so with an almost timeless clarity that makes his responses seem at once local and national, principled as well as practical, and somehow both political and spiritual.[24]

The main topic of discussion for the evening was "matters related to the freedmen of the state of Georgia," which everyone took to mean the burgeoning refugee crisis gripping Savannah. But rather oddly, Stanton began by asking for definitions. It was an attempt, perhaps, to feel Frazier out and see if the old man knew what he was talking about. He first asked if Frazier understood the details of the Emancipation

Proclamation; Frazier said he did and quickly explained. Stanton then asked an astounding, if oddly phrased, follow-up question: "State what you understand by Slavery and the freedom that was to be given by the President's proclamation." Frazier responded by offering perhaps the most concise definition of human bondage ever given. "Slavery," he said, is "receiving by *irresistible power* the work of another man, and not by his *consent*. The freedom," as outlined in the Emancipation Proclamation, he then explained, "is taking us from under the yoke of bondage, and placing us where we could reap the fruit of our own labor, take care of ourselves and assist the Government in maintaining our freedom."[25]

Slavery, freedom, the yoke of bondage, and the fruits of labor. With some provocation and in his own special way, Frazier managed to include in his answer the two defining ideas of the war and the central crux of American history. On top of that, in answering the question as he did, he framed the rest of the discussion, ensuring that whatever came next would reach beyond Savannah and speak to the nation as a whole. Thus, when Stanton followed up by asking Frazier how he thought freed people could best take care of themselves, the wily old stouthearted minister took that narrow sliver of an opening and made a much larger statement. His answer was *land*: "The way we can best take care of ourselves is to have land, and turn it and till it by our own labor," he told his two interviewers, adding that he thought that women, children, and the elderly could start preparing the ground while the young men enlisted "in the service of the Government." But the critical piece of the puzzle was landownership: not just *having* land but *owning* it. He emphasized, "We want to be placed on land until we are able to buy it and make it our own."[26]

Frazier wasn't answering Stanton so much as outlining a vision of freedom. Landownership, he recognized, would be the great equalizer. It would be the source of independence, wealth, and industry, and it would be the surest way for freed people to claim a stake in society. Landowning could provide an entry into politics or local government.

It offered business opportunities and was a source of credit. Aside from that, land was inheritable, which meant it had generational value and was as good as a future investment; one's children and one's children's children could continue to reap its rewards for years. Landowership, in other words, was the building block around which freed people could begin building new lives out of bondage. It was also, from where Frazier sat, the only plausible long-term solution to the problem both Sherman and Stanton needed solving: What to do about the thousands of displaced refugees who had followed Sherman to Savannah? We know that was on Frazier's mind because at one point he told the two men that he had formed his opinion during talks with the refugees. He then registered his amazement at what he'd seen, saying that their numbers had surpassed his own expectation.[27]

If landownership was the primary foundation, Frazier's vision also rested on at least two other ideas. One was autonomy. That point came up most substantially when Frazier told Stanton that he preferred to live separately from Southern whites for the time being because, as he put it, "there is a prejudice against us in the South that will take years to get over." For Frazier, that was a matter of pragmatism. He didn't know how freed people would otherwise be able to get the fresh start they deserved given the prevailing prejudice against them; all but one of his peers spoke up in agreement. Frazier then answered an insulting question from Stanton by insisting that freed people were more than capable of living together as a community: when asked whether he thought freed people had the "intelligence" to "maintain themselves under the Government of the United States, and maintain good and peaceable relations among yourselves and with your neighbors?," Frazier gave his most direct answer of the evening: "I think there is sufficient intelligence among us to do so," he replied. He said nothing more, as if he didn't want to dignify the question with any further response.[28]

The other idea central to Frazier's vision was that freed people had a right to American citizenship. Despite his talk of separatism, that idea was the underlying assumption behind all his answers. The war had made the case for him: Not only had freed people been loyal to the government and faithful to the army, they'd served in the army. Freedmen had put on uniforms, fixed bayonets, and fought and died storming parapets and siege lines; women, similarly, had been the army's laundresses, cooks, and nurses. Freed people had been the latent force behind so much of the army's operations and had helped kill the Confederacy by destroying it from within. As far as Frazier was concerned, he and his peers would continue doing their part: he told Stanton that he and the other ministers would recruit Black troops and that to even think of helping the rebels would amount to "suicide." "If the prayers that have gone up for the Union army could be read out," he said at one point, "you would not get through them [in] these two weeks." That alone—that freed people supported the Union and had fought for the Union while Southern whites had fought to destroy it—was reason enough, he felt, to forge a new South on the basis of Black citizenship and inclusion.[29]

After Stanton and Frazier parried questions back and forth, the mood in the room suddenly shifted. With the lamps burning low and the conversation drawing to a close, Stanton excused Sherman so he could speak with the ministers alone. Everyone must have known what was coming. There was thus probably an awkward pause as Sherman exited and the ministers shuffled in their seats; Stanton then likely cleared his throat and looked at his notes before proceeding: "State what is the feeling of the colored people in regard to Gen. Sherman," he said before asking if they considered him "friendly to their rights and interests, or otherwise?" Stanton, a nationally known attorney with years of experience, was being coy. He didn't ask about Ebenezer Creek specifically. Nor did he ask about the refugees in general. He might not have needed to. The freed ministers might have heard the reports and known that Sherman's conduct had provided the subtext to the entire evening. Or maybe they didn't know about the incident or hadn't heard the reports. It is also possible that Stanton didn't want to know the specifics and was perhaps happy to leave Savannah having only skimmed the surface of the issue. In any case, instead of being specific, he asked the question and waited for a response.[30]

"We looked upon Gen. Sherman prior to his arrival as a man in the Providence of God specially set apart to accomplish this work," Frazier said, "and we unanimously feel inexpressible gratitude to him, looking upon him as a man that should be honored for the faithful performance of his duty." Many of the ministers had called on the general just after the army had arrived, and Sherman had treated them courteously, which had convinced them that he was both "a friend and a gentleman." Frazier then offered the affirmative statement Stanton wanted and Sherman hoped to get: "We have confidence in Gen. Sherman, and think that what concerns us could not be under better hands." One of the ministers, James Lynch, said that he had only "limited acquaintance" with the general and thus had no real opinion on the matter, but all the other ministers agreed with Frazier. No one pressed the issue any further and there was nothing else said on the subject, which was all Stanton needed. Once he had sailed to Savannah, confronted Sherman, and mounted a mostly perfunctory investigation, the case was effectively closed. The inquiry was over.

And with that, so was the meeting. The aide who took the only known record of what was said noted that further comments were made relating to the March more generally, but no one made any special note of them. The two parties then probably shook hands and exchanged pleasantries. Everyone involved, except maybe Sherman—who, when he wrote his memoirs nearly a decade later, still grumbled about Stanton having asked him to leave the room—seemed to consider the conference a great success. The staff officers had been impressed by the ministers and their comportment. James Lynch likewise wrote that he and the ministers had walked away "blessing the Government, Mr. Secretary Stanton, and General Sherman" and their hearts had been "buoyant with hope and thankfulness." Stanton was even said to have commented afterward that history had just been made—that for the first time in American history representatives of the US government had consulted people of color and inquired what they wanted for themselves.[31]

Understandably, hope started to mount. The consensus was that that historic summit in Savannah couldn't have been for nothing and that either Sherman or Stanton must have some plan. The odds supported land reform. The soldiers seemed to expect it. The freed people did, too. A correspondent from Washington also reported that after the January 12 meeting at the Green House "it is understood here that the country will be electrified in a few days by an order from him [Sherman] partitioning" the abandoned plantations—which, the reporter went on, would establish "new freeholds" and lay "the foundation for a new social condition in the South." That, however, was about it. No one knew anything for sure. Stanton and Sherman kept their plans close to the vest, and the ministers didn't have any particular insight, either. Yet none of that stopped anyone from assuming that whatever the plan was, it was going to be big, a momentous and fitting end to the monumental March.[32]

The rumors were true. On January 16, four days after meeting with the ministers, Sherman issued Special Field Order No. 15, which set aside a strip of land extending thirty miles in from the coast between Charleston, South Carolina, and the St. Johns River in Florida for exclusively African American homesteading. The land, some 400,000 acres in all, was to be divided into equal plots of about forty acres apiece, and furthermore, no white person—except military or government officials—would be allowed into the area. In a separate order issued days later, Sherman even mentioned furnishing freed families with the army's "partially broken down" pack animals, thus the origins of the phrase "forty acres and a mule." As of yet, Sherman's orders represented the most drastic escalation in Reconstruction policy to date—in effect, a formal, military-backed mandate that the federal government would confiscate Confederate property, redistribute it to freed families, and provide the materials needed to make something of it. It was a sign of how radical Reconstruction could become.[33]

The problem was that Sherman didn't see it that way. To him and everyone in the War Department, the Special Field Orders were mostly a matter of strategic self-interest. Sherman, for one, had already begun planning his next move. In only a matter of days, his entire army would wake from its winter slumber and embark on a new campaign north through the Carolinas. A large body of freed refugees following the army out of Savannah would only encumber what he hoped would be the last campaign of the war. He also knew that Georgia was just the beginning. The ten to twenty thousand refugees who had followed the army to Savannah might be a conservative estimate of what awaited the army in the Carolinas. Part of the calculation was that in settling freed people along the coast, the army might discourage future refugees from following the columns and instead convince them to head to the Sea Islands, where they could find homesteads of their own.[34]

Sherman was finally doing what he had always been reluctant to do: playing politics. While he had received an important vote of confidence from Frazier and the other ministers, there was still a lingering sense that he needed to do more to cover his flanks and assuage his critics by settling the refugee situation more permanently. Moreover, though Frazier and the other ministers had given him positive reviews, who's to say that prominent Black leaders elsewhere felt the same? What about Northern abolitionists or freed people more generally? Also, what might the emerging narrative of Sherman's March and the reports that Sherman had turned his back on the refugees do to the army's recruitment of Black troops? With the war still raging and the news of Ebenezer Creek, those were critical questions, and both Sherman and Stanton realized that something would have to be done to shore up public perception.[35]

The order has always been called Sherman's Special Field Order No. 15, but the reality is that it wasn't necessarily original to Sherman. Stanton had a hand in drawing it up, offering revisions and edits. Also, recall that Henry Halleck had urged Sherman weeks earlier to adopt something similar in an effort to quiet his critics and put the business of the March to rest. The initial contours of Sherman's order also map onto what Frazier outlined during the conference at the Green House. The order endorsed African American homesteading, the core of Frazier's vision; it excluded whites from the surrounding vicinity, another of Frazier's key ideas; and it included a provision whereby families of enlisted men could claim their homesteads while their husbands and sons still served in the army, which was yet another issue Frazier had raised in the conference. One way to look at the origins of Special Field Order No. 15, then, is as something not specific to Sherman but rather as an amalgam of what Halleck and Frazier had proposed with what Sherman and Stanton would allow.[36]

On the topic of origins, there is also a point to be made about historical precedent. While redistributing confiscated plantations to freed slaves was a novel idea, giving away land was not. If anything, land schemes like that had been among the most American of traditions. For more than two centuries, cheap, available land had driven settlers westward, and from lotteries to preemptions, the federal government had actively promoted western settlement. A perfect case in point: the Homestead Act of 1862. Passed by the same US Congress that legislated the war and emancipation, the Homestead Act offered settlers 160-acre tracts of cheap western land if they agreed to settle on and improve the land for five years; they didn't even need to be citizens to apply. They just had to be over twenty-one years of age, make a small down payment, and, if a recent immigrant, state their intention to become a permanent US citizen. Nevertheless, the point is that Special Field Order No. 15 appeared at a time when federal land programs weren't utopian dreams but American realities. They were the internal gears powering the United States' "manifest destiny."[37]

For a brief moment, Special Field Order No. 15 seemed like a similar promise. It was a symbol, if nothing else, of the government's commitment to righting the wrongs of slavery and rebuilding American society in a new, brighter, and more equitable image. Thus the excitement and celebrations: On the evening of February 2, about two weeks after Sherman issued the order and about a week after the army left town, close to a thousand freed people gathered at the Second African Baptist Church of Savannah off Greene Square; apparently several hundred more arrived but had to be turned away because the church was packed to the rafters. Organized by Rufus Saxton, the gathering was one part town meeting and two parts camp revival. A freed organist played old hymns; the choir sang patriotic songs; and pastors preached and prayed, bringing their listeners to tears. Saxton then read the order aloud and encouraged everyone in attendance to head to the islands to claim their homesteads. It seemed that even the most serious of skeptics could believe that the Day of Jubilee had truly arrived.[38]

At the same time, cynicism was alive and well. The first signs of doubt came during a meeting in the new schoolhouse located on the former site of A. Bryan's Negro Mart just days after the celebration at the Second African Baptist Church. Prospective freeholders—likely a mix of refugees and locals from Savannah—raised valid objections: Why should they leave Savannah for some unknown homestead? What if they had better prospects finding work in the city and didn't want to have to try to grow a crop on some abandoned plantation? Freed people had also read the fine print. Critically, Sherman's order granted only *possessory* claims to the land, not a full legal title, which raised all sorts of concerns about how permanent an arrangement the so-called Sherman Reserve would be. "I can get a good living here, and don't want to go to the islands unless I can be assured of a title to the land," a prospective settler announced during the meeting, which elicited the only response the white agents could give: that they couldn't guarantee deeds, but that on the "faith and honor" of the United States, Sherman's order was airtight and incontrovertible.[39]

The concerns about obtaining legal title to the lands echoed the concerns coming out of the North. The reactions to Sherman's order among Northern free Black leaders and antislavery agitators had been surprisingly muted—and mostly for that very reason. Most saw the scheme for what it was: a temporary fix to a strategic problem; a naked attempt to "colonize" freed people; not a step toward the full reconstruction of the South but a punting of the issue down the road. The chorus of people criticizing the order grew so loud that James Lynch had to write from Savannah and say that while the order wasn't ideal, it received his "highest gratification" because it met "the exigencies of the present condition of the thousands of homeless, who, without it," he explained, "would remain . . . in a terrible chasm between freedom and slavery, or else crowd [ed] at military posts" totally "demoralized." That was the consensus of those on the ground: the order was not a universal panacea, but at least in theory, it would provide a sense of security.[40]

In all, nearly forty thousand people eventually settled on the roughly 400,000 acres outlined in Special Field Order No. 15. Their experiences varied. Some settled as individual families; others pooled their resources and settled as communities. Some resettled in their old home places, taking over land on which they had lived, worked, and buried loved ones; others settled in places new and foreign to them. Some took up homesteads almost immediately; many others took longer, and some undoubtedly got caught up in the tangled web of the settlement process—the slow workings of paperwork, confusion over whose land was whose, and a general lack of administrative wherewithal. Some also managed to buy their land and hold on to it permanently; others held on for as long as they could, but because the order was meant as a Band-Aid and never a solution, because it granted possessory titles only, and because President Andrew Johnson later pardoned Confederate planters and gave them their land back, the dream of reconstructing the South on the basis of Black landowning remained elusive.[41]

It was also a dream that many of the freed refugees had trouble accessing. Sherman had issued Special Field Order No. 15 because of their presence. The refugees were the intended beneficiaries. But the order was also the pretext the army needed to move out of Savannah, which had the effect of leaving the refugees out in the cold: when the army marched away into South Carolina, the transports to Port Royal slowed, which stranded thousands of displaced people around King's Bridge with little choice but to press on into Savannah. In addition, with the army gone, the main authority in the region was suddenly absent, which created a command vacuum that slowed the settlement process, reduced the available resources, and made providing relief more difficult. Furthermore, without the army there to flex its muscles and flash its guns, local whites felt empowered to do as they pleased. They could resist Sherman's order, and returning planters in particular often took advantage of freed people by signing them to unfair labor contracts. Put simply, the army's leaving Savannah created a situation that left the refugees to suffer.

The suffering was fairly widespread. It is one thing to announce a land scheme such as Special Field Order No. 15; it is quite another to implement it. For one, settling takes time. Those who managed to acquire homesteads didn't get them overnight, nor were the homesteads always operable upon arrival. The sad reality was that for many of the refugees, the time needed to make them so was time they didn't have. Their feet hurt. Their bodies ached. They had been living in the elements for weeks, if not months. Food was hard to come by, as were clothes and shoes. Sickness ravaged the camps. Even those on the first steamers bound for Port Royal faced at least a day or two in the camp at King's Bridge, maybe a day or two at sea, and then several days waiting on the islands before settling somewhere. Those who settled in Georgia likewise had to migrate and begin building new homes, a task more difficult when done on an empty stomach with empty pockets and a bad case of the chills. Special Field Order No. 15 addressed none of those challenges, which is to say that while landownership was a building block of freedom, it was not enough in itself. The refugees needed more resources and never quite got what they needed.

The situation was arguably worse at Port Royal. Teams of missionaries were on hand, ready to teach schools, administer aid, and provide whatever help was needed. The islands around Port Royal had been a haven for freed refugees from the surrounding islands throughout much of the war. But that was then. For about a month—from Christmas 1864 to late January 1865—as many as seventeen thousand freed refugees arrived on the islands, a number that more than matched the roughly fifteen thousand freed men and women already there under the aegis of the Port Royal Experiment. The presence of so many new inhabitants destabilized the entire region. The arrival of the Georgia refugees transformed the once small, self-contained freedmen's colony at Port Royal into the center of a sprawling crisis that stretched up and down the coast and engulfed freed people from across the region. In one sense, what happened on the South Carolina coast mirrored what was happening in Georgia and was but a constitutive piece of the March's long aftermath. At the same time, Port Royal was its own unfolding story—indeed, its own tragedy.

Brigadier General Rufus Saxton. Saxton served as the military governor of the Department of the South and spent most of his military career on the Sea Islands.

Chapter Six

PORT ROYAL AND THE REFUGEE STRUGGLE OF RECONSTRUCTION

On Christmas Day 1864, Rufus Saxton spent his holiday pacing the docks along the Beaufort River. As the first seven hundred refugees from Sherman's army descended the gangway, Saxton and his staff became aware of the severity of the refugee crisis that would soon take over the islands. H. G. Judd, the superintendent of freedmen and one of Saxton's chief subordinates, reported that most of the arrivals were "women, old men and children" and that "half of them had traveled from Macon, Atlanta, and even Chattanooga." While some carried a collection of pots, pans, and other utensils, most possessed little more than the clothing on their back. "They were all utterly destitute of blankets stockings or shoes," Judd noted, adding that "all were foot-sore and weary," which underscored the urgency of finding relief. Hence the scramble. On that first night, only through a "vigorous effort on the part of all the friends [Northern agents]" did he and his team find suitable, though not ideal, accommodations: "They [the refugees] were housed—packed—in a disused commissary building through the rainy night that followed."[1]

As daylight broke the next morning, the search for more permanent accommodations continued. Saxton and his staff made what later became a grave mistake. In his letter to the editor, Judd wrote that four hundred of the seven hundred freed people who had arrived the day before had been marched out with a guard detail to a location some three miles from Beaufort, where tents had been set up. That campsite would serve as yet another temporary home until more permanent accommodations became available. The plan, Judd explained, was to scatter the refugees among the plantations already housing freed families, but there weren't enough vacant tenements to go around. Until then, the refugees would sit and wait and live on the makeshift campsite until something more permanent became available.[2]

The problem was that there was little time to spare. At the moment, food wasn't the issue. With the Port Royal Experiment in place and the army now stationed on the islands, there were generally enough provisions to go around. The issue was a lack of blankets, clothing, and other items that might ameliorate the effects of sleeping out in the cold. The situation had apparently become so desperate that Saxton and his staff resorted to handing out linsey, a linen-and-woolen fabric, so that the freedwomen could make their own coverings. For some it was too little, too late. Most if not all of the refugees had already spent weeks, even months, living out in the elements, and the fatigue of such a debilitating journey with only the barest necessities had started to take its toll, which was why placing the refugees in the temporary camp was such a grave mistake. In only a matter of days, large numbers of the new arrivals—as many as half, Judd said—started to fall sick from "exposure," leaving him to report that "coffins go out each day to bury the dead."[3]

Given the seriousness of the situation and given especially the expectation that many more thousands of refugees would arrive in the coming days, Saxton and his staff knew they needed help. Luckily, the project at Port Royal had flush friends in the Northern aid societies. The philanthropic organizations operated mostly out of New York, Boston, and Philadelphia and had names such as Freedmen's Aid Society and National Freedman's Relief Association. Their purpose had initially been to hire and train teachers and missionaries, but as the war continued, the scope of their activities expanded. They started raising relief money, purchasing food or supplies, and fitting out steamships to carry the goods to those in need; for all across the country, wherever freed communities were, the Northern aid societies raised funds to support them. However, the situation at Port Royal was a special case: it was the initial occupation of the Sea Islands back in 1862 that had called many of the organizations into existence, so in asking them for support, Saxton tapped trusted friends and reliable donors, men and women who had been supporting the Port Royal Experiment since its inception.[4]

It helped Saxton's case that the funders of the freedmen's aid societies were the same donors who had recently raised a small fortune earmarked for the suffering citizens of Savannah. The leaders of the various organizations appealed to guilty consciences. "The very last cause for which we drew our purse-strings make it impossible for us to tighten them against this," wrote representatives of New York City's National Freedmen's Relief Association. "We have fed with abundant liberality the people of Savannah," they went on. "Let us match that act of politic philanthropy to those who but a moment since were our enemies, by at least an equal generosity to those who never for a moment have been anything but our friends." The New England Freedmen's Aid Society responded in kind, asking "Will not Boston, which has so generously contributed $30,000 for the relief of the white population of Savannah—friends and enemies—give at least one-third as much for black people, whose sufferings are much more severe, and *all* of whom are our friends?" Though it's unclear how much money was actually raised, at least some of the societies procured a sizable cargo—and kept at it.

More supplies arrived later in February and into early spring, becoming a lifeline for a project teetering on the brink of failure.[5]

As the various Northern aid societies kick-started their fundraising drives, the great refugee movement to Port Royal proceeded. Successive waves of refugees arrived by the day. Saxton and his staff continued their scramble to find adequate shelter. "Another great crowd of negroes has come from Sherman's army," wrote Laura Towne, the white teacher from Philadelphia, on January 8, fourteen days after the first group had arrived on Christmas Day. By now Saxton and his team had abandoned their earlier plan to house the refugees in the makeshift camp and begun simply dispersing them across the islands to find shelter wherever they could. At St. Helenaville, a small village on the tip of St. Helena Island, Towne reported that arriving refugees had either crowded inside a local church or found refuge within the homes of freed people already there.[6]

This effort to relocate the refugees captures one of the key transformations happening on the islands: old barriers had broken down, and the influx of refugees into Port Royal was bringing folks from various corners of the South into the same general location, which suddenly made reunions possible. In one instance, Elizabeth Hyde Botume, another white teacher, met two freed women while boarding a steamer bound for Savannah. The women were going there to search for old friends whom they suspected might still be there, and for the first time ever, they had the chance to do so. While Port Royal was becoming a mini-melting pot of people from across the region, so was Savannah. When Botume arrived there later in February, she found it full of fresh faces and completely changed from only a month or so earlier. Large numbers of freed people had apparently left with the army; others had moved out onto homesteads; while those who remained were mostly folks who had pressed in from the "'sand hills' and low lands" outside the city. So many moving people produced a social geography that shifted and changed.[7]

Part of the general dislocation stemmed from the incredible social force of Sherman's March and the varying refugee movements it caused.

But part of it was also by design. Saxton and his subordinates were still trying to figure out where to settle the Georgia refugees. The problem of finding permanent accommodations for them was no more resolved in mid- to late January than it had been on that cool Christmas afternoon when the first refugees had arrived. As Saxton seemed to understand quite clearly, the somewhat stopgap policy of placing refugees in the homes of freed families already on the islands worked only up to a point. There was only so much space available, and as more refugees arrived, that policy would prove untenable. The only viable option was to seek out more space. So instead of cramming freed refugees into the existing settlements, where shelter was already at a premium, Saxton's staff extended their search beyond Port Royal and started settling refugees on more peripheral islands.

One such island was Morgan Island, just northeast of Beaufort. Though abandoned and not all that far from St. Helena, its location—somewhat detached and in the middle of St. Helena Sound—made it difficult to supply and left it open to Confederate raids from up the Combahee River, a contested artery into the South Carolina interior. Nonetheless, Edward Philbrick recalled a friend and colleague who had gone there to "receive and stow away one hundred and fifty Georgia refugees," most of whom "came from the shore counties near to Savannah." Hilton Head Island would presumably have been another landing spot. Hilton Head, a large, shoe-shaped island on the south side of Port Royal Sound, had been part of the project at Port Royal (and indeed, its historic Mitchellville community had been one of the first freedmen's communities formed during the war). A similar, albeit smaller, attempt to resettle refugees occurred on Daufuskie Island, a sparsely settled island nestled between Hilton Head and Savannah, where by midsummer nearly half the freed population consisted of refugees from Georgia's interior.[8]

Yet the primary target for expansion remained Edisto Island. Located north of Port Royal on the opposite end of St. Helena Sound,

Edisto had been occupied by federal troops earlier in the war but had been abandoned in 1862 following the withdrawal of US forces from Charleston. When that had happened, the freed people on the island had been evacuated and resettled throughout the project at Port Royal, becoming the first group of refugees to arrive there en masse. With Sherman in Savannah and the Confederates now on the run, plans were made in early 1865 to reoccupy Edisto and turn it into a haven for the Georgia refugees. James P. Blake, a Northern agent from New Haven, Connecticut, and later the general superintendent of operations on the island, quickly became the point man for the project. He wrote the aid societies in early January, saying "it is in contemplation to colonize Edisto Island, S.C. with the Georgia refugees" and that he already had a "plan of colonization." In what was likely an attempt to raise money and support for the venture, a colleague would write again days later, describing Edisto as the "gem of the Sea Islands" and listing the conditions that made it an ideal place for a new settlement. Blake's efforts paid off. The plan moved forward, and by April, he found himself the general superintendent of an island that was now home to as many as five thousand freed men and women.[9]

While Edisto, Daufuskie, and Hilton Head were all islands on the South Carolina coast, relocation there was far from easy. For freed refugees from the interior of Georgia, landing on the islands would have been like landing in another world—a place culturally distinct, far from home, and with its own wartime history, including a history as part of the Port Royal Experiment. On top of that, each day spent traveling to some unknown location meant another day marching or another boat ride, which likely meant more time spent sleeping in the elements and more time exposed to the stiff winter wind. And because most of the places had been abandoned—or, like Daufuskie, were sparsely settled and accessible only by water—there was little infrastructure. There were only a few cabins, little food and few utensils, and dilapidated docks. Nearly everything needing to be built or provided from scratch. To the Georgia refugees, men and women who had followed Sherman's army for weeks, it was as if their experience was never ending, as if the March had never stopped and freedom kept coming into and fading out of reach.

It is also important to consider what the various movements meant for the islands as a whole. Refugees from Georgia landed and tried to settle in new, sometimes faraway locations. Freed people from one island relocated to another. Communities with ties running generations deep were shuffled and reconstituted—and in some cases, moved and reconstituted elsewhere. Not only that, but new settlements sprang up out of the ashes of the old. As a distinct microregion, the Sea Islands were effectively refashioned in the shadow of Sherman's March. The federal occupation had initiated some of the changes back in 1861, and the region's unique history of emancipation via the Port Royal Experiment had given it its wartime shape. But it was Sherman's March and the crisis it unleashed that transformed the region, proving that what came *after* the March was as much a crucible, as much an ordeal, as the March itself. That was true not only for the refugees but for the Sea Islands as a whole.

Back in Beaufort, the city's sandy streets were full of hoofprints and boot marks. Starting on January 3, the day after the Emancipation Day parade, blue-coated soldiers began marching in. The first regiments were followed by more soldiers, who were followed by still more, and before long, it seemed as though the long blue lines just kept coming. "The troops continue to come by the thousands," wrote Willard Saxton, noting that with all the new troops stalking the streets, it was high times for the city's merchants. "Troops continue to arrive, and the town is full of activity," he wrote again two days later. Everything was hustle and bustle. "There is so much life along the Shell Road & on each side; & this island never saw such life," Saxton wrote, now a little frustrated that the increased street traffic disturbed his routine jaunts around the island. All in all, two full army corps—Sherman's entire right wing, a force of about thirty thousand men—marched through Beaufort and its vicinity during the month of January 1865, enough for Saxton to declare that "this island has never seen such life."[10]

The soldiers were all Howard's men, members of the Army of the Tennessee. A Bowdoin man with a long beard and warm, gentle eyes, Oliver Otis Howard had commanded Sherman's rightward flank during the March to the Sea. Up until now, he had had a brutal war. He had been hit twice in his right arm on the Virginia Peninsula in 1862 and had had to have his arm amputated; his sleeve hung pinned up and empty for the rest of his life. To add insult to his otherwise obvious injury, two successive poor showings at Chancellorsville and Gettysburg had nearly ruined his reputation and left him feeling humiliated. It was his men whom Stonewall Jackson had flanked at Chancellorsville, a historic ride-around that had collapsed the Union line and forced a full-scale retreat. Months later, those same troops had fled through town on the first day at Gettysburg, a mortifying and some would suggest unnecessary flight that had gotten Howard transferred to Chattanooga, a move that wasn't styled as a face-saving reassignment but very much was. From then on, it was clear that if he wanted redemption, he'd have to find it with Sherman.[11]

Despite those setbacks, however, Howard never lost his sensibility. Known as "the Christian general," he was pious and evangelical, and he hated profanity about as much as whiskey. He had once even considered leaving the military and joining the ministry. His piety made him a warmhearted foil for some of the less savory members of Sherman's high command—men such as Jefferson C. Davis and the reckless cavalryman Hugh Judson Kilpatrick, known by the pejorative nickname "Kill-Cavalry." Because of those qualities and probably also because he was a fellow New Englander from southern Maine, Howard fit right in among the so-called Gideonites working on the islands. Rufus Saxton came to respect him deeply during the army's stay in Beaufort and considered him a friend and ally. Willard did, too, describing him at one point as a "very pleasant gentleman, affable and agreeable, & an exceedingly good man."[12]

Willard would have known. He and his older brother acted as Howard's unofficial hosts for the month or so the army spent stationed on the islands. The trio dined together, entertained one another, and worked closely together. It helped that Willard had his wife and two-year-old son, Eddie, with him in Beaufort, which kindled in Howard thoughts of his own family, including his children, two of whom were around Eddie's age. Howard also had his younger brother Charles—who had left on a trip home upon arriving in Savannah—serving as his aide de camp similar to the way Willard served Rufus, a coincidence that fostered a natural connection between people whose wartime spheres had converged. For Howard, that warm welcome made his time at Port Royal a pleasant experience. It was a brief respite from the drudgery of command and a much-needed rest from a campaign full of hard marching. The only problem was the weather. The Gulf Stream blew in dismal weather throughout January. It was colder than normal, or so it seemed. And the brisk wind and seemingly waterlogged air had everyone worrying about their health.[13]

Nevertheless, in between storms and when military duty didn't call, Howard joined the Saxtons and others in touring the islands. Of special interest to him were the schools. He made stops at several of them. He visited Laura Towne's school at the Oakes Plantation on St. Helena Island. One teacher tells us that his missing arm "made quite an impression on the children." He also stopped at Elizabeth Hyde Botume's school at the Old Fort Plantation about five miles from Beaufort, where he stood to the side listening earnestly as the children sang songs and learned their lessons. He then took some time at the end to make a few brief remarks, the gist of which encouraged the students to do their best. As a former Sunday school teacher and mathematics instructor at West Point, Howard found himself back in his element. The schools were a sanctuary for him and the children, and fortunately, there were plenty of them to visit; for no other place in the wider landscape of the war had as many freedmen's schools been concentrated in a single area, and nowhere else had as many teachers operating at Port Royal.[14]

Unfortunately, two of the best-known teachers were absent during Howard's stay. One was Charlotte Forten. Born free in Philadelphia to a family of prominent African American abolitionists, she had come south to the Sea Islands in 1862 as one of the first Philadelphians and the first African American to join the newly established experiment. She taught at what became the Penn School and later published a long two-part essay titled "Life on the Sea Islands" in the *Atlantic Monthly*, which documented her experiences. She wrote vividly about her teaching, her pupils, the project's successes and failures, meeting Colonel Robert Gould Shaw of the 54th Massachusetts USCT, and the immense sadness she had felt as she had tended the wounded and dying following the assault on Fort Wagner. She was one of the great documenters of the war and of African American life in general—and nowhere more so than in her journals and diaries, which run to five volumes and span 1854 to 1864 and then 1885 to 1892 after she had become a lifelong teacher and suffragette. Forten and Howard never crossed paths at Port Royal because she had sailed home sometime in 1864 after suffering a bout of ill health.[15]

It was a similar story for Susie King Taylor. Unlike Forten, who had been born free, Taylor had been born enslaved along the coast of Georgia and had received an "underground education" from a free Black teacher while living in Savannah as a child. At just fourteen years old and with her hand clasped to her uncle's wrist, she had been one of hundreds of enslaved people who had escaped to federal gunboats off the Georgia coast in 1862, and she had later found a de facto freedom living at Port Royal. She had soon married a member of the 1st South Carolina

Volunteer Infantry Regiment, the early USCT regiment founded on the islands, and had quickly become the regiment's laundress, nurse, and teacher, becoming something of a headmaster for the entire regiment. She had taught scores of adult men how to read and write in between drill sessions. After the war, she served a brief stint teaching school in Savannah and on St. Catherines Island, and she would later publish a famous memoir titled *Reminiscences of My Life in Camp with the 33d United States Colored Troops Late 1st S.C. Volunteers.* She, too, missed Howard that January because she was away with the regiment on one of the islands near Charleston waiting on the city to fall.[16]

Even so, the classrooms Howard visited and the children he spoke with left an indelible impression on him. Although he had been surprisingly ambivalent about slavery as the war began, he was making his way through a personal and political evolution that would see him become not just an antislavery general or an advocate of emancipation but a champion of Black civil and political rights. His time touring the classes at Port Royal was a revelation. To Howard, a lifelong and committed educator, the freedmen's schools were models of reconstruction in miniature. They were examples of what was possible and represented what would be key building blocks in a new and reconstructed South. Education, like landownership, had generational value, but what education had that landownership didn't was the ability to start leveling society—if not immediately, then perhaps over a single generation. It was, to some degree, the equalizer of all equalizers and the best form of personal capital anyone could have. He was so impressed with the schools that when Edwin Stanton came to visit the islands after meeting with Sherman in Savannah, Howard insisted that the secretary visit the schools. He wanted the notoriously inscrutable secretary to have the same experience as he'd had.[17]

As Howard toured the schools, elsewhere on the islands his men—all thirty thousand or so of them—were making their presence known. Armies are like tidal waves; they engulf localities and leave them shells of their former selves. Port Royal, Beaufort, and the surrounding islands were no exception. Despite being an army outpost for much of the war and despite not having any local resistance, the islands groaned from the pressure the army put on them. Consider the basic numbers: Howard's thirty thousand troops nearly doubled the arriving seventeen thousand refugees, who themselves settled among fifteen thousand freed people, plus an assortment of treasury agents, teachers, missionaries, and superintendents, not to mention Saxton's staff and the soldiers and sailors who were already there. At the time, beyond the muddy trench lines of Petersburg, Virginia, where Grant's massive Union Army had Lee's men pinned outside Richmond, Port Royal may well have been the densest, most concentrated theater of the war. And if the arrival of that many refugees threatened to overwhelm the islands, the arrival of so many soldiers made the situation worse.

It didn't help that the soldiers turned the islands into their own stomping grounds. They camped about four miles from Beaufort and were unruly guests. The pent-up anxieties of the March boiled over in sporadic acts of vandalism. The want of places to sleep and food to eat led to their taking what they pleased: they chased down and plucked chickens, plundered gardens, and ate whatever they could find. The Northern agents found them appalling. The Gideonites scorned their behavior and had a hard time grappling with even the sight of them. "The Western soldiers are rough, unkempt customers," wrote one, saying that most had long, shaggy hair and that the first days in Beaufort were "more amusing" to the mass of soldiers than to the holders of property. Willard Saxton wrote similarly. Upon seeing some of the first regiments march in, he described them as "a rough looking set," noting with some amazement that it was "as if they'd seen service, as if marching & fighting was their business instead of drilling and guard duty," which perhaps says more about Willard and how little of the war he had actually seen.[18]

It wasn't long before the general rowdiness spilled over into violence, and as was the case elsewhere, freed people faced the worst of it. John Hill Ferguson of the Illinois 10th Regiment of Volunteers described in his diary a night that reads like a miniriot:

> In a short time afterwards, a detail of 20 men and a sergeant was called for to each company to go up to town after rations. It was 10 Oclock [sic] P.M. when they reached town. I understand they broke ranks, went where they pleased, and cut up all sorts of devilment. Killed two Negro soldiers. Crippled and knocked down a number of others. A whole regt.

Another soldier from the 6th Iowa Infantry Regiment was less explicit but perhaps more revealing when he wrote that that the "changed condition and new ideas concerning the great hordes of freedmen gathered" at Port Royal were a bit too much for the men. They recognized freed people as "true and loyal friends" and had treated them "kindly and generously about the camps, but not many had learned to meet them on terms of equality in all the public and social conditions of life." For the first time, the soldiers were seeing the full fruits of the war—the endgame of this new American revolution—and they didn't like what they saw. The Iowan said as much. "The new and radical customs and conditions found in the town at once engendered severe friction between the men and the colored people," he wrote, saying somewhat euphemistically that the tension caused "considerable disturbance and some altercations." Saxton, in fact, was so fearful that something might erupt on the streets of Beaufort that he eventually prohibited freed people from entering town.[19]

The "altercations," as the soldier called them, were new versions of an old problem. From the earliest days of the Port Royal Experiment, it had been clear that the soldiers stationed on the islands resented the freed people and even scoffed at what they considered the lily-livered work of the Northern agents; hence the term "Gideonites," which the soldiers had first coined as a mocking pejorative. Saxton had been appointed for precisely that reason: he was there as a military man to manage the divisions between the army and a set of Treasury officials, on one hand, and the teachers, missionaries, and freed people, on the other. He had done well up to that point, but with so many new soldiers stalking around, tensions flared once again. Some of Howard's men thought the freed people were being pampered; others especially seethed over the fact that they were fighting while the Port Royal Experiment continued on. As one soldier put it, "there is a great many niggers here, nigger Regiments, nigger schools and churches, the eternal nigger is everywhere and the only place I care about seeing him is with a musket in his hand."[20]

It comes perhaps as no surprise that military impressment once again became a topic of concern. Laura Towne specifically mentioned an incident in which recruiting agents had shot and killed two freedmen for resisting recruiting agents. "Such things," she said, "were not uncommon." Oddly, however, it wasn't the army's recruiting agents who came under the harshest scrutiny; rather, it was Saxton. The army's recruiting abuses had long been a grievance of his. In late December 1864, just prior to Sherman's arrival, he brought it up again in an end-of-the-year report to Secretary Stanton. The situation was so bad and the freed people so disheartened—first by the land sales and then by the ongoing issues of impressment along with the army's unequal pay—that he tendered his resignation. But Stanton—a sharp, keen-thinking politician—headed him off. He let the resignation letter sit for a while. Then he gave Saxton a promotion. He then got Sherman to place Saxton in charge of recruiting by way of Special Field Order No. 15, a sly move that he figured would solve the problem and keep Saxton from resigning.[21]

He was right. Yet while Special Field Order No. 15 gave Saxton control of enlistments and kept him in line, the appointment sparked angry outcries from some of his colleagues, none more than General John G. Foster. Foster, a sort of cocommander of the Department of the South, wrote to Sherman, begging him to relieve Saxton of his command. Saxton, he said, did more to encourage settlement than enlistment and had apparently once threatened "that he could have the head cut off of any officer who opposed him [on the issue]." "He [Saxton] is crazy on the subject," added General John Porter Hatch, one of Foster's subordinates, suggesting that "the negroes misunderstand their recently acquired freedom" and that Saxton's "course is thought to encourage them in their opinions." Sherman admitted to sympathizing with the concerns but said his hands were tied. If Foster wanted the appointment changed, he'd have to take it up with Stanton, though he didn't think Stanton would budge. "I cannot modify my orders relative to General Saxton having the charge of recruiting blacks," he wrote. Foster tried to write to Sherman again, but the squabble ended later that winter when Foster, not Saxton, was reassigned.[22]

O. O. Howard was long gone by the time the recruiting controversy bubbled to the surface. By then, he was somewhere in the South Carolina interior—likely Salkehatchie or Branchville—leading the southern wing of the march through the Carolinas. But before he left the islands he took one last action that ended up altering the course of his career: he pledged Saxton his full support—and he backed it up. He wrote to the new secretary of the Treasury, William Pitt Fessenden, a former senator and fellow Bowdoin alumnus, and gave his new associate a full-throated endorsement: "Whenever [Saxton] has been untrammeled in work, he has introduced system and order and industry among these poor people, in such a manner as to afford a practical example of the best method of dealing with the negroes, as fast as they are freed." He meant it, too. He believed that Saxton's leadership at Port Royal offered freed people their best chance at a full and meaningful freedom, and what he was asking was for Fessenden to call off his Treasury agents so that Saxton could continue his work unopposed.[23]

Little did Howard know at the time, but in writing to his old friend and fellow Mainer, he put his own name forward for one of the most important positions in the country. As Congress pushed the Thirteenth Amendment toward passage in late January, it was also holding debates on a proposed Bureau of Emancipation. The idea, first proposed by the American Freedmen's Inquiry Commission, was for the government to create a body designed to help usher former slaves into freedom. The issue was how? The divisions among the commission's members mirrored those miring up the works at Port Royal. More moderate members imagined a scaled-back approach, fearing that too much federal help would lead to dependency; others advocated a more robust involvement, imagining the bureau as the federal muscle behind the wider reconstruction of the South. The initial scope of the project thus included only relief in the form of food, shelter, and assistance to displaced people. But as passage neared, the bureau's mandate expanded to include settling abandoned lands, which gave it greater latitude in handling freedman affairs. Finally, on March 3, in the waning hours of a legislative session, Congress formally established the Bureau of Refugees, Freedmen, and Abandoned Lands, an institution best known as the Freedmen's Bureau.[24]

Two months later, in early May, O. O. Howard became the bureau's first and only commissioner. After fighting a war that had taken his right arm and some of his dignity, he was now head of a federal body charged with managing emancipation. It wasn't exactly a success. The Freedmen's Bureau was always underfunded and too paternalistic, and it was never given the enforcement mechanisms it needed. Its many failings have a lot to do with why the war's revolution ultimately bent backward, not forward. Yet its failings aside, the Freedmen's Bureau also carved out spaces where Reconstruction worked. It allied itself with freed people on the ground and helped them settle on land. It created its own court system. Its agents managed plantations and mediated labor disputes. It also—and this was by far its greatest success—built hundreds of freedmen's schools across the South, many of which are still standing and represent some of America's first public school systems. Howard doesn't deserve all the credit. The bureau wasn't his alone, and he certainly didn't do all the work. But he did, as its head, mold it in the image of Port Royal. His experience that January was both a benchmark and a blueprint, which made what happened at Port Royal a basis for Reconstruction not just on the Sea Islands but across the postwar South.[25]

Land reform became part of the Freedmen's Bureau's mandate partly because the day Special Field Order No. 15 went into effect, the federal government suddenly had a lot more land—about 400,000 acres worth to be exact. In fact, the bureau's land provision—forty acres per homestead—mirrored Special Field Order No. 15, and though the provision didn't redistribute land outright, it did offer freed people the chance to preemptively purchase it. Nevertheless, most stakeholders saw it as building on the program Sherman had already put into place. Therein lies the essential irony behind Special Field Order No. 15: it was only ever an expedient, a temporary answer to the army's problems, but in first broaching the issue, it thrust land policy into the center of debates about Reconstruction. Widespread land reform suddenly seemed not just possible but perhaps appropriate. The confiscation of abandoned plantations gained increased support among Republicans, many of whom argued that it was not only morally right but the just deserts of treason. Radicals, meanwhile, clamored for more radical change, holding that the current policy didn't go far enough. Just as important, freed people everywhere started to believe that land reform was no longer a matter of *if* but *when*.[26]

Yet while Special Field Order No. 15 thrust landownership onto the national agenda, it also brought immediate changes to the day-to-day operations of the islands. First of all, it named Rufus Saxton the "inspector of settlements and plantations," which placed him in charge of the operation and made it his job to see that settlement proceeded as specified. It was one of his many recently acquired hats—including military governor, head of recruiting, and de facto leader of the Northern agents. Except he didn't want to wear that particular hat. It turns out that he, like so many others, saw right through the Special Field Order. He knew it was a half-hearted attempt to colonize freed people, not to actually settle them permanently, and he feared that it would end with freed people being more disappointed and disillusioned than they already were. Even so, he eventually agreed to take on the job. Despite his doubts, he assumed leadership over a project that was doubling, maybe even tripling, in size and a settlement program that would embody the essential work of Reconstruction.[27]

Second and perhaps most important, Sherman's decision to issue Special Field Order No. 15 gave him the cover he needed to start his next campaign. Preparations for his move into the Carolinas began almost as soon as the ink dried and the orders were posted. In about fifteen days, lightning fast by military standards, Sherman's massive Union Army leapt back into motion. Slocum's left wing moved into South Carolina, crossing the river near a place called Purrysburg. Howard's right wing moved up through the islands from the coast. The Shell Road—the main road connecting Port Royal to Beaufort—acted as the central thoroughfare. Soldiers landed via boat at Port Royal, marched up the road to Beaufort, and then moved on in columns into the interior of South Carolina. From there, the plan was to have the two wings converge near Salkehatchie, then have Slocum's and Howard's men move as one giant wall toward Columbia, the state capital and perceived heart of the rebellion.

The army's mobilization out of the islands was a sight to behold. The town was already crowded. New troops arrived daily, as US Navy steamers carrying soldiers over from Savannah landed at Port Royal in quick succession. "The greater part of the whole army seems to be coming around this way," wrote Edward Philbrick. "It has the look of success to see such an army in motion," wrote Willard Saxton, describing an early advance movement off the islands. He thought that seeing Sherman's large army move with such power and force made all the other expeditions on the islands seem insignificant by comparison. Of course, as the army moved, it also consumed. Howard would even write back to Saxton, practically apologizing for his men's behavior as they moved, a gentle nod to all the stolen chickens reported by freed people and all the looted fence rails used for firewood.[28]

The real problem with the army's move out of Beaufort wasn't so much the force of its movements but the fact that it left people behind. So long as Union troops remained on the islands and Sherman still had his headquarters in Savannah, there was a steady flow of steamers full of refugees and supplies back and forth between the two. After the army moved out, the convoys stopped. Priorities changed. The naval forces there to support the army redirected their attention to operations further up the coast at places such as Charleston and Wilmington, and Beaufort was left behind. The same was true for the camp at King's Bridge, the army's unofficial depot and point of departure for transports to the islands. The army left thousands of refugees stranded in Georgia on the banks of the Ogeechee with nowhere to go. James P. Blake, the future superintendent on Edisto, who would die in a boating accident off the island a year later, estimated that only a small number of refugees who arrived on the islands did so by the time the army left, implying that the rest came later and at a much slower pace. Tragically, of those stranded in Georgia, he believed that at least a thousand must have died from "disease and exposure," revealing once again that the greatest threat to the refugees was the elements.[29]

As the army moved into the interior, the borders of the once confined and self-contained project at Port Royal expanded. "Sherman's operations have opened a wider sphere for negro work and thrown a great number of refugees into our hands," wrote William C. Gannett, one of the Northern teachers. It was partly an administrative result of Special Field Order No. 15 in that it grouped the entire coastline from Charleston to St. Johns River into a single unit—or colony, as the agents called it. But the real effects of the mandate came only after the army shoved off. Without the army's presence in Savannah, the onus of keeping the peace, administering aid, and overseeing freedmen's affairs fell squarely on Saxton's team of underresourced agents and subordinates along with what military forces they could muster. The islands south of Savannah on the Georgia coast were suddenly part of their purview, which stretched their resources even thinner. In fact, in early March, after setting up what he described as a "colonization office" in Savannah, Gannett wrote exasperatedly, "First, no steamer! then no coal! And when one can be had, the other can't," admitting also that they had run woefully short on food. He later wrote that only a few of those who had fled to King's Bridge for help would ever receive any rations. There weren't any.[30]

Moreover, Charleston fell within weeks of the army's advance. The Stars and Stripes flying over the city where secession was born galvanized those at Port Royal, including the freed people, some of whom had relatives living in the city or on surrounding plantations; many of the Northern agents even attended the ceremonial flag raising over Fort Sumter, a celebration full of speakers and celebrities, including the abolitionist William Lloyd Garrison and the once enslaved riverboat captain turned national hero Robert Smalls. But the fall of Charleston also signaled that the project had an even wider sphere of influence. The islands south of Charleston—Johns, James, Wadmalaw, Seabrook—all fell within Saxton's ambit, and by early March, James Blake would write to the New England Aid Society, asking that a "principal part" of its relief shipments be redirected to Charleston, where destitution "was found to be extreme, not only among the old and infirm residents of the place, but also among the many refugees from the interior." Even more, evidence suggests that as the army moved into North Carolina, it sent some of the freed refugees down from Wilmington or Elizabeth City to Port Royal or Savannah, an extended ocean voyage that stretched the project's reach beyond the land outlined in Sherman's orders.[31]

Meanwhile, the crisis continued. During the army's push into the interior and as more islands fell within the bounds of the project, the situation worsened. By now, the settlements were close to filling to their limits. One such settlement was a place called Montgomery Hill. The settlement had originally been built to house refugees from the so-called Montgomery Raid back in 1863. It now housed anywhere from three to four hundred refugees from Georgia. Elizabeth Hyde Botume, whose school on the Old Fort Plantation wasn't too far away, described it as having a row of small houses. Within each house were four rooms, each room holding a family of four to fifteen persons. Each room had a shelf, a window, and a fireplace. Bunk beds—or berths—had been built into the walls, making each room a sort of "one-roomed cabin," as Botume put it, describing the rooms as representing "the poorest and most meagre animal existence." Another settlement not far from Montgomery Hill was Battery Plantation, where about thirty-one refugees had piled into a six-room house. A widowed father who had just lost his wife lived there with his four sons, all occupying one room. The detached kitchen had also been turned into living quarters. Botume remembered two sick women lying on the kitchen floor, resting on a bed of moss and corn husks to ease their pain.[32]

By late January, the situation was close to the breaking point. "The Georgia refugees are coming along by hundreds and thousands," wrote Edward Philbrick, the private landholder on the islands. William C. Gannett, the Northern teacher, thought the situation so bad that he personally wrote north begging for assistance. "If there is any movement afoot in Boston for the assistance of the negro refugees that Sherman's operations throw into our hands, it can be of the greatest benefit," he claimed. He remembered the aid given three years before when the occupation had begun and acknowledged that "too much was given." "But now hundreds are coming in, shivering, hungry, so lean and bony," he reported, adding:

> Old men of seventy and children of seven years have kept pace with Sherman's advance, some of them for two months and over, from the interior of Georgia; of course little or nothing could be brought but the clothing on their backs and the young children in arms. Since their arrival in comparatively comfortable quarters, great sickness has prevailed, and numbers and numbers have died.

The government was working to distribute rations and blankets, he assured them, but he told his audience that if "Northern friends" could also send aid, "nowhere can generosity be better extended."[33]

Over at The Oaks on St. Helena, where Laura Towne lived, the story was much the same. After she had welcomed some of the first arrivals back in early January, successive groups arrived not long afterward. Many of the men and women arrived from the estate of Pierce Butler. Butler, once the second largest slaveholder in the state of Georgia, who owned a small island empire near the coastal town of Darien, was notorious. Not only had he married a famous British actress named Fanny Kemble, who had divorced him and later exposed the horrors of his plantation in a widely read journal published in 1863, but he was the perpetrator of the largest recorded slave sale in American history. In 1859, in an effort to settle his many debts, Butler, whose father had been a signer of the US Constitution, sold 436 men, women, and children in a slave auction so large it took two days to complete and had to be held at a local horse track near Savannah. It apparently rained so hard during those two days that the enslaved people believed that even God was weeping; enslaved communities likewise remembered the auction as the "Weeping Time," as family and friends were sold away from one another and a tight-knit plantation community was splintered. The refugees who arrived at Port Royal were likely those who had remained with the Butler estate.[34]

To her dismay, Towne could do little for them. "We have no clothes to give these poor shivering creatures," she wrote, admitting "and I never felt so helpless." Quite a few apparently arrived sick, and according to Towne, "nearly all" were "broken down with fatigue, privation of food, and bad air at night." All she could do was hand out hot tea to the ill, whom she described as "such a weary, sick, and coughing set." Conditions would only get worse before getting better. The way she described the situation, her village may well have become a hot spot in an emerging epidemic. The "poor refugees from Georgia," she wrote, were "frightfully destitute, sickly, and miserable." They were apparently all "homesick too," she explained, saying that most had expected to "stay and enjoy their freedom in Savannah, or their back-country homes in Georgia" but instead "pine in this uncomfortable and strange place, where they die so fast." Disease ravaged the settlements. "The poor negroes die as fast as ever," she wrote again a few days later, noting that "the children are all emaciated to the last degree, and have such violent coughs and dysenteries that few survive." Worse, the deaths had started separating families. Parents looked for their lost children. Children looked for their parents. One child recovered from "typhoid pneumonia" only to discover that her mother, brother, and aunt had all succumbed to the same disease, with another of her aunts "just [now] dying."[35]

Conditions improved a bit by mid-February. Relief shipments began arriving. Clothes and blankets were dispersed among those in need, and even more important, the weather improved, which reduced the number of deaths. "The terrible sickness and mortality among those in this village is much less now that the severe cold weather is over," Towne wrote, which brought to light the sad reality that most had died simply from exposure to the elements. Towne knew it, too. "[The] Government gave each family a blanket or two," she wrote. ". . . I really think many actually died from cold." Others, she knew, might have improved but still had such "severe coughs" that she wondered if they would ever truly recover. "Nearly all who are ill take the dropsy as they get better," she explained; they would get up and walk about until their lungs filled, and then they would "take to the floor" and pass a day or so later. That was likely the case for most of the children, as Towne wrote that as of mid-February, "Nearly all the children are dead, or a very large proportion of them."[36]

To make matters even worse, even though the weather cleared by early February, March threw a new wrench into the ongoing crisis: a terrible storm delayed the flow of rations to the islands—possibly the result of ships being unable to refuel at coaling stations. In any case, food suddenly became scarce, causing Towne to record that at St. Helena Village "there has been something very like starvation here." The Georgia refugees bore the brunt of the shortages. "Being nearly reduced to starvation, for the want of rations, which were stopped by want of the means of transportation (coal for steamers)," she explained, the refugees from Georgia had taken to stealing "whatever was eatable" on the islands. That didn't matter all that much, though, because everyone, she wrote, was "for a time reduced to salt food entirely"—meaning food that had been salted and dried and thus stripped of important nutrients such as vitamin C, which caused some in the village to develop scurvy. "It was trying enough for a week, —indeed, for three or four weeks, —but for one week they were almost laid up," she wrote.[37]

The March was also only part of the equation. What happened on the islands during those long winter months was partly a product of the project's own making. Indeed, no matter how well intentioned the Northern agents were, no matter how feverishly they wrote north, no matter how sad they all were to see more coffins being built and buried, the project's contradictory goals persisted. Take Towne as an example. When the weather began to break in mid-February, she knew that the expectation was for the refugees to start working as soon as their bodies would allow it. Some had already started. But Towne didn't know what good that would do. As she wrote, rations had dwindled and "at the present low rate of wages and high prices of provisions," she didn't know how they could buy both food and clothing, thus keeping them deprived of even the most basic necessities. Edward Philbrick had also begun assessing the refugees as potential laborers and felt that the "Georgia negroes" were a "superior-looking set to those of these islands."[38]

Philbrick was without a doubt the worst offender. His doctrinaire approach to the free labor ethic kept freed people locked in a vise grip. "When I take my leetle bit money and go to the store," a woman said to him once, ". . . the money all gone and leave chillun naked." The woman and her sons had worked for him for three years, she said, and they were tired of never having enough. Philbrick responded by telling her that if anyone didn't like his wages they were free to leave, though he wouldn't allow them to plant corn or potatoes on what he called *his* land. Moments later, another woman spoke up and said that though she'd recovered from smallpox, she expected to work, wanted to work, and would work for him, but she implied that it was only because she wanted to "lay my bones in dat air bush," she said, pointing to the family cemetery. Philbrick replied that that was all well and good, but he affirmed what he had said earlier. "I told them, too," he wrote, "that if some of those people who made such noise did n't look out, they would get turned off the place." That was his threat, and he seemed happy with it, writing that the women were only "trying to play brag" about their work and that "they will all go to work in a few days, I feel sure."[39]

Philbrick's heavy-handed approach to the women who protested his wages demonstrates the baseline paradox that pervaded the Port Royal Experiment. The paradox was this: the project's founding ideas and rationales, its underlying logic, all ran counter to the basic spirit of humanitarianism. Instilling such a strong free labor ethic—promoting ideas of thrift, discipline, and the market—required threatening pain and suffering as the proverbial sticks that would enable the project's wage system to work. To eliminate hardship with too much charity or relief was to undermine the basic market logic on which the project had been based. That fundamental tension pressed down on the islands from all angles and was ever present. Freed people thus found themselves trapped in a contrived and seemingly endless state of insecurity, perpetually caught somewhere between nearly starving and lacking basic needs and working for their freedom. That paradox in some ways explains why what happened at Port Royal was so tragic: as much as the agents wrung their hands over the dire state of affairs, at least some of the suffering was orchestrated and controlled, the results of a labor system working as it had been designed to.

In March and early April 1865, the settling of abandoned lands revved into motion. Initial fears had been assuaged by the formation of the Freedmen's Bureau, which signaled that the federal government intended to honor their "possessory" claims and make them permanent. The future, in other words, seemed bright. Despite the death and despair, despite the cold January, the sickness of February, and the hungry weeks of early March, it looked as if freedom was finally coming within reach. The Port Royal Experiment had also evolved, though it remained beset by contradictions. It was no longer serving as an experiment to prod the government into a wider embrace of emancipation; it was now using settlement as a blunt-force mechanism to try to pound out space for a truly radical reconstruction to take hold. Everything centered on land-ownership and the kind of future it could bring.

One of the men who struck off to settle the land was a Savannah pastor named Ulysses L. Houston. Houston had been one of the twenty ministers to join Frazier in meeting with Stanton and Sherman. He was the pastor of the Third African Baptist Church, now the First Bryan Baptist Church on Bryan Street, and was one of the several pastors at the famous meeting who had still been enslaved when Sherman's army had arrived in Savannah. He had apparently bought his time from his enslaver—meaning that for a fee of about $50 a month, he had leased himself and his labor from the man who had owned him—and worked as a pastor on Sundays and a provisions dealer during the week. His home and store happened to be in the same building as the old A. Bryan's Negro Mart turned schoolhouse, which meant that before the war he had spent his nights listening to the cries of enslaved men and women on the verge of being sold. "It was hell, sir!" he told Charles Coffin, who took a shine to Houston and his story. "The wailings of the damned can never be more heart-rending," he added, noting that the worst was hearing mothers cry for their lost children and listening as traders shuffled bonded men and women up the stairs, their chains clanking as they went.[40]

In early 1865, Houston led a contingent of freed people out to Skidaway Island, a marshy intracoastal island just southeast of Savannah, to start a new community of freeholders. Coffin, who was already on good terms with Houston, reported: "They laid out a village, also farm lots of forty acres, set aside one central lot for a church, another for a school-house; then placing numbers in a hat, made the allotment . . . [and] agreed that if any others came to join them they should have equal privileges." Coffin described it as being like "Plymouth Colony repeating itself." "So the Mayflower was blooming on the islands of the South Atlantic!" he wrote, obviously agreeing with the idea that Houston and company were busy planting a new society and undergoing a new type of founding. The settlers claimed close to five thousand acres, and due to the want of ready cash, Houston arrived with goods from his provision store and was prepared to sell the rest—in effect, mortgage his future—in order to raise money for the community.[41]

In March, Tunis G. Campbell launched a similar venture on St. Catherines Island farther to the south. Born free in New Jersey, Campbell had spent most of his early life in New York working in hotels as a headwaiter and steward; he had even published a manual on hotel management. Yet when he wasn't pouring water or serving wine, he was an active member of the Colored Convention Movement, an annual meeting of free Black leaders, and in the early 1830s, he founded his own *anti*-colonization society, a group that opposed efforts at relocating African Americans outside the United States. He was said to have pledged "never to leave this country until every slave was free on American soil." Because of his zeal as well as his sterling reputation, he was tapped in 1865 to head up a branch of the newly minted Freedmen's Bureau, which was how he wound up leading a group of freed homesteaders on the islands surrounding Ossabaw Sound.[42]

The group left in early spring. Some were likely freed refugees from elsewhere in Georgia; some were likely natives of the coast. The community stretched across Colonel's, Ossabaw, and Sapelo islands, but the base of operations was on St. Catherines Island, one of coastal Georgia's barrier islands. Campbell's job was to allocate homesteads and manage the settlement process as outlined in Special Field Order No. 15, but that understates what actually happened: Campbell and company created their own self-sustained community. The settlers allocated tracts of land, formed a new village, and established a system of civil governance. For all intents and purposes, it was a self-governing, autonomous community, and it became a model of what a wider reconstruction of the South could look like.[43]

By the first week of April, close to twenty thousand freed people had been settled on about 100,000 acres of land throughout the Lowcountry. Edisto was also in the process of being resettled. Most of the initial settlers were those who had lived there prior to the war, though hundreds of Georgia refugees joined them as well. Settlement generally proceeded like this: the land nearest to Port Royal went to native islanders, many of whom had already laid claims to the land in the auctions of 1863 and '64. Some of the families had already purchased their plots and were therefore the legal titleholders. The lands on the periphery were typically reserved for refugees and other newcomers. The program had its issues, as the land farthest from Beaufort tended to be rougher and in need of the most work; Saxton's team remained underresourced and understaffed; and the arrival of new refugees meant that there were always new claimants, so the staff could never get ahead. At one point, they resorted to handing out certificates outlining details of people's land claims to try to expedite the settlement process. Nevertheless, by the first of June, nearly forty thousand families had been settled on close to 400,000 acres of land, an enormous feat given the circumstances.[44]

Fortunes turned, however, in mid-April. On April 9, 1865, after fleeing the siege lines of Petersburg, Robert E. Lee surrendered his Army of Northern Virginia at a place called Appomattox. Five days later, on the fourteenth, the Union Army held a celebratory flag raising over Fort Sumter. The next morning, around half past seven, President Abraham Lincoln died from an assassin's bullet. All of Washington searched for the assailants and buzzed with frenzied questions: Was the president really dead? Had Confederate agents been involved? Had there been one assassin or two? A nation that had been breathing a sigh of relief suddenly reeled. In less than six days in April, Lee had surrendered his army, Lincoln had been shot dead, a killer was on the loose, a new president was sworn in under a state of emergency, and tens of thousands of Confederate soldiers began journeying home.

The evidence of the last development first appeared on the islands near the end of spring. Former slaveholders started filtering back to their old plantations—often without a dollar on them but with big plans for the future. One former planter, Dr. Clarence Fripp, moved into a home not a stone's throw away from Laura Towne's place on St. Helena. Another moved back to Hilton Head but refused to bring his family on account of the Northern agents and the freed people present there; the changes repulsed him, and he didn't think the place fit for his wife. At first, freed people feigned sympathy for the impoverished state of their former masters, and some even tried to help the families that had once owned them. But that was partly strategic: freed people didn't fully trust that the land was theirs and wanted to curry at least a little favor with their former owners, just in case they lost the land and suddenly needed a place to go or somewhere to work. But even then, hardly any freed person did more than talk or offer kind regards. Few, if any, agreed to work for their old masters, despite the former masters' asking, sometimes begging, and sometimes threatening freed people to do so. The freed people simply refused.[45]

It turned out that the returning planters had a powerful friend in the new president. Andrew Johnson had been chosen as Lincoln's vice president as an appeal to unity, as he was the one Southern senator not to have withdrawn from Congress back in 1861. Since then, he had served as the military governor of Tennessee, where he'd been tasked with administering Lincoln's plan for Reconstruction. But while he had served Lincoln ably as a governor, that's not what our seventeenth president is often remembered for. While historians have debated how much he drank on a daily basis, Johnson showed up at Lincoln's second inauguration in such a wobbly stupor that he could barely perform his part of the proceedings, which won him the nickname "the drunken tailor from Tennessee." As it suggests, Johnson was the prototypical poor boy who had made good. He had apprenticed as a tailor, he had been illiterate until adulthood, and though he had once been a slaveholder himself, he identified as a small farmer and based his politics around a populism that abhorred the South's plantation elite.[46]

Though Johnson had initially said that "treason must be made odious," sometime around midsummer he changed his mind. His true colors came out. Instead of making good on his pledge, he began pardoning ex-Confederates at an impressive clip. Granted, Lincoln had signaled a preference for leniency before his death and considered a general proclamation of amnesty for ex-Confederates willing to take an oath of allegiance. But Johnson took the pardons to another level. He kept in place many of Lincoln's exemptions—which denied amnesty, for example, to high-ranking officials, generals, and others—and even added a new exemption for Confederates who owned over $20,000 worth of property. However, so long as people applied for a pardon and sufficiently groveled at his feet, he usually pardoned them. By June 1866, just over a year after the end of the war, Johnson had issued more than twelve thousand pardons to former Confederates; people had literally lined up outside the White House for a chance to plead their case. Worst of all, part of receiving a pardon, in Johnson's mind, meant having one's property (excepting enslaved people) restored, which opened the door for ex-Confederates to reclaim their land.[47]

The first battle over postwar land claims occurred in September 1865 on Edisto Island. By then Johnson's pardoning spree was in full swing. Ex-Confederates demanded their land back, and Johnson informed O. O. Howard, the head of the Freedmen's Bureau, that, where possible, he intended to restore Confederate property to its previous owners. It would be Howard's job, he said, to break the news and broker an arrangement between freed people and the restored landholders. Howard bristled at the thought. Neither he nor Stanton wanted to see the property restored; Stanton told several of the teachers on the islands that "it would be a thousand years before the rebels would repossess the land if he could have his way." Rufus Saxton also raised a ruckus. Just as he had done during the Port Royal land auctions of 1863 and 1864, he appended protests to his official reports demanding that the government stand by its promise. To him, Sherman's original land order was as "binding as a statute," and he argued that the government had a duty to honor its promises. But as president, Johnson had the final say. So in September 1865, Howard had no choice but to go south, first to Edisto, and tell freed families that the land was no longer theirs.[48]

Howard had been backed up against a wall. On July 28, he had released a document, Circular No. 13, which instructed bureau agents to start settling freed people on land as fast as possible. He could see where Johnson was going, and the circular was his attempt to get ahead of the president's plans for restoration. Johnson, however, caught wind of the circular and had Howard write a new one, Circular No. 15, the document that marked the government's initial retreat from land reform on the Sea Islands. It was, in Howard's view, a compromise measure: He described it as a conditional plan to restore Confederate property only after the ex-Confederates set aside lands for freed people to work as their own. It turned out to be anything but a compromise. Not only did the plan place the onus for allocating lands on the ex-Confederates, it also implicitly drew back from the idea that freed people had a right to the land. Howard saw the circular as a compromise, a kind of best deal available given the circumstances, but it was an ominous first sign that land reform was losing.[49]

The backlash was understandably swift and intense. Freed people on Edisto, many of whom had been evacuated from the island in 1863 and were finally back in their homes, erupted in protest. They objected to everything Howard said, a chorus of voices telling him that they would never work for their masters again. Then they organized. A committee of three—Henry Brown, Ishmael Moultrie, and Yates Sampson—wrote to Howard privately. They told him that they wanted land, that they wanted homesteads, and that the present situation threatened to make them "landless and Homeless." "This," they said, "Is not the condition of really freemen." One even wrote that while the general could perhaps forgive the man who had maimed his arm, the freedman could never forgive "the man who tied me to a tree & gave me 39 lashes & who stripped and flogged my mother & my sister & who will not let me stay In His empty Hut except I will do His planting & be Satisfied with his price." He then wrote that even if he forgave his former master, the man would only conspire against him. That was why they needed land, so that they could be neither slaves "nor compelled to work for those who would treat us as such."[50]

Next, the committee of three took what they had written to Howard, added more, and sent it in a petition to President Johnson on October 28. It read in part: "This is our home, we have made These lands what they are . . . we have been always ready to strike for Liberty and humanity yea to fight if needs be To preserve this glorious union. Shall not we who Are freedman [*sic*] and have been always true to this Union have the same rights as are enjoyed by Others? Have we broken any Law of these United States? Have we forfieted [*sic*] our rights of property In Land—If not then! are not our rights as A free people and good citizens of these United States To be considered before the rights of those who were Found in rebellion against this good and just Goverment [*sic*]." The petition went on to say that no one objected to purchasing the land and that they would buy it if they needed to. After all, none of them needed all that much, just a home and a few acres. They went on to insist that after being encouraged to take up homesteads, that was exactly what they had done and with great success. Thus as "freedmen of this Island and of the state of South Carolina," they therefore looked to the US government for "protection and Equal Rights" and asked for the "privilege of Purchasing A Homestead right here in the Heart of South Carolina."[51]

Johnson likely never read the petition. It probably wouldn't have mattered if he had. By the fall of 1865, he was dead set on rolling back the repercussions of the war and thwarting the pace of change. At the time, he had extraordinary power to do so because Congress wasn't in session. The Thirty-eighth Congress, which had passed both the Thirteenth Amendment and the Freedmen's Bureau Bill in the same session, had adjourned in early March. Though the next Congress, the Thirty-ninth, met in a short, eight-day special session from March 4 to March 11, right after the previous Congress adjourned, the next full legislative session wasn't slated to begin until December. That wide legislative vacuum in the spring, summer, and fall of 1865 gave Johnson control of the federal government and all its power.

The trio of Stanton, Howard, and Saxton, however, recognized Johnson's intentions early on and hatched a plot of their own. To be fair, calling it a plot may overstate it. They simply stalled, obstructed, and did their best to maintain the status quo. When there were legal appeals to make, they made them; when there was no other option but to restore

tracts of land, they did so, but they reclaimed others and tried to relocate families elsewhere (in October, for instance, they restored eighty
plantations to their original owners but claimed another thirty-six).
Where there was the slightest room to maneuver—whether it was in
slowing land restoration, helping freed people buy more land outright, or
retarding negotiations—they did what they could. Howard was especially
bothered by his role in the land restorations and promised the people
of Edisto that he would do everything in his power to make sure they
kept the land. The idea was to stall long enough for Congress to come
back into session by the end of the year and, he hoped, step in—ideally
by reauthorizing the Freedmen's Bureau for at least another year and
beefing up its mandate to include an enlarged set of powers.[52]

But although there was some support in Congress for providing freed
people with the land they had been promised, a bill for relicensing the
Freedmen's Bureau didn't come to the floor until the first of the year. It
took nearly a month to debate. The final vote came on January 25, 1866.
It passed and went to the president for his approval on February 13, but
Johnson sent it back to the stunned Congress with a veto. He refused
to sign it, arguing that it was too expensive, that it favored Blacks over
whites, that it increased the size of the government, and that it infringed
on the rights of both individuals and states. For him, the war was over,
slavery had been abolished, the Southern states were rejoining the Union,
and there was nothing more to do. The veto, though, was as much about
sending a message as halting a piece of legislation; Johnson was inviting
Congress into a contest over who would control Reconstruction.

The wrangling over Johnson's veto throughout the spring of 1866
doomed the prospects of halting the land restorations. Congress dith-
ered. It let the issue sit, and when it finally gathered the requisite number
of votes to override Johnson's veto, it was already mid-July. By then
hundreds of plantations had been restored, and all the momentum,
all the legal challenges, all the realities on the ground had tilted back
toward the planters. The first major development had come in January

1866, when Johnson had removed Rufus Saxton from his post. Saxton had become a nuisance to the president. He had refused to restore land granted by Sherman's order, so Johnson sacked him. That had removed the freed people's most consistent and credible ally. Even worse, with Saxton gone, the job of adjudicating and enforcing land claims fell to the military forces in the area, which meant that freed people who refused to comply could be forced off the islands by the army.[53]

It was perhaps at that time—the late winter and early spring of 1866—that the great refugee movement of Sherman's March came to a close. When Johnson removed Saxton and gave the army the authority to force people off the land, the Georgia refugees were some of the first people displaced. Unlike those native to the coast and unlike those freed people who had already purchased homesteads or had solid land claims, the refugees had comparatively weak claims to the land and were thus left stranded. Moreover, they were people with no existing relationship to the planters who were returning; no real, earthbound attachment to the land, as they might have had to their own homes; and perhaps no friends or family in the area. Most were likely miles away from their traditional networks of support, miles away from the lands they had once known, and miles away from any local connections who might help. So they left; not everyone, but instead of signing labor contracts, many of the refugees set out on a new and dispiriting journey back to Georgia.[54]

The efforts to stem the tide and reverse course on the land restorations received what seemed like one last boost when Congress finally passed the new Freedmen's Bureau bill in July 1866. Yet the new bill wasn't quite what most of its proponents had hoped it would be. Instead of offering a blanket provision securing titles to the original Sherman land, halting restoration outright, and finding a way to make widespread land reform possible, the bill moved in the opposite direction. While it offered freed people a chance to purchase land, it limited the land available for purchase to twenty acres per family, half of the original forty. It also mandated that those purchasing the land lease it for a fixed term first, ostensibly to prove that they could successfully farm it and pay their bills. Most critically, it made no concessions to those who had lost land through the restoration process. The central issue roiling the islands was ignored. Although the second Freedmen's Bureau bill renewed the agency, which was no small feat and was an important step in the course of Reconstruction, when it came to landownership, the bill signaled that the federal government didn't have the stomach for widespread reform. Despite a veto override and a congressional rebuke to the president, the land was lost.[55]

After marching for the better part of three months through the thick Georgia countryside, after crossing rivers and streams and eluding Confederate patrols, after shivering through the winter and foraging off the land, after arriving in Savannah and surviving the death-filled days at Port Royal, the story of the Georgia refugees ends with their making a long walk home. It's not that so many walked home that's so tragic; it's that they walked home perhaps alone, empty handed, and no more certain of freedom than they had been when they had left. The great dream of one day owning land and the independence that would come with it ran aground on the beaches around Port Royal; the sense of hope and excitement that was so alive in the Savannah winter dissipated by the first days of spring; and the great efforts they had made to define freedom and make it more meaningful while on the March now seemed like the beginning of a story that had somehow gone wrong.

EPILOGUE

O n the morning of May 23, 1865, Sherman's army received a hero's welcome in Washington, DC. The war was over. The Confederacy had been defeated, and to celebrate, the US government organized one last review, a Grand Review, as it was called, so that the American people could pay their respects to the boys in blue. For two full days, thousands of Americans thronged the streets of the nation's capital. "Washington has been filled as it never was filled before," wrote the *New York Times*. Hotels ran out of room, and packed grandstands surrounded soldiers, around 145,000 in all, as they marched down Pennsylvania Avenue to the White House, where President Johnson, General Ulysses S. Grant, and other officials waited to give them one final salute. "Such a spectacle as no other continent ever saw" and one "this continent will never see again" read one article. Even the criminal trial of the surviving conspirators involved in the Lincoln assassination adjourned until after the two-day parade.[56]

General George Meade's Army of the Potomac, which had battled that of Robert E. Lee in Virginia, went first. The eighty-thousand-man army wove its way through the capital for most of the day on the twenty-third. Flags shone in the sun. Banners sported the names of victories—Shiloh! Vicksburg! Atlanta!—while Meade's men marched to sporadic cheers of "Gettysburg, Gettysburg." Spectators who couldn't get a seat in the grandstands lined the hills around the Capitol or spilled out onto the

Mall. "With many it is the greatest epoch of their lives," wrote the *Times*, referring to all those in attendance who had come out to celebrate and support the army. For an America that had just suffered through four years of war, the event felt like a grand finale. Within weeks, the armies would be dissolved and the soldiers would go home. To mark the occasion, Johnson had the White House flag raised from half-staff, where it had been since Lincoln's death.[57]

While the first day attracted large crowds, those on the second were even larger. To all the easterners in attendance, Sherman's army was a great mystery; men and women thronged into DC just to a catch glimpse of the famed Army of the West. The men didn't disappoint. Whereas Meade's army marched with drill-like precision and wore fresh new uniforms, the soldiers of Sherman's army looked like the western pioneers that many of them were. They were dirty and rough looking, and most of the regiments sported their shabby, clearly used colors of old. One report described them as "thin, sunbrowned and war worn. Their clothes and banners are worn and bullet torn." And though they marched well, as one might expect, the rigid respect for rank and hierarchy had been replaced by a casual equality and sense of comradery. The striking difference between the two armies was noticeable enough that it became one of the day's headlines. Onlookers in the worst of seats could see it. Newsmen reported it. Sherman himself even reportedly worried that his army might cut a crude figure compared to that of its peers from the east.[58]

In spite of its ragtag appearance, Sherman's army stole the show. The marching men of the West mesmerized onlookers and peers alike. General Joshua Lawrence Chamberlain, a native of Maine, who had survived the horrors of Fredericksburg, fought bravely on the second day at Gettysburg, and presided over Lee's surrender at Appomattox, knew that he and the rest of the Army of the Potomac had been eclipsed. "The prestige of this army that had marched from the Great River to the Sea, and thence up half the Atlantic coast, bringing the fame of mighty things done afar" had stirred more hearts than his own army had, he would write, noting that the crowd "preferred [them] before us." He even found himself gawking at his western peers and the medley of foragers, bummers, pack mules, and regimental pets that marched along with Sherman and his men.[59]

But for Chamberlain, the most remarkable feature of Sherman's army and the most poignant part of the whole two-day review came at the very end. "As a climax, with significance which one might ponder," he wrote, families of freed slaves marched along at the rear of Sherman's army. Many of them had marched with the army as servants; some had traveled with small children. Most were likely from somewhere in the Carolinas, but more than a few might have been with the army from as far back as Atlanta or Savannah. For all the differences of appearance and comportment between the two armies, the presence of those freed families was perhaps the most important distinction of all, with Chamberlin describing the scene as "more touching in some ways than the proud passing column [of soldiers]."[60]

The freed families marching at the end of the line had likely followed the army straight from the battlefield. After leaving Savannah, Sherman led his army up into South Carolina. He had bypassed Charleston in favor of Columbia, the state capital. Many of the soldiers had been excited to enter South Carolina, seeing it as a chance to punish the state for its leading role in starting the war. Not only had it been the first state to secede, but the war had begun at Fort Sumter in the mouth of Charleston Harbor, and many of the leading secessionists had been South Carolinians. Some historians have argued that the devastation wrought there was worse than in Georgia, which may well have been true. It may also be true that the march through South Carolina was an emancipation event as large as, if not larger than, the March through Georgia, as enslaved people responded to the army's movements in South Carolina just as they had done when it had been en route to the sea.[61]

Indeed, wherever the army moved, enslaved people followed. Regiments reported that enslaved people were following them by the hundreds. Corps commanders estimated the number as into the thousands. Alpheus Williams of Sherman's Twentieth Corps reported that as many as two thousand freed people had followed his army and that he had sent a portion over to the coast. As had happened in Georgia, enslaved people had acted as scouts and lookouts, informing the army of when and where Confederate forces had been seen. When the army eventually made its way into Columbia in mid-February, the city's enslaved people greeted it with open arms. In one instance, an Iowa colonel remembered leaving his men for an hour so that he could put an American flag atop the South Carolina statehouse only to return to find that many of his men were already drunk. "Hundreds" of enslaved people had celebrated the army's arrival by giving his men "all kinds of liquors from buckets, bottles, demijohns, &c." And since the men hadn't eaten or slept much in the preceding days, the liquor had had a "speedy effect," the colonel wrote.[62]

Like Atlanta, Columbia was eventually burned. While generations of Southerners have blamed Sherman for starting the fires, the real culprit was a combination of drunken soldiers, heavy winds, and the burning of cotton bales. Nevertheless, Sherman and his army left Columbia smoldering behind them. From there, the army moved into North Carolina, where it met the heaviest resistance it had seen in months. Confederate general Joseph Johnston, whom Sherman's troops had already bested outside Atlanta, consolidated several different Confederate armies in what amounted to one last gasp. Johnston attacked Sherman at the Battle of Bentonville, just south of Raleigh, in March 1865, but he had just over a third of the men that Sherman had and could only hope that he might splinter Sherman's moving army. That didn't happen. Instead, Johnston withdrew further to the west toward Greensboro while Sherman kept his army moving toward Goldsboro.[63]

Though the soldiers didn't know it, that would be the finish line. Following Lee's surrender at Appomattox on April 9, 1865, Johnston surrendered to Sherman just over a week later, bringing the last chapter of the war to a close. An invasion that had begun outside Chattanooga and included the fall of Atlanta, Savannah, and Columbia was now over. After marching somewhere in the range of two thousand miles and traversing farms and plantations across the heart of the South, Sherman's soldiers could stop and celebrate and begin planning their journey home. Most knew almost immediately that they had been a party to history. Not only were they there in the field when Johnston surrendered and the Confederacy collapsed, they had taken part in one of the great military movements of the nineteenth century, a campaign of such ambition and scope it felt almost Napoleonic in scale, something that generations would surely remember. Yet as epic as the movement may have been, Chamberlain was correct in recognizing that perhaps the real meaning of Sherman's great March lied with those traveling at the army's rear.

Sherman's March was more than a military movement. Savannah's Primus Wilson stated it succinctly: "I was born in Liberty County, Ga, a slave, [and] became free after Sherman's army came through here." "I was born in Tattnall County, State of Georgia, a slave, and remained so till the Yankee army came to Savannah," related Boson Johnson, a freed person from Liberty County. Scipio King likewise testified that he had been born enslaved, but added, "I was freed when Sherman's army came through." Cato Keating told a similar story. While speaking with an agent of the Southern Claims Commission after the war, he narrated his personal history, saying "I was born a slave and became free after Sherman's army came through." That common refrain—"I was a slave till the army came"—captures America's rebirth, our pivot from slavery to freedom, and the lasting legacy of our Civil War. It also captures in the clearest, most succinct way possible why the March lives on and why the story of American freedom runs through Atlanta, Savannah, and the islands along the coast.[64]

Wilson, Johnson, King, and Keating told their stories sometime in the early 1870s, five years or so after the March and the end of the war. By then the nation had come out of the Johnson years and experienced a flowering of rights and freedoms rivaled by few periods in our history. Congressional Reconstruction—otherwise known as Radical Reconstruction—began in the waning days of 1866. Outraged by Johnson's vetoes of the Freedmen's Bureau bill and the Civil Rights Act of 1866, Republicans in Congress reasserted control over Reconstruction after gaining the requisite two-thirds majority in the midterm elections that year. They tried (and narrowly failed) to remove Johnson from office, refused ex-Confederates' taking seats in Congress, and reset the entire process of Reconstruction. Whereas Johnson was willing to let Southern states rejoin the Union without consequences or penalties, congressional Republicans divided the region into military districts, appointed military governors, and outlined a step-by-step process through which states could officially rejoin the Union.[65]

Alongside that reassertion of congressional control, Republicans in Congress passed one of the most critical pieces of legislation in US history. To better support the Thirteenth Amendment, which had been passed in 1865 and formally abolished slavery, Congress passed the Fourteenth Amendment, which contained expansive provisions staking out an official position on civil rights. It defined citizenship for the first time ever, granting birthright citizenship to anyone born in America (except, ironically, Native Americans). It ensured citizens the right to due process and equal protection under the law. It also forced states to accept universal manhood suffrage or risk losing representation in Congress—which was Congress's way of establishing voting rights via a big and powerful stick. Later, in 1870, Congress would try to bolster the provision by passing the Fifteenth Amendment, the last of the three so-called Reconstruction amendments.[66]

The result was a groundbreaking period of biracial democracy. Black Georgians voted for the first time in 1867, and in the elections of 1868, African Americans went to the polls in incredible numbers. They elected

Black legislators, officials, and local leaders, including city commissioners and justices of the peace, and they served as delegates to state constitutional conventions. Backed by institutions such as the Republican Party, the US Army, local Union Leagues, and grassroots organizations that mobilized Republican voters, Black Americans became a force in southern politics, and it didn't end there. Voters would elect small cohorts of African Americans to the House of Representatives in 1871 and '72, and in 1871, Hiram R. Revels of Mississippi was sworn in as the first African American senator. Everywhere across the South the political landscape had changed, creating for the first time an active and participatory democracy in which African Americans had a loud and sometimes decisive voice.[67]

Socially, some of the changes were just as great. While thousands of formerly enslaved people saw the dream of landownership slip from their grasp, in some pockets African American landownership flourished. Freed towns, or freedmen's towns, sprang up as independent communities; southern cities likewise witnessed the emergence of an urban and propertied Black elite. Perhaps most of all, schools spread like wildfire. State legislatures established formal systems of public education. Freedmen's schools that had operated on an ad hoc basis during the war blossomed into formal centers of education. Thousands of teachers spread across the South, sometimes teaching in primary and secondary schools and sometimes teaching night classes for eager adults or training other teachers. And with the support of organizations such as the American Missionary Association and the Freedmen's Bureau, some of the first historically black colleges and universities opened their doors, welcoming some of the first cohorts of black college students.[68]

Yet that period of rapid social and political change wouldn't last. Starting in the early 1870s, as more and more southern states returned to white home rule, ex-Confederates launched a counterrevolution designed to roll back the transformations that had come out of the war. Fueled by torrents of violence, led by ex-Confederates, and aimed at restoring white supremacy in southern life, that reactionary wave whittled away at Reconstruction until there was little left. It didn't help that as night-riding vigilantes terrorized African American voters, the white North retreated from Reconstruction. The pangs of the war, the power of sectional and white reconciliation, and pervasive American racism all proved inimical to lasting change. The same northern constituencies that had once celebrated the war and embraced emancipation eventually turned their back on programs meant to reform southern society and sold out freed people in the process. The last act of the sordid drama came in 1876. In an attempt to settle a disputed presidential election, the Republican winner, Rutherford B. Hayes, removed the remaining federal troops from the South, which ended federal oversight and put a final, inglorious end to Reconstruction.[69]

In all that time, the question of landownership never really reentered the equation. Beyond the initial attempts to settle freed people on new homesteads in 1865 and 1866, the urgency of land reform as both a federal prerogative and a matter of reparative justice fell by the wayside. Congressional power brokers considered it politically impossible and treated it as low priority. Indeed, if a guiding idea ruled Reconstruction, establishing citizenship—that is, granting civil and political rights while reconstructing our national body politic—prevailed. As such, notions that fell outside that general framework—ideas about economic justice, material security, and a basic right to land—lost their political currency. Thus, after a war in which ideas of freedom had collided on battlefields, on plantations, and alongside lines of marching soldiers, Reconstruction defined freedom within the bounds of the state and citizen, leaving the promise of Jubilee, of a wider freedom, largely unfulfilled

This brings us back to the March and its legacy. As a matter of sheer force, Sherman's March through Georgia made the redefinition of American freedom possible. It was as if two great forces met and converged. The army and its sixty thousand–plus marching soldiers stomped out the dying embers of a slave regime, and through the sum of their individual movements, freed people made the new idea of freedom a central consequence of the campaign. One fueled the other, and in tandem, the two forces combined in Georgia to make the American Civil War not just a war between two sections or a war that would end slavery but a war that would shape the meaning of freedom for the next century or more—a war, if you will, for an American Jubilee. In the end, that—not the burning of Atlanta, Sherman's tactics, or Sherman himself, not the grievances of the white South, and certainly not the concept of "total war"—is why and how we should remember the March, for, like Yorktown, Gettysburg, and Selma, Alabama, Sherman's March to the Sea was a landmark moment in the history of American freedom.

At the risk of sounding inconsistent, if the March was a great watershed, it was also a missed opportunity. The freedom it produced was never conclusive. Freed refugees suffered at Port Royal; the idea of meaningful land reform ended with the war; and the winds of change that came to life in that long Savannah winter eventually died out. The March created space for people to imagine a more expansive freedom and turned the nation toward a free future, but because Sherman preferred being a flywheel to being a mainspring, because soldiers turned freed people away while on the main road, and because no one stopped to listen to the freed refugees or try to see the world as they did, this more expansive vision of freedom never got the support it needed. As a result, the Jubilee came and went with only a few of its promises fulfilled, making the months and years following the March seem at times less like a great dawning of freedom and more like an early eclipse. Despite our wishes to the contrary, this unresolved story is a legacy, too.

ACKNOWLEDGMENTS

For all intents and purposes, I began working on this book as a PhD dissertation in early March of 2020, about two weeks before the world came to screeching halt. Little did I, or anyone, know just how much life would change in only a matter of weeks. As schools closed, libraries shuttered, and the word "Zoom" became a new part of our daily vocabulary, I wasn't sure how, when, or whether I would ever finish, especially once a novel outbreak morphed into a global pandemic.

Luckily, I did, and for that reason I want to start by thanking all the library staff and administrators who worked tirelessly to make online research possible. This book could not have been written without the folks at Yale's Sterling Library, who ushered in remote access. I also want to thank the folks at Internet Archive, the Haithi Digital Trust, Jstor, Project Muse, and countless other online resources for expanding access at a time of such great uncertainty and doubt.

On that note, I also had the pleasure of visiting several top-notch archives while working on this project. The library specialists and curators at the Georgia Historical Society, the Abraham Lincoln Presidential Library, the Library of Congress, the National Archives, the Indiana State Historical Society, the Ohio History Connection, the Massachusetts Historical Society, the Boston Athenaeum, Yale Manuscripts and Archives, the Huntington Library, the Bienecke Rare Book and Manuscript Library, and the Houghton Library at Harvard all have my gratitude.

I also want to say a special thank you to the Yale University History Department. Despite the pandemic and despite the cold of New Haven, which never ceased to shock me, my five years there as a graduate fellow were some of the best I've ever had. Not only was it an excellent place to work, write, and think about history, I made many dear friends. I want to a give a special shoutout to the history department's co-ed softball team, the Field Historians, otherwise known as the Hobs-bombers, for several successful seasons. I also want to thank Pranav Jain, Patrick Barker, Elle Nye, Hannah Greenwald, and Tiraana Bains for their feedback on chapter drafts in our Zoom writing group. Their comments gave me real direction and a much-needed sense of comradery during the most isolating days of 2020–21. The same for Taylor Rose, James Shinn, Emily Yankowitz, Kate Birkbeck, Teanu Reid, and Connor Williams, all friends who read sections, chapters, whole drafts, or shared many conversations with me about the project. Holden Zimmerman, Zaib un Nisa Aziz, Elizabeth Buckheit, and John D'Amico also deserve my many thanks.

My time at Yale would not have been the same without Michelle, Melissa, Daniel, Tom, and all the folks at the GLC. I benefited immensely from getting to know them—and from taking part in all their sponsored events. I want to especially thank all the folks who took part in the Yale Race and Slavery Working Group, which was one of the highlights of my time in New Haven. I also want to thank Edward Rugemer and Crystal Feimster for serving as dissertation readers. Their comments and feedback were always generous and first rate. Paul Anderson, Rod Andrew, and Lee Wilson also read very, very early versions of this project as M.A. advisors at Clemson University.

Speaking of advisors, I have been blessed to have two of the best mentors in the business, David Blight and Vernon Burton. When I think about who I want to be as a teacher, writer, and person, I think of them. Both have supported this project from the start, and I owe them both so much, more than I could ever dream of putting in words. It has been a real privilege of mine to learn from them. I especially want to thank David, who, as a PhD advisor, was everything I could have asked for and more, particularly as the pandemic turned teaching and writing upside down.

Over the years, I have also benefited from anonymous readers, who read versions of this project published in *The Georgia Historical Quarterly*, *The Journal of the Civil War Era*, and *Civil War History*. Larry Rowland and Steve Wise also deserve thanks for their feedback. So does Paul Escott, who offered invaluable comments on a full draft. When I signed up for the Southern Historical Association's mentorship program, I couldn't have asked for a better, more gracious match. I also owe a very large thank-you to the Yale University History Department and Yale's Ethnicity, Race, and Migration Program for their generous financial support and fellowship programs.

Pat Lentz also was generous to share her home during an invaluable stay in California while finishing the book. Many thanks go to her for her extraordinary kindness in welcoming us to Pasadena.

I also want to say a special thank you to all my colleagues in the Georgia Southern University History Department, along with Maxine Bryant and the team at the Center for Africana Studies. I have felt the warmest welcome since starting at GSU, and it has been a wonderful place to teach and work. My colleague and office neighbor Kurt Knoerl produced two model maps for the project while colleagues Drew Swanson, Lisa Denmark, and Alan Downs all read and offered incisive comments on the full manuscript. They most certainly made this a better book.

The same is undoubtedly true for Bob Bender, my editor at Simon & Schuster. I could tell Bob knew exactly what this project was about barely a minute into our very first phone conversation. He asked the very best questions and has since been a wonderful editor and teacher. I am grateful to have been able to work together. I also want to thank Johanna Li, Jonathan Jao, and Jennie Miller for their work on the book as well as Wendy Strothman and her team at Aevitas Creative. Like Bob, Wendy has been a steadfast believer in the book, and I am especially grateful for her wisdom.

Last but certainly not least, I want to thank my family: Mom (Jill), Dad (Bill), Drew, and Chappel along with Nana, Leigh-Ann, Haley, and Heather. My parents have always supported me, even if it meant me moving from Georgia to Connecticut. My mother, in particular, spent countless hours on trips to Boston, Gettysburg, and so many monuments in between. I would also be remiss if I didn't mention my late grandmother, Ruth Parten, for whom this book is jointly dedicated. A lifelong educator and storyteller, she was a top-notch historian and an even better person to have coffee with.

Finally, I want to thank Hannah, my lovely wife, who has lived with this book for as long as I have. She's done it all: listened, read, edited, given feedback, and has been a true partner every step of the way.

This book is for her.

NOTES

1. John Potter, *Reminiscences of the Civil War in the United States* (Oskaloosa, IA: The Globe Presses, 1897), 109.

2. Potter, *Reminiscences of the Civil War in the United States.*

3. James Austin Connolly, *Three Years in the Army of the Cumberland: The Letters and Diary of Major James A. Connolly* (Bloomington: Indiana University Press, 1959), 311.

4. The term *total war* was first applied to Sherman's march in an article in *Journal of Southern History* by John Bennett Walters; see John Bennett Walters, "General William T. Sherman and Total War," *Journal of Southern History* 14, no. 4 (1948): 447–80. See also John Bennett Walters, *Merchant of Terror: General Sherman and Total War* (Indianapolis, IN: Bobbs-Merrill, 1973). Recent scholarship, however, suggests that Sherman's march and the Civil War at large were not a display of total war. See Mark Grimsley, *The Hard Hand of War: Union Military Policy Toward Southern Civilians, 1861–1865* (Cambridge, UK: Cambridge University Press, 1995); Mark E. Neely, "Was the Civil War a Total War?," *Civil War History* 50, no. 4 (2004): 434–58. Historians now typically opt for the term *hard war* instead of *total war*, which carries certain twentieth-century connotations. For these recent exceptions, see Lisa Tendrich Frank, *The Civilian War: Confederate Women and Union Soldiers During Sherman's March* (Baton Rouge, LA: LSU Press, 2015); Anne Sarah Rubin, *Through the Heart of Dixie: Sherman's March and American Memory* (Chapel Hill: University of North Carolina Press, 2014). For the best book on the soldiers' experience, see Joseph Glatthaar, *The March to the Sea and Beyond: Sherman's Troops in the Savannah and Carolina Campaigns* (Baton Rouge: University of North Carolina Press, 1985). On the Sherman quote, see his letter to Grant from Vicksburg, 261, in *The War of the Rebellion: A Compilation of the Official Records of the Union and Confederate Armies*, ser. 1, vol. 17 (Washington, DC: U.S. Government Printing Office), 261.

5. See Willie Lee Rose, *Rehearsal for Reconstruction: The Port Royal Experiment* (Oxford, UK: Oxford University Press, 1964).

6. See William Sherman Letter to George Thomas in Simpson, October 2, 1864, in Berlin, eds., *Sherman's Civil War: The Selected Correspondence of William Tecumseh Sherman, 1860–1865* (Chapel Hill: University of North Carolina Press, 1999), 730.

7. See T. W. Connelly, *History of the Seventieth Ohio Regiment: From Its Organization to Its Mustering Out* (Cincinnati, OH: Peak Bros., 1902), 131; Henry Clay Work, "Marching Through Georgia," in *Songs of Henry Clay Work*, compiled by Bertram G. Work (New York: J. J. Little & Ives Co., 1920 [?]), 18.

8. Potter, *Reminiscences of the Civil War in the United States*, 110, 111.

9. The quote comes from Higginson's January 8, 1863, entry in his diary, later published as *Army Life in a Black Regiment* (Boston: Fields, Osgood, & Co., 1869). Higginson was a well-known New England abolitionist who later went to the South Carolina Sea Islands to serve as an officer in the 1st South Carolina Volunteer Infantry Regiment, a United States Colored Troops regiment made up of formerly enslaved people.

Chapter One: The View from Atlanta

1. Sam Richards, diary entry, September 1, 1864, in Samuel Pearce Richards, *Sam Richards's Civil War Diary: A Chronicle of the Atlanta Home Front*, ed. Wendy Hamand Venet (Athens: University of Georgia Press, 2009), 233.

2. William T. Sherman, letter to Henry Halleck, September 3, 1864, in William T. Sherman, *Sherman's Civil War: Selected Correspondence of William T. Sherman, 1860–1865*, ed. Brooks D. Simpson and Jean V. Berlin (Chapel Hill: University of North Carolina Press, 1999), 696.

3. Sam Richards, diary entry, September 2, 1864, in *Sam Richards's Civil War Diary*, 234–35; Sam Richards, diary entry, September 4, 1864, in *Sam Richards's Civil War Diary*, 235–36.

4. Sam Richards, diary entry, September 9, 1864, in *Sam Richards's Civil War Diary*, 235–36.

5. James M. Wells, *"With Touch of Elbow," or Death Before Dishonor: A Thrilling Narrative of Adventure on Land and Sea* (Philadelphia: John C. Winston, 1909), 216–17.

6. Wells, *"With Touch of Elbow,"* 216–18.

7. See Lee Kennett, *Marching Through Georgia: The Story of Soldiers and Civilians During Sherman's Atlanta Campaign* (New York: Harper Perennial, 1995), 134–35. See also David Evans, *Sherman's Horsemen: Union Cavalry Operations in the Atlanta Campaign* (Bloomington: Indiana University Press, 1996).

8. Kennett, *Marching Through Georgia*, 134–35; Evans, *Sherman's Horsemen*.

9. Dolly Sumner Lunt, *A Woman's Wartime Journal: An Account of the Passage over a Georgia Plantation of Sherman's Army on the March to the Sea, as Recorded in the Diary of Dolly Sumner Lunt* (New York: Century Co., 1918), 9–11; Fannie A. Beers, *Memories: A Record of Personal Experience and Adventure During Four Years of War* (Philadelphia: J. B. Lippincott Company, 1891), 140.

10. S.E.D. Smith, *The Soldier's Friend; Being a Thrilling Narrative of Grandma Smith's Four Years' Experience and Observation, as Matron, in the Hospitals of the South During the Late Disastrous Conflict in America* (Memphis, TN: Bulletin Publishing Company, 1867), 132; W. L. Sanford, *History of Fourteenth Illinois Cavalry and the Brigades to Which It Belonged* (Chicago: R. R. Donnelly and Sons, 1898), 194. See also Kennett, *Marching Through Georgia*, 146; Mohr, "The Atlanta Campaign and the African American Experience of Civil War Georgia,"

in *Inside the Confederate Nation: Essays in Honor of Emory M. Thomas*, ed. Lesley J. Gordon and John C. Inscoe (Baton Rouge, LA: LSU Press, 2005), 272–94, 283–85; Evans, *Sherman's Horsemen*, 227–28.

11. Clarence L. Mohr, "The Atlanta Campaign and the African American Experience in Civil War Georgia," in *Inside the Confederate Nation: Essays in Honor of Emory M. Thomas*, ed. Lesley J. Gordon and John C. Inscoe (Baton Rouge, LA: LSU Press, 2005), 272–94.

12. Kate Stone, *Brokenburn: The Journal of Kate Stone, 1861–1868*, ed. John Q. Anderson (Baton Rouge, LA: LSU Press, 1955), 28; see Charles Colcock Jones to Charles C. Jones, Jr., July 21, 1862, in *The Children of Pride: A True Story of Georgia and the Civil War*, ed. Robert Manson Myers (New Haven: Yale University Press, 1972), 932; Kennett, *Marching Through Georgia*, 146.

13. See Joseph T. Glatthaar, "Black Glory: The African-American Role in Union Victory," in *Why the Confederacy Lost*, ed. Gabor S. Boritt (Oxford, UK: Oxford University Press, 1992), 142. The Freedmen and Southern Society Project suggests a similar figure. Work on the enslaved experience of the war began with W.E.B. Du Bois's famous *Black Reconstruction in America*, published in 1935, and has since spawned an impressive bibliography. For an overview, see Ira Berlin, "Who Freed the Slaves? Emancipation and Its Meaning," in *Union and Emancipation: Politics and Race in the Civil War Era*, ed. David W. Blight and Brooks D. Simpson (Kent, OH: Kent State University Press, 1997).

14. James Oakes, *Freedom National: The Destruction of Slavery in the United States, 1861–1865* (New York: W. W. Norton & Sons, 2014), 95–97.

15. See "CHAP. LX.—*An Act to Confiscate Property Used for Insurrectionary Purposes*," First Confiscation Act, https://freedmen.umd.edu//conact1.htm. See also Chandra Manning, *Troubled Refuge: Struggling for Freedom in the Civil War* (New York: Vintage, 2016), 176.

16. See Manning, *Troubled Refuge*; Amy Murrell Taylor, *Embattled Freedom: Journeys Through the Civil War's Slave Refugee Camps* (Chapel Hill: University of North Carolina Press, 2018).

17. Manning, *Troubled Refuge*; Taylor, *Embattled Freedom*. See also Ira Berlin et al., eds., *Free at Last: A Documentary History of Slavery, Freedom, and the Civil War* (New York: New Press, 2007), 34–35.

18. Oakes, *Freedom National*, 236–40.

19. Adam Guelzo, *Lincoln's Emancipation Proclamation: The End of Slavery in America* (New York: Simon & Schuster, 2005), 132–34.

20. Guelzo, *Lincoln's Emancipation Proclamation*, 172–73.

21. See Eric Foner, *Reconstruction: America's Unfinished Revolution, 1863–1877* (New York: Harper and Row, 1988), 3–4; Oakes, *Freedom National*, 370–73.

22. William T. Sherman, letter to John Sherman, December 9, 1860, in William T. Sherman, *Sherman's Civil War: Selected Civil War Correspondence of William T. Sherman, 1860–1865*, ed. Brooks D. Simpson and Jean V. Berlin (Chapel Hill: University of North Carolina Press, 1999), 16; Sherman, *Memoirs of General William T. Sherman*, vol. 1 (New York: D. Appleton & Company, 1875), 177; William T. Sherman, letter to D. F. Boyd, April 4, 1861, in Walter L.

Fleming, ed., *General W. T. Sherman as College President: A Collection of Letters, Documents, and Other Material, Chiefly from Private Sources, Relating to the Life and Activities of General William Tecumseh Sherman, to the Early Years of Louisiana State University, and to the Stirring Conditions Existing in the South on the Eve of the Civil War, 1859–1861* (Cleveland: Arthur H. Clarke Company, 1912), 76; William T. Sherman, letter to Thomas Ewing, Jr., January 21, 1860, in ibid., 124–25; William T. Sherman, letter to John Sherman, April 15, 1861, in Rachel Sherman Thorndike, ed., *The Sherman Letters: Correspondence Between General and Senator Sherman from 1837 to 1891* (New York: Charles Scribner's Sons, 1894), 114.

23. For Sherman biographies, see John F. Marszaleck, *Sherman: A Soldier's Passion for Order* (New York: Free Press, 1993); Michael Fellman, *Citizen Soldier: A Life of William Tecumseh Sherman* (New York: Random House, 1995); James Lee McDonough, *William Tecumseh Sherman: In the Service of My Country: An American Life* (New York: W. W. Norton & Company, 2016).

24. William T. Sherman, letter to John Sherman, September 22, 1862, in Sherman, *Sherman's Civil War*, 161–62.

25. See "Secretary Cameron's Visit to Kentucky," *New-York Daily Tribune*, October 30, 1861. See also quotes in McDonough, *William Tecumseh Sherman*, 286–92. On "absolutely sacrificing," see Sherman's letter to John, November 21, 1861, in Thorndike, ed., *The Sherman Letters*, 135. See also Marszaleck, *Sherman*, 161–63.

26. William T. Sherman, letter to John Sherman, October 1, 1862, in Sherman, *Sherman's Civil War*, 311–12; William T. Sherman, letter to John Sherman, September 3, 1862, in Thorndike, ed., *The Sherman Letters*, 161; McDonough, *William Tecumseh Sherman*, 338–41, 423.

27. William T. Sherman to John Sherman, October 1, 1862, in Sherman, *Sherman's Civil War*, 311–12; William T. Sherman to John Sherman, September 3, 1862, in Thorndike, ed., *The Sherman Letters*, 161.

28. See Marszaleck, *Sherman*, 191–93. See also McDonough, *William Tecumseh Sherman*, 342–44; Noel C. Fisher, "Prepare Them for My Coming: General William T. Sherman, Total War, and the Pacification of West Tennessee," *Tennessee Historical Quarterly* 51, no. 2 (Summer 1992): 75–86.

29. James M. McPherson, *The Negro's Civil War: How American Blacks Felt and Acted During the War for the Union* (New York: Vintage Books, 2003). *See also* Benjamin Quarles, *The Negro in the Civil War* (New York: Da Capo Press, 1989); John David Smith, ed., *Black Soldiers in Blue: African Americans in the Civil War Era* (Chapel Hill: University of North Carolina Press, 2014); Joseph T. Glatthaar, *Forged in Battle: The Civil War Alliance of Black Soldiers and White Officers* (Baton Rouge, LA: LSU Press, 2000).

30. William T. Sherman, letter to John Sherman, April 22, 1864, William Tecumseh Sherman Papers, Manuscripts Division, Library of Congress, Washington, DC, quoted in McDonough, *William Tecumseh Sherman*, 470; William T. Sherman, letter to Ellen Sherman, April, 17, 1863, in William T. Sherman, *Home Letters of General Sherman*, ed. M. A. DeWolfe Howe (New York: Charles Scribner's Sons, 1909), 249; William T. Sherman, letter to John Sherman, April 26, 1863, in Sherman, *Sherman's Civil War*, 459–61. See also Michael Fellman, "A White Man's War," *Civil War Times*, December 2009.

Notes

31. See Mohr, "The Atlanta Campaign and the African American Experience in Civil War Georgia," 281–82.

32. William T. Sherman, letter to Lorenzo Thomas, June 26, 1864, in Sherman, *Sherman's Civil War*, 658; *The War of the Rebellion*, ser. 1, vol. 39, 132.

33. *The War of the Rebellion*, ser. 1, vol. 38, 210. See also Mohr, "The Atlanta Campaign and the African American Experience in Civil War Georgia," 281–82.

34. William T. Sherman, letter to John Spooner, July 30, 1864, in Sherman, *Sherman's Civil War*, 677; Sherman, letter to William M. McPherson, circa September 15–30, 1864, in Sherman, *Sherman's Civil War*, 727.

35. James McPherson, *Battle Cry of Freedom: The Civil War Era* (Oxford, UK: Oxford University Press, 1988), 724–37, 756–60.

36. William T. Sherman, letter to Ulysses S. Grant, November 2, 1864, in Sherman, *Sherman's Civil War*, 748; Sherman, letter to Ulysses S. Grant, October 1, 1864, in Sherman, *Sherman's Civil War*, 732–33; Sherman, letter to George Thomas, October 2, 1864, in Sherman, *Sherman's Civil War*, 729–30; Sherman, letter to Henry Halleck, October 19, 1864, in Sherman, *Sherman's Civil War*, 735.

37. See McPherson, *Battle Cry of Freedom*, 807–10.

38. William T. Sherman, letter to George Thomas, October 2, 1864, in Sherman, *Sherman's Civil War*, 729–30; Sherman, letter to Henry Halleck, October 19, 1864, in Sherman, *Sherman's Civil War*, 735–36; Sherman, letter to Ulysses S. Grant, October 9, 1864, in Sherman, *Sherman's Civil War*, 731.

39. William T. Sherman, letter to Ulysses S. Grant, November 6, 1864, in Sherman, *Sherman's Civil War*, 749–52. See also John Bennett Walters, *Merchant of Terror: General Sherman and Total War* (New York: Bobbs-Merrill, 1973); Anne J. Bailey, *War and Ruin: William T. Sherman and the Atlanta Campaign* (New York: Rowan and Littlefield, 1993); Mark A. Grimsley, *The Hard Hand of War: Union Military Policy Toward Southern Civilians, 1861–1865* (Cambridge, UK: Cambridge University Press, 2008).

40. William T. Sherman, letter to James Calhoun, September 12, 1864, in Sherman, *Sherman's Civil War*, 707. On the new strategy, see McPherson, *Battle Cry of Freedom*, 722.

41. William T. Sherman, letter to James Calhoun, September 12, 1864, in Sherman, *Sherman's Civil War*, 707. The war's hard turn has been well documented. Perhaps the best account is in Grimsley, *The Hard Hand of War*.

42. *The War of the Rebellion*, ser. 1, vol. 39, 679; William T. Sherman, letter to Ulysses S. Grant, October 11, 1864, in Sherman, *Sherman's Civil War*, 732; McDonough, *William Tecumseh Sherman*, 754–55.

43. "Special Field Order No. 120," in *The War of the Rebellion*, ser. 1, vol. 39, 713–14.

44. "Special Field Order No. 120," in *The War of the Rebellion*.

45. Harvey Reid, *The View from Headquarters: Civil War Letters of Harvey Reid*, ed. Frank L. Byrne (Madison: State Historical Society of Wisconsin, 1965), 202; John J. Hight, *History of the Fifty-eighth Regiment of Indiana Volunteer Infantry. Its Organization, Campaigns and Battles from 1861 to 1865* (Princeton: Press of the Clarion, 1895), 411; *The War of the Rebellion*, ser. 1, vol. 39, 681, 741; Sherman, *Memoirs of General William T. Sherman*, vol. 2, 111; David P. Conyngham, *Sherman's March Through the South* (New York: Sheldon and Company, 1865), 238; Kennett, *Marching Through Georgia*, 241–42.

46. William T. Sherman, letter to Henry Halleck, September 4, 1864, in Sherman, *Sherman's Civil War*, 697. See also Stephen Davis, *What the Yankees Did to Us: Sherman's Bombardment and Wrecking of Atlanta* (Macon, GA: Mercer University Press, 2012).

47. Sherman, *Memoirs of General William T. Sherman*, vol. 2, 177; Conyngham, *Sherman's March Through the South*, 238; Kennett, *Marching Through Georgia*, 241–42.

Chapter Two: The Politics of the Plantation

1. Henry Hitchcock, *Marching with Sherman: Passages from the Letters and Campaign Diaries of Henry Hitchcock, Major and Assistant Adjutant General of Volunteers, November 1864–May 1865*, ed. M. A. DeWolfe Howe (Lincoln: University of Nebraska Press, 1995), 30.

2. Hitchcock, *Marching with Sherman*, 49–50.

3. Hitchcock, *Marching with Sherman*, 139.

4. George Sharland, *Knapsack Notes of Gen. Sherman's Grand Campaign Through the Empire State of the South* (Springfield, IL: Johnson & Bradford, 1865), 34; S. F. Fleharty, *Our Regiment. A History of the 102d Illinois Infantry Volunteers, with Sketches of the Atlanta Campaign, the Georgia Raid, and the Campaign of the Carolinas* (Chicago: Brewster & Hanscom, 1865), 121.

5. See Anne J. Bailey, *War and Ruin: William T. Sherman and the Savannah Campaign* (Wilmington, DE: Scholarly Resources, 1992). On Georgia's slave population: in 1860 Georgia reported a slave population of 462,198. The counties that had seen the most drastic expansion of slavery in the years leading up to the Civil War were those located in the central Georgia cotton belt. See Watson Jennison, *The Cultivation of Race: The Expansion of Slavery in Georgia, 1750–1860* (Lexington: University of Kentucky Press, 2012); Joseph P. Reidy, *From Slavery to Agrarian Capitalism in the Cotton Plantation South: Central Georgia, 1800–1880* (Chapel Hill: University of North Carolina Press, 1992); Ralph Betts Flanders, *Plantation Slavery in Georgia* (Chapel Hill: University of North Carolina Press, 1933).

6. Hitchcock, *Marching with Sherman*, 61. On the chattel principle, see Walter Johnson, *Soul by Soul: Life Inside the Antebellum Slave Market* (Cambridge, MA: Harvard University Press, 1999), 20–21.

7. Hitchcock, *Marching with Sherman*, 66.

8. Hitchcock, *Marching with Sherman*, 70–71.

9. Hitchcock, *Marching with Sherman*, 72. On slave drivers, see John W. Blassingame, *The Slave Community: Plantation Life in the Antebellum South* (Oxford, UK: Oxford University Press, 1972), 258–60, 316.

Notes

10. Joseph A. Saunier, ed., *A History of the Forty-seventh Regiment Ohio Veteran Volunteer Infantry, Second Brigade, Second Division, Fifteenth Army Corps, Army of the Tennessee* (Hillsboro, OH: Lyle Printing Company, 1903), 352; "One of the Boys" [H. W. Rood], *Story of the Service of Company E, and of the Twelfth Wisconsin Regiment, Veteran Volunteer Infantry, in the War of the Rebellion* (Milwaukee: Swain & Tate Co., 1893), 360; Hartwell Osborn et al., *Trials and Triumphs: The Record of the Fifty-fifth Ohio Volunteer Infantry* (Chicago: A. C. McClurg & Co., 1904), 177; J. E. Brant, *History of the Eighty-fifth Indiana Volunteer Infantry, Its Organization, Campaigns and Battles* (Bloomington, IN: Cravens Bros., 1902), 78; John Richards Boyle, *Soldiers True: The Story of the One Hundred and Eleventh Regiment Pennsylvania Veteran Volunteers, and of Its Campaigns in the War for the Union 1861–1865* (New York: Eaton & Mains, 1903), 262.

11. On slave religion, see Albert J. Rabateau, *Slave Religion: The Invisible Institution in the Antebellum South* (New York: Oxford University Press, 2004). See also Lawrence Levine, *Black Culture and Black Consciousness: Afro-American Folk Thought from Slavery to Freedom* (New York: Oxford University Press, 2007); Sylvia R. Frey and Betty Wood, *Come Shouting to Zion: African American Protestantism in the American South and British Caribbean to 1830* (Chapel Hill: University of North Carolina Press, 1998).

12. Boyle, *Soldiers True*, 262; Adin B. Underwood, *The Three Years' Service of the Thirty-third Mass. Infantry Regiment, 1862–1865* (Boston: A. Williams & Co. 1881), 243; William T. Sherman, *Memoirs of General William T. Sherman*, vol. 2 (New York: D. Appleton & Company, 1875), 180; William T. Sherman, *Home Letters of General Sherman*, ed. M. A. DeWolfe Howe (New York: Charles Scribner's Sons, 1909), 319.

13. George Ward Nichols, *The Story of the Great March, from the Diary of a Staff Officer* (New York: Harper & Brothers, 1865), 72; "Sherman and the 'Georgia Negroes,'" *Anti-Slavery Reporter: Under the Sanction of the British and Foreign Anti-slavery Society* (London, England), February 1, 1865; G. S. Bradley, *The Star Corps; or, Notes of an Army Chaplain, During Sherman's Famous "March to the Sea"* (Milwaukee: Jermain & Brightman, 1865), 195; Samuel H. Hurst, *Journal-History of the Seventy-third Ohio Volunteer Infantry* (Chillicothe, OH: Samuel H. Hurst, 1866), 156.

14. Hitchcock, *Marching with Sherman*, 110; H. H. Orendorff et al., *Reminiscences of the Civil War from Diaries of Members of the 103d Illinois Volunteer Infantry, 1904* (Chicago: J. F. Learning & Co., 1904), 148.

15. Lee Kennett, *Marching Through Georgia: The Story of Soldiers and Civilians During Sherman's Atlanta Campaign* (New York: Harper Perennial, 1995), 267–68.

16. Sarah Byrd, in *Born in Slavery: Slave Narratives from the Federal Writers' Project, 1936–1938*, vol. 4, *Georgia*, part 1, 171; T. W. Connelly, *History of the Seventieth Ohio Regiment: From Its Organization to Its Mustering Out* (Cincinnati, OH: Peak Bros., 1902), 126; H. I. Smith, *History of the Seventh Iowa Veteran Volunteer Infantry. During the Civil War* (Mason City, IA: E. Hitchcock, 1903), 304. See also Joseph T. Glatthaar, *The March to the Sea and Beyond: Sherman's Troops in the Savannah and Carolina Campaigns* (Baton Rouge: Louisiana State University Press, 1995). The one arguable exception was Sheridan's Valley Campaign, though his numbers were not quite as large.

17. Quoted in Kennett, *Marching Through Georgia*, 266. See also Special Field Order No. 120 in *The War of the Rebellion: A Compilation of the Official Records of the Union and Confederate Armies*, ser. 1, vol. 39 (Washington, DC: U.S. Government Printing Office), 713–14.

18. Special Field Order No. 120 in *The War of the Rebellion*; Hitchcock, *Marching with Sherman*, 69. See also Kennett, *Marching Through Georgia*, 296.

19. Fleharty, *Our Regiment*, 118; Harvey Reid, *Uncommon Soldiers: Harvey Reid and the 22nd Wisconsin March with Sherman*, ed. Frank L. Byrne (Knoxville: University of Tennessee Press, 2001), 203.

20. Emma Hurley, in *Born in Slavery: Slave Narratives from the Federal Writers' Project, 1936–1938*, vol. 4, *Georgia*, part 2, 277.

21. Nichols, *The Story of the Great March*, 59. See also Kennett, *Marching Through Georgia*, 289. On rumors, see Steve Hahn, "Extravagant Expectations of Freedom: Rumor, Political Struggle, and the Christmas Insurrection Scare of 1865 in the American South," *Past & Present* 157, no. 1 (November 1997): 122–58.

22. F. Y. Hedley, *Marching Through Georgia. Pen-Pictures of Every-day Life in General Sherman's Army, from the Beginning of the Atlanta Campaign Until the Close of the War* (Chicago: R. R. Donnelley & Sons, 1887), 312–13; Hitchcock, *Marching with Sherman*, 81, 128. On Confederate efforts to arm slaves, see Bruce Levine, *Confederate Emancipation: Confederate Efforts to Free and Arm Slaves During the Civil War* (Oxford, UK: Oxford University Press, 2006).

23. Charles J. Brockman, Jr., "The John Van Duser Diary of Sherman's March from Atlanta to Hilton Head," *Georgia Historical Quarterly* 53, no. 2 (June 1969): 222; Nichols, *The Story of the Great March*, 59; Hitchcock, *Marching with Sherman*, 66, 122.

24. John K. Duke, *History of the Fifty-third Regiment Ohio Volunteer Infantry, During the War of the Rebellion, 1861 to 1865* (Portsmouth, OH: Blade Printing Company, 1900), 166.

25. W. H. Forbis, quoted in Albion W. Tourgée, *The Story of a Thousand. Being a History of the Service of the 105th Ohio Volunteer Infantry, in the War for the Union, from August 21, 1862 to June 6, 1865* (Buffalo, NY: S. McGerald & Son, 1896), 356; Bradley, *The Star Corps*, 188.

26. George H. Puntenney, *History of the Thirty-seventh Regiment of Indiana Infantry Volunteers: Its Organization, Campaigns, and Battles—Sept. '61–Oct. '64* (Rushville, IN: Jacksonian Book and Job Department, 1896), 189; Brockman, "The John Van Duser Diary," 223.

27. H. H. Tarr, quoted in John W. Storrs, *The "Twentieth Connecticut": A Regimental History* (Ansonia, CT: Press of the "Naugatuck Valley Sentinel," 1886), 151–53.

28. Tarr, quoted in Storrs, *The "Twentieth Connecticut,"* 151–52.

29. Tarr, quoted in Storrs, *The "Twentieth Connecticut,"* 153–54.

30. Stephanie Camp, *Closer to Freedom: Enslaved Women and Everyday Resistance in the Plantation South* (Chapel Hill: University of North Carolina Press, 2004), 6–7.

31. On the existence of such spaces, see also Anthony E. Kaye, *Joining Places: Slave Neighborhoods in the Old South* (Chapel Hill: University of North Carolina Press, 2009).

32. A Committee of the Regiment, *The Story of the Fifty-fifth Regiment Illinois Volunteer Infantry in the Civil War, 1861–1865* (Clinton, MA: W. J. Coulter, 1887), 401; D. Leib Ambrose,

Notes

History of the Seventh Regiment Illinois Volunteer Infantry, from Its First Muster into the U.S. Service, April 15, 1861, to Its Final Muster Out, July 9, 1865 (Springfield: Illinois Journal Company, 1868), 285. See also Camp, *Closer to Freedom*, 135–36; Kennett, *Marching Through Georgia*, 262.

33. Boyle, *Soldiers True*, 263; *Ninety-second Illinois Volunteers* (Freeport, IL: Journal Steam Publishing House and Bookbindery, 1875), 181; Camp, *Closer to Freedom*, 138.

34. Ambrose, *History of the Seventh Regiment Illinois Volunteer Infantry*, 280; Fleharty, *Our Regiment*, 121; Edwin W. Payne, *History of the Thirty-fourth Regiment of Illinois Volunteer Infantry, September 7, 1961–July 12, 1865* (Clinton, IA: Allen Printing Company, 1903), 169; F. M. McAdams, *Every-day Soldier Life, or a History of the One Hundred and Thirteenth Volunteer Infantry* (Columbus: Chas. M. Cott & Co., 1884), 120.

35. Ira Berlin, *Generations of Captivity: A History of African-American Slaves* (Cambridge, MA: Harvard University Press, 2004), 3.

36. Charles E. Belknap, *Recollections of a Bummer*, Military Order of the Loyal Legion of the United States, War Papers no. 28, 7; Henry H. Wright, *A History of the Sixth Iowa Infantry* (Iowa City: State Historical Society of Iowa, 1924), 372; Thomas M. Stevenson, *History of the 78th Regiment O.V.V.I. from Its "Muster-In" to Its "Muster-Out"* (Zanesville, OH: Hugh Dunne, 1865), 317; Hitchcock, *Marching with Sherman*, 143. See also Tyler D. Parry and Charlton W. Yingling, "Slave Hounds and Abolition in the Americas," *Past & Present* 246, no. 1 (February 2020): 69–108.

37. Orendorff et al., *Reminiscences of the Civil War from Diaries of Members of the 103d Illinois Volunteer Infantry*, 164; Tarr, quoted in Storrs, *The "Twentieth Connecticut,"* 154.

38. Hitchcock, *Marching with Sherman*, 82.

39. Hitchcock, *Marching with Sherman*, 82.

40. See Dylan Penningroth, "Slavery, Freedom, and Social Claims to Property Among African Americans in Liberty County, Georgia, 1850–1880, " *Journal of American History* 84, no. 2 (September 1997): 405–35; Philip D. Morgan, "Work and Culture: The Task System and the World of Lowcountry Blacks, 1700–1880," *William and Mary Quarterly* 39, no. 4 (October 1982): 563–99.

41. Oscar L. Jackson, *The Colonel's Diary: Journals Kept Before and During the War by the Late Colonel Oscar L. Jackson of New Castle, Pennsylvania, Sometime Commander of the 63rd Regiment O.V.I.* (Sharon, PA, 1922), 192–94; Hitchcock, *Marching with Sherman*, 114–15; Dolly Sumner Lunt, *A Woman's Wartime Journal: An Account of the Passage over a Georgia Plantation of Sherman's Army on the March to the Sea, as Recorded in the Diary of Dolly Sumner Lunt* (New York: Century Co., 1918), 23–24; Frances Thomas Howard, *In and Out of the Lines: An Accurate Account of Incidents During the Occupation of Georgia by Federal Troops in 1864–65* (New York: Neale Publishing Company, 1905), 24.

42. Sharland, *Knapsack Notes of Gen. Sherman's Grand Campaign Through the Empire State of the South*, 46; Rice C. Bull, *Soldiering: The Civil War Diary of Rice C. Bull, 123rd New York Volunteer Infantry*, ed. K. Jack Bauer (New York: Berkley Books, 1988), 181; John Potter, *Reminiscences of the Civil War in the United States* (Oskaloosa, IA: The Globe Presses, 1897), 108.

43. Lucy McCullough, in *Born in Slavery: Slave Narratives from the Federal Writers' Project, 1936–1938*, vol. 4, *Georgia*, part 3, 68; Lunt, *A Woman's Wartime Journal*, 23–24.

44. See Kennett, *Marching Through Georgia*, 291.

45. John R. McBride, *History of the Thirty-third Indiana Veteran Volunteer Infantry During the Four Years of Civil War, from Sept. 16, 1861, to July 21, 1865; and Incidentally of Col. John Coburn's Second Brigade, Third Division, Twentieth Army Corps, Including Incidents of the Great Rebellion* (Indianapolis, IN: Wm. B. Burford, 1900), 163; Hitchcock, *Marching with Sherman*, 171; David Bittle Floyd, *History of the Seventy-fifth Regiment of Indiana Infantry Volunteers, Its Organization, Campaigns, and Battles (1862–65)* (Philadelphia: Lutheran Publication Society, 1893), 351.

46. See Kennett, *Marching Through Georgia*, 256; Bailey, *War and Ruin*, 70–74.

47. H. H. Orendorff et al., *Reminiscences of the Civil War from the Diaries of Members of the 103rd Illinois Volunteer Infantry*, 152–53; Theodore F. Upson, *With Sherman to the Sea: The Civil War Letters, Diaries & Reminiscences of Theodore F. Upson*, ed. Oscar Osburn Winther (Millwood, NY: Kraus, 1985), 138. See also Bailey, *War and Ruin*, 70–74.

48. Edwin E. Bryant, *History of the Third Regiment of Wisconsin Volunteer Infantry, 1861–1865* (Madison, WI: Veteran Association of the Regiment, 1891), 282–83; William Grunert, *History of the One Hundred and Twenty-ninth Regiment Illinois Volunteer Infantry* (Winchester, IL: R. B. Dedman, 1866), 128.

49. Bryant, *History of the Third Regiment of Wisconsin Volunteer Infantry*, 283; Grunert, *History of the One Hundred and Twenty-ninth Regiment Illinois Volunteer Infantry*, 129.

50. Hitchcock, *Marching with Sherman*, 89. For the story about the Georgia State House, see Noah Andre Trudeau, *Southern Storm: Sherman's March to the Sea* (New York: Harper Perennial, 2009), 222–23.

51. Sherman, *Memoirs of General William T. Sherman*, vol. 2, 185; Hitchcock, *Marching with Sherman*, 84.

52. Hitchcock, *Marching with Sherman*, 84–85; Nichols, *The Story of the Great March*, 58–59.

53. Hitchcock, *Marching with Sherman*, 85.

Chapter Three: On the March

1. Henry Hitchcock, *Marching with Sherman: Passages from the Letters and Campaign Diaries of Henry Hitchcock, Major and Assistant Adjutant General of Volunteers, November 1864–May 1865*, ed. M. A. DeWolfe Howe (Lincoln: University of Nebraska Press, 1995), 78.

2. Quoted in Noah Andre Trudeau, *Southern Storm: Sherman's March to the Sea* (New York: Harper Perennial, 2009), 146; Samuel H. Hurst, *Journal-History of the Seventy-third Ohio Volunteer Infantry* (Chillicothe, OH: S. H. Hurst, 1866), 155; Charles Smith, *A View within the Ranks*, quoted in Trudeau, *Southern Storm*, 124; John R. McBride, *History of the Thirty-third Indiana Veteran Volunteer Infantry During the Four Years of Civil War, from Sept. 16, 1861, to July 21, 1865; and Incidentally of Col. John Coburn's Second Brigade, Third Division, Twentieth*

Army Corps, Including Incidents of the Great Rebellion (Indianapolis, IN: Wm. B. Burford, 1900), 152.

3. G. S. Bradley, *The Star Corps; or, Notes of an Army Chaplain, During Sherman's Famous "March to the Sea"* (Milwaukee: Jermain & Brightman, 1865), 195; J. R. Kinnear, *History of the Eighty-sixth Regiment Illinois Volunteer Infantry, During Its Term of Service* (Chicago: Tribune Company's Book and Job Printing Office, 1866), 81; Thomas M. Stevenson, *History of the 78th Regiment O.V.V.I. from Its "Muster-In" to Its "Muster-Out"* (Zanesville, OH: Hugh Dunne, 1865), 314.

4. See entry, November 15, 1864, in Robert Hale Strong, *A Yankee Private's Civil War*, ed. Ashley Halsey (Chicago: Henry Regnery Company, 1961), 113–14.

5. Hitchcock, *Marching with Sherman*, 126–27.

6. Hitchcock, *Marching with Sherman*, 127–28.

7. Hitchcock, *Marching with Sherman*, 127–28.

8. Kinnear, *History of the Eighty-sixth Regiment, Illinois Volunteer Infantry*, 80–81; McBride, *History of the Thirty-third Indiana Veteran Volunteer Infantry*, 154.

9. John Potter, *Reminiscences of the Civil War in the United States* (Oskaloosa, IA: The Globe Presses, 1897), 109–11; T. W. Connelly, *History of the Seventieth Ohio Regiment: From Its Organization to Its Mustering Out* (Cincinnati, OH: Peak Bros., 1902), 133.

10. Stephanie Camp, *Closer to Freedom: Enslaved Women and Everyday Resistance in the Plantation South* (Chapel Hill: University of North Carolina Press, 2004), 6–7. On the feel of freedom, see 118. See also Leon F. Litwack, *Been in the Storm So Long: The Aftermath of Slavery* (New York: Vintage, 1980), 292.

11. James A. Connolly, *Three Years in the Army of the Cumberland: The Letters and Diary of Major James A. Connolly*, ed. Paul M. Angle (Bloomington: Indiana University Press, 1959), 311.

12. See Chandra Manning, *Troubled Refuge: Struggling for Freedom in the Civil War* (New York: Vintage, 2016); Amy Murrell Taylor, *Embattled Freedom: Journeys Through the Civil War's Slave Refugee Camps* (Chapel Hill: University of North Carolina Press, 2018).

13. Eric Foner, *The Second Founding: How the Civil War and Reconstruction Remade the Constitution* (New York: W. W. Norton, 2019), 184.

14. Allen Morgan Greer, *The Civil War Diary of Allen Morgan Greer, Twentieth Regiment, Illinois Volunteers*, ed. Mary Ann Anderson (Tappan, NY: Appleman, 1977), 177; Charles F. Hubert, *History of the Fiftieth Regiment Illinois Volunteer Infantry in the War of the Union* (Kansas City, MO: Western Veteran Publishing Company, 1894), 324; Hitchcock, *Marching with Sherman*, 80–81.

15. A Committee of the Regiment, *The Story of the Fifty-fifth Regiment Illinois Volunteer Infantry in the Civil War, 1861–1865* (Clinton, MA: W. J. Coulter, 1887), 389–91.

16. A Committee of the Regiment, *The Story of the Fifty-fifth Regiment Illinois Volunteer Infantry in the Civil War, 1861–1865.*

Notes

17. Henry H. Wright, *A History of the Sixth Iowa Infantry* (Iowa City: State Historical Society of Iowa, 1924), 363. See also Special Field Order No. 120, in *The War of the Rebellion*, ser. 1, vol. 39, 713–14.

18. Wright, *A History of the Sixth Iowa Infantry*, 363; Special Field Order No. 120, in *The War of the Rebellion*.

19. Bradley, *The Star Corps*, 196, 200–1; Samuel Storrow, letter to his mother, Samuel Storrow Papers, Civil War Correspondence, Diaries, and Journals, Massachusetts Historical Society, call no. P-376.

20. Bradley, *The Star Corps*, 196; Edwin W. Payne, *History of the Thirty-fourth Regiment of Illinois Volunteer Infantry, September 7, 1961–July 12, 1865* (Clinton, IA: Allen Printing Company, 1903), 177; Payne, *History of the Thirty-fourth Regiment Illinois Volunteer Infantry*, 174.

21. George Ward Nichols, *The Story of the Great March from the Diary of a Staff Officer* (New York: Harper & Brothers, 1865), 71; Henry Fales Perry, *History of the Thirty-eighth Regiment Indiana Volunteer Infantry, One of the Three Hundred Fighting Regiments of the Union Army in the War of the Rebellion, 1861–1865* (Palo Alto, CA: F. A. Stuart, 1906), 185.

22. Payne, *History of the Thirty-fourth Regiment of Illinois Volunteer Infantry*, 108; Hight, *History of the Fifty-eighth Regiment of Indiana Volunteer Infantry*, 425; Stevenson, *History of the 78th Regiment O.V.V.I. from Its "Muster-In" to Its "Muster-Out,"* 312–13; Samuel Storrow, letter to his mother, December 29, 1864, Samuel Storrow Papers.

23. "One of the Boys" [H. W. Rood], *Story of the Service of Company E, and of the Twelfth Wisconsin Regiment, Veteran Volunteer Infantry, in the War of the Rebellion* (Milwaukee: Swain & Tate Co., 1893), 366.

24. David P. Conyngham, *Sherman's March Through the South* (New York: Sheldon and Company, 1865), 277.

25. Charles D. Kerr, "From Atlanta to Raleigh," in *Glimpses of the Nation's Struggle*, vol. 1 (St. Paul, MN: St. Paul Book and Stationery Company, 1887), 214; Enoch D. John, "'With Tears in Their Eyes' On the Road to the Sea: Shannon's Scouts," *Civil War Times Illustrated* 21 (January 1983): 28, quoted in Trudeau, *Southern Storm*, 185; *The War of the Rebellion: A Compilation of the Official Records of the Union and Confederate Armies*, ser. 1, vol. 44 (Washington, DC: U.S. Government Printing Office), 410.

26. Kinnear, *History of the Eighty-sixth Regiment, Illinois Volunteer Infantry*, 84; William Wirt Calkins, *The History of the One Hundred and Fourth Regiment Illinois Volunteer Infantry. War of the Great Rebellion, 1862–1865* (Chicago: Donohue & Henneberry, 1895), 259–60.

27. Rice C. Bull, *Soldiering: The Civil War Diary of Rice C. Bull, 123rd New York Volunteer Infantry*, ed. K. Jack Bauer (New York: Berkley Books, 1988), 197; Connolly, *Three Years in the Army of the Cumberland*, 332–33.

28. McBride, *History of the Thirty-third Indiana Veteran Volunteer Infantry*, 154. On the language, see the E. P Failing Diary, November 29, 1864, in the Failing-Knight Papers, Ms. N-1211, Box 1, Massachusetts Historical Society.

Notes

29. Hight, *History of the Fifty-eighth Regiment of Indiana Volunteer Infantry*, 425; S. F. Fleharty, *Our Regiment. A History of the 102d Illinois Infantry Volunteers, with Sketches of the Atlanta Campaign, the Georgia Raid, and the Campaign of the Carolinas* (Chicago: Brewster and Hanscom, 1865), 120.

30. A Committee of the Regiment, *The Story of the Fifty-fifth Regiment Illinois Volunteer Infantry in the Civil War, 1861–1865*, 396; Hight, *History of the Fifty-eighth Regiment of Indiana Volunteer Infantry*, 425; Alfred H. Trego, diary entry, 1864, Manuscripts Collection, Chicago Historical Society, quoted in Trudeau, *Southern Storm*, 349.

31. H. H. Orendorff et al., *Reminiscences of the Civil War from Diaries of the 103d Illinois Volunteer Infantry, 1904* (Chicago: J. F. Learning & Co., 1904), 164; John Henry Otto, *Memoirs of a Dutch Mudsill: The "War Memories" of John Henry Otto, Captain, Company D, 21st Regiment, Wisconsin Volunteer Infantry*, ed. David Gould and James B. Kennedy (Kent, OH: Kent State University Press, 2004), 306; *Ninety-second Illinois Volunteers* (Freeport, IL: Journal Steam Publishing House and Bookbindery, 1875), 196.

32. Connolly, *Three Years in the Army of the Cumberland*, 339; Hight, *History of the Fifty-eighth Regiment of Indiana Volunteer Infantry*, 426–27.

33. Quoted in Nathaniel Cheairs Hughes, Jr., and Gordon D. Whitney, *Jefferson Davis in Blue: The Life of Sherman's Relentless Warrior* (Baton Rouge: Louisiana State University Press, 2002), 112.

34. Hughes and Whitney, *Jefferson Davis in Blue*.

35. Michael H. Fitch, *Echoes of the Civil War as I Hear Them* (New York: R. F. Fenno & Company, 1905), 236; *The War of the Rebellion*, ser. 1, vol. 44, 502.

36. Hight, *History of the Fifty-eighth Regiment of Indiana Volunteer Infantry*, 426–27.

37. Hight, *History of the Fifty-eighth Regiment of Indiana Volunteer Infantry*, 427; Fitch, *Echoes of the Civil War as I Hear Them*, 236; John Henry Otto, *Memoirs of a Dutch Mudsill*, 306.

38. Hight, *History of the Fifty-eighth Regiment of Indiana Volunteer Infantry*, 427.

39. Connolly, *Three Years in the Army of the Cumberland*, 353; John Henry Otto, *Memoirs of a Dutch Mudsill*, 310–11.

40. Connolly, *Three Years in the Army of the Cumberland*, 356–57.

41. William B. Miller, diary entry, Gibson County Civil War Papers, Indiana Historical Society, Indianapolis, IN, quoted in Trudeau, *Southern Storm*, 382. See also Trudeau, *Southern Storm*, 382–83.

42. William Passmore Carlin, *The Memoirs of Brigadier General William Passmore Carlin, U.S.A.*, ed. Robert I. Girardi and Nasthaniel Cheairs Hughes, Jr. (Knoxville: University of Tennessee Press, 2005), 197; Conyngham, *Sherman's March Through the South*, 277.

43. *Ninety-second Illinois Volunteers*, 197–98.

44. Carlin, The *Memoirs of Brigadier General William Passmore Carlin, U.S.A.*, 157–58; Calkins, *The History of the One Hundred and Fourth Regiment Illinois Volunteer Infantry*, 259; Kerr, "From Atlanta to Raleigh," 216.

45. Hight, *History of the Fifty-eighth Regiment of Indiana Volunteer Infantry*, 432; *Ninety-second Illinois Volunteers*, 200; Robert G. Athern, "An Indiana Doctor Marches with Sherman: The Diary of James Comfort Patten," *Indiana Magazine of History* 49, no. 4 (December 1953): 419–20; Connolly, *Three Years in the Army of the Cumberland*, 355.

46. *Ninety-second Illinois Volunteers*, 197; Jacob D. Cox, *Campaigns of the Civil War*, vol. 10, *The March to the Sea: Franklin and Nashville* (New York: Charles Scribner's Sons, 1892), 38.

47. Charles D. Kerr, "From Atlanta to Raleigh," 215–16. See also Trudeau, *Southern Storm*, 382.

48. H. I. Smith, *History of the Seventh Iowa Veteran Volunteer Infantry. During the Civil War* (Mason City, IA: E. Hitchcock, 1903), 209; Payne, *History of the Thirty-fourth Regiment of Illinois Volunteer Infantry*, 177.

Chapter Four: The Pivot to Port Royal

1. S. Willard Saxton, diary entry, December 14, 1864, Rufus and S. Willard Saxton Papers, Yale University Library, Manuscripts and Archives. See also Roger S. Durham, *Guardian of Savannah: Fort McAllister, Georgia, in the Civil War and Beyond* (Columbia: University of South Carolina Press, 2008).

2. Mary Mallard, journal entries, December 17 and 19, 1864, in Robert Manson Myers, ed., *The Children of Pride: A True Story of Georgia and the Civil War* (New Haven, CT: Yale University Press, 1972), 512; Mary Jones, journal entry, January 7, 1865, in Myers, *The Children of Pride*, 524. See also Erskine Clarke, *Dwelling Place: A Plantation Odyssey* (New Haven, CT: Yale University Press, 2005), 433–37.

3. See Noah Andre Trudeau, *Southern Storm: Sherman's March to the Sea* (New York: Harper Perennial, 2009), 413.

4. "One of the Boys" [H. W. Rood], *Story of the Service of Company E, and of the Twelfth Wisconsin Regiment, Veteran Volunteer Infantry, in the War of the Rebellion* (Milwaukee: Swain & Tate Co., 1893), 375; Oscar L. Jackson, *The Colonel's Diary: Journals Kept Before and During the War by the Late Colonel Oscar L. Jackson of New Castle, Pennsylvania, Sometime Commander of the 63rd Regiment O.V.I.* (Sharon, PA, 1922), 173. On rice, see Peter H. Wood, *Black Majority: Negroes in Colonial South Carolina from 1670 Through the Stono Rebellion* (New York: Alfred A. Knopf, 1974); Judith A. Carney, *Black Rice: The African Origins of Rice Cultivation in the Americas* (Cambridge, MA: Harvard University Press, 2002).

5. "One of the Boys," *Story of the Service of Company E, and of the Twelfth Wisconsin Regiment, Veteran Volunteer Infantry, in the War of the Rebellion*, 375; Samuel Merrill, *The Seventieth Indiana Volunteer Infantry in the War of the Rebellion* (Indianapolis: The Bobbs-Merrill Company, 1900), 219; John Potter, *Reminiscences of the Civil War in the United States* (Oskaloosa, IA: The Globe Presses, 1897), 115–16; J. R. Kinnear, *History of the Eighty-sixth Regiment, Illinois Volunteer Infantry, During Its Term of Service* (Chicago: Tribune Company's Book and Job Printing Office, 1866), 88.

Notes

6. Samuel Toombs, *Reminiscences of the War: Comprising a Detailed Account of the Experiences of the Thirteenth Regiment New Jersey Volunteers in Camp, on the March, and in Battle* (Orange, NJ: The Journal Office, 1878), 182; S. F. Fleharty, *Our Regiment. A History of the 102d Illinois Infantry Volunteers, with Sketches of the Atlanta Campaign, the Georgia Raid, and the Campaign of the Carolinas* (Chicago: Brewster and Hanscom, 1865), 125; Kinnear, *History of the Eighty-sixth Regiment Illinois Volunteer Infantry*, 88. See also Gerald Horne, *The Deepest South: The United States, Brazil, and the African Slave Trade* (New York: New York University Press, 2007); Ernest Obadele-Starks, *Freebooters and Smugglers: The Foreign Slave Trade in the United States After 1808* (Fayetteville: University of Arkansas Press, 2007); Leonardo Marques, *The United States and the Transatlantic Slave Trade to the Americas, 1776–1867* (New Haven, CT: Yale University Press, 2016); John A. E. Harris, "Circuits of Wealth, Circuits of Sorrow: Financing the Illegal Transatlantic Slave Trade in the Age of Suppression, 1850–1866," *Journal of Global History* 11, no. 3 (November 2016): 409–29. For a Georgia example of the illicit trade, see Jonathan M. Bryant, *Dark Places of the Earth: The Voyage of the Slave Ship* Antelope (New York: W. W. Norton, 2015).

7. William Dusinberre, *Them Dark Days: Slavery in the American Rice Swamps* (Oxford, UK: Oxford University Press, 1996), 4. Manigault inherited Silk Hope from his father-in-law, Nathaniel Heyward. Heyward was one of the largest slaveholders in the country. At the time of his death, he owned more than seventeen plantations run by as many as twenty-three hundred enslaved people.

8. Manigault Plantation, journal, 39–40, in Manigault Family Papers, no. 484, Southern Historical Collection, Wilson Library, University of North Carolina at Chapel Hill. See also Dusinberre, *Them Dark Days*, 3.

9. Manigault Plantation Journal, 38–40, in Manigault Family Papers, no. 484; Mary Jones, journal entry, January 11, 1865, in Robert Manson Myers, ed., *The Children of Pride: A True Story of Georgia and the Civil War* (New Haven, CT: Yale University Press, 1972), 1244.

10. See Trudeau, *Southern Storm*, 491–92. See also Nathaniel Cheairs Hughes, Jr., *General William J. Hardee: Old Reliable* (Baton Rouge: Louisiana State University Press, 1992).

11. Reuben Williams, *General Reub Williams's Memories of Civil War Times: Personal Reminiscences of Happenings That Took Place from 1861 to the Grand Review* (Westminster, MD: Heritage Books, 2004), 219–20. See also Trudeau, *Southern Storm*, 512.

12. James M. Simms, *The First Colored Baptist Church in North America. Constituted at Savannah, Georgia, January 20, A.D. 1788* (Philadelphia: J. B. Lippincott Company, 1888), 137; Merrill, *The Seventieth Indiana Volunteer Infantry in the War of the Rebellion*, 233–35; For quote to Sherman, see Jacqueline Jones, *Saving Savannah: The City and the Civil War* (New York: Vintage, 2008), 208.

13. See Jones, *Saving Savannah*, 205–09. See also William T. Sherman, *Memoirs of General William T. Sherman*, vol. 1 (New York: D. Appleton & Company, 1875), 231.

14. See Edwin W. Payne, *History of the Thirty-fourth Regiment of Illinois Volunteer Infantry, September 7, 1961–July 12, 1865* (Clinton, IA: Allen Printing Company, 1903), 178. See also Joseph S. Reynolds, letter to Sister, December 28, 1864, Joseph S. Reynolds Papers, no. 5060-z, Southern Historical Collection, Wilson Library, University of North Carolina at Chapel Hill; Trudeau, *Southern Storm*, 512.

15. Special Field Order No. 133, in *The War of the Rebellion: A Compilation of the Official Records of the Union and Confederate Armies*, ser. 1, vol. 44 (Washington, DC: U.S. Government Printing Office), 729–30.

16. *The War of the Rebellion*, ser. 1, vol. 44, 729–30, 159; *The War of the Rebellion*, ser. 1, vol. 44, 211; William T. Sherman, letter to Salmon Chase, January 11, 1865, in William T. Sherman, *Sherman's Civil War: Selected Civil War Correspondence of William T. Sherman, 1860–1865*, ed. Brooks D. Simpson and Jean V. Berlin (Chapel Hill: University of North Carolina Press, 1999), 794.

17. On Colerain, see *The War of the Rebellion*, ser. 1, vol. 44, 729–30, 159. See also Charles E. Smith, *A View from the Ranks: The Civil War Diaries of Charles E. Smith, Citizen Soldier, 32nd O.V.I. Delaware County, Ohio* (Delaware, OH: Delaware County Historical Society, 1999), 465.

18. Leslie M. Harris and Daina Ramey Berry, eds., *Slavery and Freedom in Savannah* (Athens: University of Georgia Press, 2014).

19. See Willie Lee Rose, *Rehearsal for Reconstruction: The Port Royal Experiment* (Oxford, UK: Oxford University Press, 1964).

20. *The War of the Rebellion*, ser. 1, vol. 44, 701–02, 840. See also *The War of the Rebellion*, ser. 1, vol. 44, 819.

21. *The War of the Rebellion*, ser. 1, vol. 44, 787.

22. Smith, *A View from the Ranks*, 466.

23. Rose, *Rehearsal for Reconstruction*, 16–18; Wise et al., *The History of Beaufort County, South Carolina*, vol. 2, 17.

24. E. L. Pierce, *The Negroes at Port Royal. Report of E. L. Pierce, Government Agent, to the Hon. Salmon P. Chase, Secretary of the Treasury* (Boston: R. F. Wallcut, 1862), 26–28. See also Edward L. Pierce, "The Contrabands at Fortress Monroe," *Atlantic Monthly*, November 1861, 626–40.

25. Pierce, *The Negroes at Port Royal*, 28.

26. Pierce, *The Negroes at Port Royal*, 28. See also Rose, *Rehearsal for Reconstruction*; Eric Foner, *Free Soil, Free Labor, Free Men: The Ideology of the Republican Party Before the Civil War* (Oxford, UK: Oxford University Press, 1995); Thomas C. Holt, *The Problem of Freedom: Race, Labor, and Politics in Jamaica and Britain, 1832–1938* (Baltimore: Johns Hopkins University Press, 1991).

27. See Rose, *Rehearsal for Reconstruction*, 20–24. See also Wise et al., *History of Beaufort County*, vol. 2, 72–74.

28. Quoted in Rose, *Rehearsal for Reconstruction*, 43, 45. See also Wise et al., *History of Beaufort County*, vol. 2, 73–74.

29. Quoted in Rose, *Rehearsal for Reconstruction*, 334. On divisions, see also Wise et al., *History of Beaufort County*, vol. 2, 75.

30. See Rose, *Rehearsal for Reconstruction*, 89.

Notes

31. [William C. Gannett and E. E. Hale], "Education of the Freedmen," *North American Review* 101, no. 209 (October 1865): 533. The authors of this article are unknown, though John R. Rachel suggests that it was cowritten by Gannett and Hale. See also John R. Rachal, "Gideonites and Freedmen: Adult Literacy Education at Port Royal, 1862–1865," *Journal of Negro Education* 55, no. 4 (Autumn 1986): 453–69; Orville Vernon Burton with Wilbur Cross, *Penn Center: A History Preserved* (Athens: University of Georgia Press, 2014).

32. See Rose, *Rehearsal for Reconstruction*, 144–51; Wise et al., *History of Beaufort County*, vol. 2, 109–13; Stephen V. Ash, *Firebrand of Liberty: The Story of Two Black Regiments That Changed the Course of the Civil War* (New York: W. W. Norton, 2008).

33. See Julie Saville, *The Work of Reconstruction: From Slave to Wage Laborer in South Carolina, 1860–1870* (Cambridge, UK: Cambridge University Press, 1994).

34. Laura M. Towne, *Letters and Diary of Laura M. Towne: Written from the Sea Islands of South Carolina, 1862–1884*, ed. Rupert Sargent Holland (Cambridge, MA: Riverside Press, 1912), 9, 20. See also Saville, *The Work of Reconstruction*.

35. See Akiko Ochiai, "The Port Royal Experiment Revisited: Northern Visions of Reconstruction and the Land Question," *New England Quarterly* 74, no. 1 (March 2001): 94–95.

36. See Rose, *Rehearsal for Reconstruction*, 152–53.

37. See Saville, *The Work of Reconstruction*, 40–41; Rose, *Rehearsal for Reconstruction*, 212. See also Ochiai, "The Port Royal Experiment Revisited," 94–95.

38. Ochiai, "The Port Royal Experiment Revisited," 99–100.

39. Quoted in Rose, *Rehearsal for Reconstruction*, 218. See also Saville, *The Work of Reconstruction*, 41–42; Ochiai, "The Port Royal Experiment Revisited," 99–100. Ochiai pointed out that preemption, as a policy, had its roots in the western settlement of the Homestead Act of 1862. At the time, some members of Congress were working to extend the provisions of the bill to include all abandoned land in the South.

40. Rose, *Rehearsal for Reconstruction*, 296. See also Saville, *The Work of Reconstruction*, 59–60.

41. Rufus Saxton, letter to Prof. F. J. Child, March 15, 1864, Rufus Saxton Letter book, 89, Rufus and S. Willard Saxton Papers, Yale University Library, Manuscripts and Archives.

42. Rufus Saxton, letter to Edward Philbrick, June 15, 1864, Rufus Saxton Letter book.

43. Rufus Saxton, letter to Edward Philbrick, June 15, 1864, Rufus Saxton Letter book.

44. Rufus Saxton, letter to Edward Philbrick, June 15, 1864, Rufus Saxton Letter book.

45. See Rose, *Rehearsal for Reconstruction*, 296. See also Saville, *The Work of Reconstruction*, 59–60.

46. Willard Saxton, diary entries, December, 24, 25, and 30, 1864, Rufus and S. Willard Saxton Papers.

47. Willard Saxton, diary entries, January 2–3, Rufus and S. Willard Saxton Papers.

Notes

Chapter Five: The Savannah Winter

1. Charles Carleton Coffin, *The Boys of '61: or, Four Years of Fighting. Personal Observation with the Army and Navy. From the First Battle of Bull Run to the Fall of Richmond* (Boston: Estes and Lauriat, 1885), 429–30.

2. See Jacqueline Jones, *Saving Savannah: The City and the Civil War* (New York: Vintage, 2008), 213; Frances Thomas Howard, *In and Out of the Lines: An Accurate Account of Incidents During the Occupation of Savannah by Federal Troops in 1864–65* (New York: The Neale Publishing Company, 1905), 204; Coffin, *The Boys of '61*, 416.

3. See George Ward Nichols, *The Story of the Great March from the Diary of a Staff Officer* (New York: Harper & Brothers, 1865), 107.

4. See Jones, *Saving Savannah*, 213.

5. See Jonathan M. Bryant, "'We Defy You!' Politics and Violence in Reconstruction Savannah," in *Slavery and Freedom in Savannah*, ed. Leslie M. Harris and Daina Ramey Berry (Athens: University of Georgia Press, 2014), 161–84; William A. Byrne, "'Uncle Billy' Sherman Comes to Town: The Free Winter of Black Savannah," *Georgia Historical Quarterly* 79, no. 1 (Spring 1995): 108–09.

6. See Bryant, "'We Defy You!,'" 161; Special Field Order No. 143, in William T. Sherman, *Memoirs of General William T. Sherman*, vol. 2 (New York: D. Appleton & Company, 1875), 233.

7. G. S. Bradley, *The Star Corps; or, Notes of an Army Chaplain, During Sherman's Famous "March to the Sea"* (Milwaukee: Jermain & Brightman, 1865), 244; Coffin, *The Boys of '61*, 406; Nichols, *The Story of the Great March from the Diary of a Staff Officer*, 107. See also James David Griffin, "Savannah, Georgia, During the Civil War," PhD diss., University of Georgia, 1963.

8. Bradley, *The Star Corps*, 244. See also Griffin, "Savannah, Georgia, During the Civil War," 279.

9. See John P. Dyer, "Northern Relief for Savannah During Sherman's Occupation," *Journal of Southern History* 19, no. 4 (November 1953): 457–72; Coffin, *The Boys of '61*, 417. See also Byrne, "'Uncle Billy' Sherman Comes to Town," 110.

10. Sherman, *Memoirs of General William T. Sherman*, vol. 2, 243–44.

11. Sherman, *Memoirs of General William T. Sherman*, vol. 2, 243–44.

12. Henry Halleck, letter to William T. Sherman, December 30, 1864, in *The War of the Rebellion: A Compilation of the Official Records of the Union and Confederate Armies*, ser. 1, vol. 44 (Washington, DC: U.S. Government Printing Office), 836–37.

13. Henry Halleck, letter to William T. Sherman, December 30, 1864, in *The War of the Rebellion*.

14. Henry Halleck, letter to William T. Sherman, December 30, 1864, in *The War of the Rebellion*.

15. Quoted in Nathaniel Cheairs Hughes, Jr., and Gordon D. Whitney, *Jefferson Davis in Blue: The Life of Sherman's Relentless Warrior* (Baton Rouge: Louisiana State University Press, 2002), 312. Hitchcock said this in a long letter to the noted military theorist and scholar Francis Lieber; see Hughes and Whitney, *Jefferson Davis in Blue*, 211.

Notes

16. William T. Sherman, letter to Salmon P. Chase, January 11, 1865, in William T. Sherman, *Sherman's Civil War: Selected Civil War Correspondence of William T. Sherman, 1860–1865*, ed. Brooks D. Simpson and Jean V. Berlin (Chapel Hill: University of North Carolina Press, 1999), 794–95.

17. See Sherman, letter to Salmon P. Chase, January 11, 1865, in Sherman, *Sherman's Civil War*, 794–95. Sherman laid out a defense of himself in great detail in his letter to Chase.

18. William T. Sherman, letter to Salmon P. Chase, January 11, 1865, in Sherman, *Sherman's Civil War*, 794–95; William T. Sherman, letter to Ellen, January 15, 1865, in William T. Sherman, *Home Letters of General Sherman*, ed. M. A. DeWolfe Howe (New York: Charles Scribner's Sons, 1909), 328.

19. See *The War of the Rebellion*, ser. 1, vol. 47, 87.

20. William T. Sherman, letter to Henry Halleck, January 12, 1865, in Sherman, *Sherman's Civil War*, 795–96.

21. William T. Sherman, letter to Henry Halleck, January 12, 1865, in Sherman, *Sherman's Civil War*, 795–96.

22. See "Minutes of an Interview Between the Colored Minsters and Church Officers at Savannah with the Secretary of War and Major-Gen. Sherman," in Ira Berlin et al., eds., *Free at Last: A Documentary History of Slavery, Freedom, and the Civil War* (New York: New Press, 2007), 310–13.

23. See Eric Foner, *Freedom's Lawmakers: A Directory of Black Officeholders During Reconstruction* (Baton Rouge, LA: LSU Press, 1996). See also Vernon Lane Wharton, *The Negro in Mississippi, 1865–1890* (Chapel Hill: University of North Carolina Press, 1965).

24. James M. Simms, *The First Colored Baptist Church in North America. Constituted at Savannah, Georgia, January 20, A.D. 1788* (Philadelphia: J. D. Lippincott Company, 1888), 128.

25. See "Minutes of an Interview Between the Colored Ministers and Church Officers at Savannah with the Secretary of War and Major-Gen. Sherman."

26. "Minutes of an Interview Between the Colored Ministers and Church Officers at Savannah with the Secretary of War and Major-Gen. Sherman."

27. "Minutes of an Interview Between the Colored Ministers and Church Officers at Savannah with the Secretary of War and Major-Gen. Sherman."

28. "Minutes of an Interview Between the Colored Ministers and Church Officers at Savannah with the Secretary of War and Major-Gen. Sherman."

29. "Minutes of an Interview Between the Colored Ministers and Church Officers at Savannah with the Secretary of War and Major-Gen. Sherman."

30. "Minutes of an Interview Between the Colored Ministers and Church Officers at Savannah with the Secretary of War and Major-Gen. Sherman."

31. See James Lynch, "Highly Important Letter from Georgia. Letter from James Lynch," *Christian Recorder*, February 4, 1865; "Gen. Sherman Taking Advice from the Negroes: Report

of the Conference Between Secretary Stanton, Gen. Sherman, and the Colored People of Savannah," *National Anti-Slavery Standard*, February 18, 1865.

32. See "Reported Cruelty to the Negroes by Sherman's Army," *National Anti-Slavery Standard*, January 28, 1865. On soldiers' expecting a land plan, see Byrne, "'Uncle Billy' Sherman Comes to Town," 111.

33. *The War of the Rebellion*, ser. 1, vol. 47, 60–63. On "forty acres and a mule," see *The War of the Rebellion*, ser. 1, vol. 47, 115. See also Eric Foner, *Reconstruction: America's Unfinished Revolution, 1863–1877* (New York: Harper and Row, 1988), 70–71; Claude F. Oubre, *Forty Acres and a Mule: The Freedman's Bureau and Black Land Ownership* (Baton Rouge, LA: LSU Press, 1978); Edward Magdol, *A Right to the Land: Essays on the Freedmen's Community* (Westport, CT: Greenwood Press, 1977). Howard C. Westwood, "Sherman Marched—and Proclaimed 'Land for the Landless,'" *South Carolina Historical Magazine* 85, no. 1 (January 1984): 33–55.

34. See Foner, *Reconstruction*, 70–71; Jones, *Saving Savannah*, 219–20. See also Sherman, *Memoirs of General William T. Sherman*, vol. 2, 250.

35. See Sherman, *Memoirs of General William T. Sherman*, vol. 2, 250. Sherman never said that publicly. But recruitment was a major issue during his time in Savannah, and it was made more of an issue by his reputation and previous statements. The need to shift perception was alluded to by Henry Halleck in his initial letter to Sherman letting him know about the "certain classes" that were speaking ill of him.

36. Sherman later wrote in his memoir that he had written the official order in conjunction with Stanton, but Northern papers speculated that Stanton had been the real force behind the order. See "Letters from New York," *Liberator*, February 17, 1865. See also "Minutes of an Interview Between the Colored Ministers and Church Officers at Savannah with the Secretary of War and Major-Gen. Sherman."

37. Douglas W. Allen, "Homesteading and Property Rights; or, 'How the West Was Really Won,'" *Journal of Law & Economics*, vol. 34, no. 1 (April 1991), 1–23. See also Trina Williams Shanks, "The Homestead Act: A Major Asset-Building Policy in American History," paper commissioned for Inclusion in Asset Building: Research and Policy Symposium, Center for Social Development, Washington University in St. Louis, September 21–23, 2000; Kerri Leigh Merritt, "Race, Reconstruction, Reparations," *Black Perspectives*, February 9, 2016.

38. Coffin, *The Boys of '61*, 420–23. See also Jones, *Saving Savannah*, 225; Byrne, "'Uncle Billy' Sherman Comes to Town," 112.

39. See Byrne, "'Uncle Billy' Sherman Comes to Town," 112–13; Coffin, *The Boys of '61*, 433.

40. See James Lynch, "A Black Man's Opinion of Gen. Sherman's Order," *National Anti-Slavery Standard*, February 11, 1865. See also "Letters from New York," *Liberator*, February 17, 1865.

41. See Foner, *Reconstruction*, 70–71; Oubre, *Forty Acres and a Mule*; Magdol, *A Right to the Land*.

Chapter Six: Port Royal and the Refugee Struggle of Reconstruction

1. H. G. Judd, "Appeal for Aid to the National Freedmen," letter to the editor, *New-York Daily Tribune*, January 17, 1865.

Notes

2. Judd, "Appeal for Aid to the National Freedmen."

3. Judd, "Appeal for Aid to the National Freedmen."

4. See Richard B. Drake, "Freedmen's Aid Societies and Sectional Compromise," *Journal of Southern History* 29, no. 2 (May 1963): 175–86.

5. "Sherman's Freedmen," *New York-Daily Tribune*, January 17, 1865; "The Freedmen of Georgia," *Liberator*, January 20, 1865; "Acknowledgements," *Freedmen's Record* 1, no. 2 (February 1865); "Incidents," *Freedmen's Record* 1, no. 3 (March 1865); "Aid for Savannah—Departure of the Daniel Webster," *New-York Daily Tribune*, January 17, 1865. See also John P. Dyer, "Northern Relief for Savannah During Sherman's Occupation," *Journal of Southern History* 19, no. 4 (1953): 457–72.

6. Laura M. Towne, *Letters and Diary of Laura M. Towne: Written from the Sea Islands of South Carolina, 1862–1884*, ed. Rupert Sargent Holland (Cambridge, MA: Riverside Press, 1912), 148.

7. Elizabeth Hyde Botume, *First Days Amongst the Contrabands* (Boston: Lee and Shepard Publishers, 1893), 168–69.

8. Edward S. Philbrick, letter to Elizabeth Ware Pearson, in Elizabeth Ware Pearson, ed., *Letters from Port Royal Written at the Time of the Civil War* (Boston: W. B. Clarke Company, 1906), 295–96.

9. James P. Blake, letter to Mrs. Stevenson, January 7, 1865, *Freedmen's Record* 1, no. 2 (February 1865); "Edisto Island," *Freedmen's Record* 1, no. 2 (February 1865); N. Blaidsdell, letter to the editor, April 24, 1865, *Freedmen's Record* 1, no. 7 (July 1865).

10. Willard Saxton, diary entries, January 5, 6, 11, and 13, 1865, Rufus and S. Willard Saxton Papers, Yale University Library, Manuscripts and Archives.

11. William S. McFeely, *Yankee Stepfather: General O. O. Howard and the Freedmen* (New York: W. W. Norton & Company, 1970); David Thomson, "Oliver Otis Howard: Reconsidering the Legacy of the 'Christian General,'" *American Nineteenth Century History* 10, no. 3 (September 2009): 273–98.

12. Willard Saxton, diary entry, January 4, 1865, Rufus and S. Willard Saxton Papers, Yale University Library, Manuscripts and Archive.

13. See, Ibid. On the weather, see Willie Lee Rose, *Rehearsal for Reconstruction: The Port Royal Experiment* (Oxford, UK: Oxford University Press, 1964), 322.

14. See McFeely, *Yankee Stepfather*, 46. See also Harriet Ware, letter to Elizabeth Ware Pearson, in Pearson, *Letters from Port Royal Written at the Time of the Civil War*, 298–99; Botume, *First Days Among the Contraband*, 112; Robert C. Morris, *Reading, 'Riting, and Reconstruction: The Education of Freedmen in the South, 1861–1870* (Chicago: University of Chicago Press, 1981).

15. See Charlotte Forten Grimké, *The Journals of Charlotte Forten Grimké*, ed. Brenda Stevenson (Oxford, UK: Oxford University Press, 1988). See also Charlotte Forten, "Life on the Sea Islands," parts 1 and 2, *The Atlantic Monthly*, May and June 1864, 587–96, 666–76.

Notes

16. Catherine Clinton, "Susie King Taylor (1848–1912): 'I Gave My Services Willingly,'" in *Georgia Women: Their Lives and Times*, vol. 1, ed. Ann Short Chirhart and Betty Wood (Athens: University of Georgia Press, 2009), 130–46. See also Susie King Taylor, *Reminiscences of My Life in Camp: An African American Woman's Civil War Memoir* (Athens: University of Georgia Press, 2006); Susie King Taylor, *Reminiscences of My Life in Camp with the 33d United States Colored Troops Late 1st S.C. Volunteers* (Boston: published by the author, 1902).

17. Oliver Otis Howard, *Autobiography of Oliver Otis Howard, Major General United States Army*, vol. 2 (New York: The Baker & Taylor Company, 1908).

18. See Stephen R. Wise and Lawrence S. Rowland with Gerhard Spieler, *The History of Beaufort County, South Carolina*, vol. 2, *Rebellion, Reconstruction, and Redemption, 1861–1893* (Columbia: University of South Carolina Press, 2015), 368–69. See also C.P.W., letter to Elizabeth Ware Pearson, January 8, 1865, in Pearson, *Letters from Port Royal Written at the Time of the Civil War*, 297; Willard Saxton, diary entry, January 4, 1865, Rufus and S. Willard Saxton Papers, Yale University Library, Manuscripts and Archives.

19. John Hill Ferguson, *On to Atlanta: The Civil War Diaries of John Hill Ferguson, Illinois Tenth Regiment of Volunteers*, ed. Janet Correll Ellison with assistance from Mark A. Weitz (Lincoln: University of Nebraska Press, 2001), 96; Henry H. Wright, *A History of the Sixth Iowa Infantry* (Iowa City: State Historical Society of Iowa, 1924), 396. On Saxton, see Wise et al., *History of Beaufort County, South Carolina*, vol. 2, 369.

20. Quoted in Joseph T. Glatthaar, *The March to the Sea and Beyond: Sherman's Troops in the Savannah and Carolina Campaigns* (Baton Rouge: Louisiana State University Press, 1995), 55. See also Rose, *Rehearsal for Reconstruction*, 323–24.

21. Towne, *Letters and Diary of Laura M. Towne*, 150. See also Rose, *Rehearsal for Reconstruction*, 329–30; McFeely, *Yankee Stepfather*, 53–54.

22. See John G. Foster, letter to William T. Sherman, January 31, 1865, in *The War of the Rebellion: A Compilation of the Official Records of the Union and Confederate Armies*, ser. 1, vol. 47 (Washington, DC: U.S. Government Printing Office), 186–87; William T. Sherman, letter to John G. Foster, February 1, 1865, in *The War of the Rebellion*, ser. 1, vol. 47, 201; John Porter Hatch, William T. Sherman, February 2, 1865, in *The War of the Rebellion*, ser. 1, vol. 47, 212. See also McFeely, *Yankee Stepfather*, 53–54.

23. Quoted in McFeely, *Yankee Stepfather*, 48.

24. See Foner, *Reconstruction*, 68–69. See also Oubre, *Forty Acres and a Mule*, 20–21.

25. On the bureau and its history, see Paul Cimbala and Randall M. Miller, eds., *The Freedmen's Bureau and Reconstruction: Reconsiderations* (New York: Fordham University Press, 1999). See also Mary Farmer-Kaiser, *Freedwomen and the Freedmen's Bureau: Race, Gender, and Public Policy in the Age of Emancipation* (New York: Fordham University Press, 2010). On Howard and his appointment, see McFeely, *Yankee Stepfather*, 61–64.

26. See Rose, *Rehearsal for Reconstruction*, 338; LaWanda Cox, "The Promise of Land for the Freedmen," *Mississippi Valley Historical Review* 45, no. 3 (December 1958), 413–40. See also Foner, *Reconstruction*, 69–70; Oubre, *Forty Acres and a Mule*, 46–47.

27. For Special Field Order No. 15, see "Order by the Commander of the Military Division of the Mississippi" in Berlin, et al., *Freedom: A Documentary History of Emancipation*, Sers. I, Vol. III, *The Wartime Genesis of Free Labor: The Lower South* (Cambridge: Cambridge University Press, 1991), 338–40. See also Rose, *Rehearsal for Reconstruction*, 330.

28. Letter from Edward S. Philbrick to Elizabeth Ware Pearson, January 9, 1865, in Pearson, *Letters from Port Royal Written at the Time of the Civil War*, 299–301; Willard Saxton, diary entry, January 13, 1865, Rufus and S. Willard Saxton Papers, Yale University Library, Manuscripts and Archives; McFeely, *Yankee Stepfather*, 56; Mary Still, "Letters from Beaufort, S.C., No. 2," *Christian Recorder*, April 29, 1865.

29. Letter from James P. Blake, February 11, 1865, "Extracts from the Teachers' Letters," *Freedmen's Record* 1, no. 3 (March 1865).

30. William C. Gannett, letter to Elizabeth Pearson Ware, January 23, 1865, in Pearson, *Letters from Port Royal Written at the Time of the Civil War*, 307–8; "Letter from William C. Gannett," *Freedmen's Record* 1, no. 6 (June 1865).

31. James P. Blake, "Report of Relief Operations for the Department of the South, for March, 1865," *Freedmen's Record* 1, no. 3 (March 1865). On family, see Botume, *First Days Amongst the Contrabands*, 154. On North Carolina, see "Letter from William C. Gannett," *Freedmen's Record* 1, No. 6 (June 1865).

32. See Botume, *First Days Amongst the Contrabands*, 50–51, 82–84, 120–21.

33. Edward S. Philbrick, letter to Elizabeth Ware Pearson, January 22, 1865, in Pearson, *Letters from Port Royal Written at the Time of the Civil War*, 306; William C. Gannett, letter to Elizabeth Ware Pearson, January 23, 1865, in Pearson, *Letters from Port Royal Written at the Time of the Civil War*, 307–8.

34. See Towne, *Letters and Diary of Laura M. Towne*, 148. See also Anne C. Bailey, *The Weeping Time: Memory and the Largest Slave Auction in American History* (Cambridge, UK: Cambridge University Press, 2017).

35. Towne, *Letters and Diary of Laura M. Towne*, 148–54.

36. Towne, *Letters and Diary of Laura M. Towne*, 154–58.

37. Towne, *Letters and Diary of Laura M. Towne*, 154–58.

38. Towne, *Letters and Diary of Laura M. Towne*, 154; Edward S. Philbrick, letter to Elizabeth Ware Pearson, January 22, 1865, in Pearson, *Letters from Port Royal Written at the Time of the Civil War*, 306.

39. Edward S. Philbrick, letter to Elizabeth Ware Pearson, January 9, 1865, in Pearson, *Letters from Port Royal Written at the Time of the Civil War*, 303–4.

40. Coffin, *The Boys of '61*, 420–24. See also Jones, *Saving Savannah*, 225–26.

41. Coffin, *The Boys of '61*, 425.

Notes

42. See Russell Duncan, *Freedom's Shore: Tunis Campbell and the Georgia Freedmen* (Athens: University of Georgia Press, 1986). See also Edmund L. Drago, *Black Politicians and Reconstruction in Georgia: A Splendid Failure* (Athens: University of Georgia Press, 1992); Eric Foner, *Freedom's Lawmakers: A Directory of Black Officeholders During Reconstruction* (Baton Rouge, LA: LSU Press, 1996); Tunis G. Campbell, *Hotel Keepers, Head Waiters, and Housekeepers' Guide* (Boston: Coolidge and Wiley, 1848).

43. T. G. Campbell, *Sufferings of the Rev. T. G. Campbell and His Family in Georgia* (Washington, DC: Enterprise Publishing Company, 1877).

44. See Oubre, *Forty Acres and a Mule*, 19, 47.

45. See Rose, *Rehearsal for Reconstruction*, 347–48.

46. See Eric L. McKitrick, *Andrew Johnson and Reconstruction* (Oxford, UK: Oxford University Press, 1989).

47. Foner, *Reconstruction*, 246–49.

48. See Oubre, *Forty Acres and a Mule*, 52–55. See also Rose, *Rehearsal for Reconstruction*, 354–55; quotes from Rose in *Rehearsal for Reconstruction*, 356; Oubre, *Forty Acres and a Mule*, 51.

49. See McFeely, *Yankee Stepfather*, 130–33; Foner, *Reconstruction*, 159–61.

50. "Committee of Freedmen on Edisto Island, South Carolina, to the Freedmen's Bureau Commissioner, October 20 or 21, 1865; and the Latter's Reply, October 22, 1865," Freedmen and Southern Society Project, November 30, 2023, https://freedmen.umd.edu//Edisto%20 petitions.htm.

51. Oubre, *Forty Acres and a Mule*, 54.

52. See Oubre, *Forty Acres and a Mule*, 56; Rose, *Rehearsal for Reconstruction*, 351–52; McFeely, *Yankee Stepfather*, 146.

53. See Oubre, *Forty Acres and a Mule*, 59; Rose, *Rehearsal for Reconstruction*, 357–58.

54. See Rose, *Rehearsal for Reconstruction*, 357.

55. See Rose, *Rehearsal for Reconstruction*, 374. See also Saville, *The Work of Reconstruction*, 80, 85.

Epilogue

1. "Review of the Armies," *New York Times*, May 24, 1865; "The Grand Review," *New-York Daily Tribune*, May 25, 1865.

2. "Review of the Armies," *New York Times*, May 24, 1865.

3. "The Review," *New York Herald*, May 25, 1865.

4. Joshua Lawrence Chamberlain, *The Passing of the Armies: An Account of the Final Campaign*

Notes

of the Army of the Potomac, Based upon Personal Reminiscences of the Fifth Army Corps (New York: G. P. Putnam's Sons, 1915), 365–69.

5. Chamberlain, *The Passing of the Armies*, 367.

6. See John G. Barrett, *Sherman's March through the Carolinas* (Chapel Hill: University of North Carolina Press, 1956).

7. See *The War of the Rebellion: A Compilation of the Official Records of the Union and Confederate Armies*, ser. 1, vol. 47 (Washington, DC: U.S. Government Printing Office), 588, 265.

8. See Barrett, *Sherman's March through the Carolinas*.

9. Claim of Primus Wilson, Southern Claims Commission, Allowed Claims, 1871–1880, Chatham County, Georgia; claim of Boson Johnson, Southern Claims Commission, Allowed Claims, 1871–1880, Liberty County, Georgia; claim of Scipio King, Southern Claims Commission, Allowed Claims, 1871–1880, Liberty County, Georgia; claim of Cato Keating, Southern Claims Commission, Allowed Claims, 1871–1880, Chatham County, Georgia.

10. See Eric Foner, *The Second Founding: How the Civil War and Reconstruction Remade the Constitution* (New York: W. W. Norton and Company, 2019).

11. Foner, *The Second Founding*.

12. See Steven Hahn, *A Nation Under Our Feet: Black Political Struggles in the Rural South from Slavery to the Great Migration* (Cambridge, MA: Harvard University Press, 2005).

13. See Heather Andrea Williams, *Self-Taught: African American Education in Slavery and Freedom* (Chapel Hill: University of North Carolina Press, 2007). See also Hilary Green, *Educational Reconstruction: African American Schools in the Urban South, 1865–1890* (New York: Fordham University Press, 2016).

14. See David W. Blight, *Race and Reunion: The Civil War in American Memory* (Cambridge, MA: Harvard University Press, 2002); Carole Emberton, *Beyond Redemption: Race, Violence, and the American South After the Civil War* (Chicago: University of Chicago Press, 2013); Douglas R. Egerton, *The Wars of Reconstruction: The Brief, Violent History of America's Most Progressive Era* (New York: Bloomsbury Press, 2014); Heather Cox Richardson, *The Death of Reconstruction: Race, Labor, and Politics in the Post–Civil War North, 1865–1901* (Cambridge, MA: Harvard University Press, 2001).

INDEX

NOTE: Page numbers in *italics* reference photographs and maps.

Index

Index

Connolly, James A.
  on Baird, 96
  at Ebenezer Creek, 100–101, 103
  on refugee experience, 82–83, 93
constitutional amendments, 206
"contraband camps," 21–22
contraband policy, 19–24, 120–21
Conyers (Georgia), 44, 54
Conyngham, David P., 38, 91, 102
Cox, Jacob D., 104

Daufuskie Island (South Carolina), 169,
  170
Davis, Jefferson Columbus (general)
  Buckhead Creek incident, 98–99
  Ebenezer Creek massacre, 100–105,
    144–47, 149
  March to the Sea route, 44, 108–9
  photograph, 39
  reputation of, 96–98
  Rocky Comfort Creek incident, 99
Davis, Jefferson Finis (Confederate
  president), 31, 32, 96
dog tracking, 61–62
Douglass, Frederick, 27–28
Du Bois, W.E.B., 217n13
Du Pont, Samuel, 120

East Hermitage (plantation in Georgia),
  111
Easton, L. C., 115, 119
Eatonton (Georgia)
  destruction in, 49
  March to the Sea route, 44, 57
  plantation system in, 63
Ebenezer Creek, 96, 99–105, 144–49,
  155–56, 158
Edisto Island (South Carolina), 119,
  169–70, 183, 192, 195–98

education programs
  by Freedmen's Bureau, 180–81
  for freed people, 140–41
  at Port Royal Experiment, 125, 173–75,
    181
  post–Civil War, 207
emancipation and freed people
  Black enlistment, 27–30, 33–35, 119,
    125, 175
  celebrating in Savannah, 113–14, 139
  citizenship issue, 27–28, 121, 154–55,
    206, 208
  collapse of Southern social order,
    139–42
  contraband policy, 19–24, 120–21 (see
    also enslaved people)
  educational programs, 207
  following Sherman's army, 75–83, 84,
    86–89, 204 (see also March to the Sea
    (refugee experience))
  freed towns, 207
  in Grand Review march, 203–4
  Jubilee felt by, 6–8, 9, 47–49, 160, 208–9
    (see also freedom movement)
  landownership for, 153–54 (see also
    homesteading)
  Lincoln's views on, 22–24, 26, 27–29,
    33–34
  as manservants, 42–43
  of Port Royal, 118–36 (see also Port
    Royal Experiment; Port Royal refugee
    crisis)
  recalling their freedom march story,
    205–6
  religious experience of emancipation,
    47–49
  Savannah's surrender and, 115–20
  Second Confiscation Act, 22, 27, 28
  separatism of, 154–55

243

Index

Index

Index

Index

Index

Index

Index

Underwood, Adin B., 48
United States Colored Troops (USCT),
    28–30, 33–34, 119, 125, 175
Upson, Theodore, 68
U.S. Constitution, 206
US Navy, 108, 120

valets (manservants), 42–43, 66, 80, 86,
    115
Van Duser, John, 54, 56
Vicksburg, siege of, 28, 33
Virginia campaign, 30–31
voting rights, 206–7, 208

Wadmalaw Island (South Carolina),
    184
Wardell, Arthur, 151

wartime emancipation; *see* emancipation
    and freed people; Emancipation
    Proclamation; Second Confiscation Act
Washington, DC, Grand Review in, 201–3
"Weeping Time" auction, 186–87
Wells, James M., 15–17, 23–24
Wheeler, Joseph
    cavalry raids by, 31–32, 61, 91
    at Ebenezer Creek, 101–4, 149
    road destruction by, 100
    treatment of refugees, 98–99
white saviorism, 48–49, 114, 147
Whitfield, Mr., 75
Williams, Alpheus, 44, 116, 204
Wilson, Primus, 205, 206
Work, Henry Clay, 7
Wright, Horatio, 97